KEY CONCEPTS IN LANGUAGE AND LINGUISTICS

Palgrave Key Concepts

Palgrave Key Concepts provide an accessible and comprehensive range of subject glossaries at undergraduate level. They are the ideal companion to a standard textbook, making them invaluable reading to students throughout their course of study, and especially useful as a revision aid.

Key Concepts in Accounting and Finance
Key Concepts in Business Practice
Key Concepts in Drama and Performance
Key Concepts in Human Resource Management
Key Concepts in Information and Communication Technology
Key Concepts in International Business
Key Concepts in Language and Linguistics (second edition)
Key Concepts in Management
Key Concepts in Marketing
Key Concepts in Operations Management
Key Concepts in Politics
Key Concepts in Strategic Management
Literary Terms and Criticism (third edition)

Further titles are in preparation

www.palgravekeyconcepts.com

Palgrave Key Concepts
Series Standing Order
ISBN 1-4039-3210-7
(*outside North America only*)

You can receive future titles in this series as they are published by placing a standing order. Please contact your bookseller or, in case of difficulty, write to us at the address below with your name and address, the title of the series and the ISBN quoted above.

Customer Services Department, Macmillan Distribution Ltd,
Houndmills, Basingstoke, Hampshire RG21 6XS, England

Key Concepts in Language and Linguistics

Second Edition

Geoffrey Finch

First published as *Linguistic Terms and Concepts* in 2000 by
PALGRAVE MACMILLAN
Houndmills, Basingstoke, Hampshire RG21 6XS and
175 Fifth Avenue, New York, N.Y. 10010
Companies and representatives throughout the world

PALGRAVE MACMILLAN is the global academic imprint of the Palgrave Macmillan division of St. Martin's Press, LLC and of Palgrave Macmillan Ltd. Macmillan® is a registered trademark in the United States, United Kingdom and other countries. Palgrave is a registered trademark in the European Union and other countries.

ISBN-13: 978 1–4039–3391–1
ISBN-10: 1–4039–3391–X

This book is printed on paper suitable for recycling and made from fully managed and sustained forest sources.

A catalogue record for this book is available from the British Library.

A catalog record for this book is available from the Library of Congress

10 9 8 7 6 5 4 3 2 1
14 13 12 11 10 09 08 07 06 05

Printed in Great Britain by
Creative Print & Design (Wales), Ebbw Vale

For Mum and Dad

Contents

General Editors' Preface

If you are studying linguistics the chances are that you are looking not only for a book that will help you to come to grips with the larger themes and issues behind linguistic study, but also for a book that will help you understand the concepts and ideas that inform the terms linguists use. The aim of *Key Concepts in Language and Linguistics* is to offer you guidance on how to gain both of these important skills by providing the sort of vital information you need to understand linguistics as a discipline.

The first two chapters provide an introduction to the range and scope of linguistics as well as offering a clear overview of the subject as a whole. The chapters are intended to help students new to the subject who are looking for a sense of the overall nature and features of linguistics.

The following three chapters deal with the core areas of linguistics: phonetics and phonology; syntax; semantics and pragmatics. Each chapter has a brief helpful introduction, which is followed by a series of discussions and definitions of the main ideas and terms used in these areas, while the final chapter explores the main branches of linguistics.

Each chapter of the book can be read separately or dipped into for information or guidance. However, in the first instance, it may well repay you to look quickly through the book as a whole so that you gain a sense of what linguistics involves and how you can best use the volume. There is an index so that you can find particular terms, while the alphabetical listing of entries in each chapter's glossary provides a simple way of finding broader topics.

At once a guide to current ideas about linguistics and a dictionary of the terms used in the modern study of language, *Key Concepts in Language and Linguistics* is an essential book for all students at all levels.

John Peck
Martin Coyle

How to Use this Guide

Key Concepts in Language and Linguistics is a practical guide to the study of linguistics. Its main intention is to offer help and advice in understanding the principal linguistic terms and concepts that you will inevitably come across as a student. The guide itself is basically a dictionary of linguistic terms. It resembles other such dictionaries in that it attempts to provide essential information on a wide range of topics and ideas. It differs from other dictionaries, however, in its overall structure which is designed so as to include as much discussion as possible of those ideas and topics.

The book is divided into six chapters: 'Linguistics: a Brief Survey', 'General Terms and Concepts', 'Phonetics and Phonology', 'Syntax', 'Semantics and Pragmatics', and 'Linguistics: the Main Branches'. If, for example, you are studying syntax, you might find a number of useful ideas simply by browsing through the syntax chapter. If you know exactly what you are looking for, the quickest way of finding the relevant entry is to consult the index at the back of the book. You may, however, also be looking for guidance on broader ideas about these areas. Chapters 3–6, therefore, begin with introductory essays discussing the characteristics of linguistics as well as introducing some of the significant debates that inevitably form a part of their study.

These introductory essays, together with the survey in Chapter 1, are intended to provide a sense of the broader picture. They are followed by more specific entries, alphabetically arranged. I should point out that this is not an all-inclusive guide. Linguistics is a subject with a considerable range of technical terms and a wealth of critical literature. To have attempted to include all of that would have resulted in an encyclopaedia rather than a guide. The approach, therefore, is selective. The great advantage of this is that it has allowed me room to concentrate on the major topics you are likely to come across. The aim is to provide helpful information that is directly relevant to your studies, rather than to cover, exhaustively, every avenue of the subject.

This idea also determined the approach adopted within each entry. I do not attempt to represent the entire history of any term; nor do I list all the linguists who have written about a topic. In their place I have substituted critical discussion, attempting to provide guidelines for your study of linguistics. Underlying many of the definitions is the idea that language is endlessly fascinating and that studying it in a systematic manner is a participatory, and open-ended, process from which no one is excluded. There are no ultimate authorities here but us, as users of language. My hope is that the definitions will show you how to get started and how to develop and express your own ideas about linguistics.

Probably the best way to use this book is to browse through it, stopping at whatever catches your attention. But, as I have said, there is an index which should enable you to find a specific term quickly (page numbers in bold type in the index indicate the main discussion of an entry). Given the nature of the subject it is inevitable that individual entries often build on other entries. Where this occurs the relevant entry is cross-referenced in the text in SMALL CAPITALS and you can look it up, should you so wish, in the index. One other convention which you should be aware of is the use of * to indicate a linguistic unit, such as a sentence or a clause, which is improperly formed, and consequently ungrammatical. It is commonly employed by linguists for this purpose.

Those readers who are real beginners in linguistics will probably find it helpful to start by reading the first two chapters to get a sense of the overall range of the subject and the features that characterise it as an area of study. This can be followed up with topics that are reasonably familiar, such as 'noun', 'verb', 'clause', and 'sentence' in Chapter 4. Readers with more knowledge can branch off into 'X-bar syntax', 'transformational grammar' and other entries of a similarly specialised nature. The major shortcoming of most guides to linguistic terms is that they so often fail to tell you what you want to know; my hope is that I have gone at least some way towards providing the kind of basic information and critical discussion you are likely to find useful, as well as stimulating you to explore further.

A Note on Phonetics

A number of entries in this book make use of the International Phonetic Alphabet. This is a special alphabet used by linguists for representing pronunciation. If you are unfamiliar with it I recommend that you read the section on it in Chapter 3. For quick reference, however, you will find it helpful to know the following symbols and the speech sounds of English to which they relate. The pronunciation represented here is the British accent known as received pronunciation (RP):

Simple vowels

/iː/	b**ea**d
/ɪ/	b**i**d
/ɛ/	b**e**d
/æ/	b**a**d
/ɑː/	b**ar**d
/ɒ/	b**o**x
/ɔː/	s**aw**
/ʊ/	p**u**t
/uː/	b**oo**t
/ʌ/	c**u**p
/ɜː/	b**ir**d
/ə/	**a**bout

Diphthongs

/eɪ/	p**ay**
/aɪ/	p**ie**
/ɔɪ/	b**oy**
/əʊ/	g**o**
/aʊ/	m**ou**th
/ɪe/	b**eer**
/ɛə/	b**ear**
/ʊə/	c**ure**

Note: the symbol ː indicates that the vowel is long.

Consonants

/p/	**p**it
/b/	**b**it
/t/	**t**ip
/d/	**d**i**d**
/k/	**k**i**ck**
/g/	**g**ive
/f/	**f**ield
/v/	**v**ine
/θ/	**th**igh
/ð/	**th**is
/s/	**s**i**g**n
/z/	**z**oo
/ʃ/	**sh**ip
/ʒ/	mea**s**ure
/h/	**h**ot
/tʃ/	**ch**ain
/dʒ/	**j**u**dg**e
/m/	**m**ouse
/n/	**n**ear
/ŋ/	pi**nk**
/l/	**l**eaf
/r/	**r**un
/j/	**y**atch
/w/	**w**et

1 Linguistics: a Brief Survey

Linguistics is the systematic study of language. Some people refer to it as the 'science of language' but I have avoided this description because it can be misleading. The popular view of language is that it is regulated by precise laws which prescribe the 'correct' use of words, a little in the manner that Newtonian physics does the operation of the solar system. But the merest acquaintance with language shows us it is not like that. Language is notoriously slippery; words change their meaning and pronunciation form continually – they never stay still. This fertile capacity of language for endless diversity means that any attempt to reduce it to a set of laws is fraught with danger.

None the less, it is true to say that linguists *approach* language in a scientific manner. First of all, they adopt an objective, or disinterested, stance. They have no axe to grind: they are not concerned, like some politicians and educators, in enforcing or promoting any 'standards' of language use. Secondly, their method is **empirical**, that is they proceed by **observation**, **description**, and **explanation**. These are the three stages of linguistic enquiry distinguished by the linguist Noam Chomsky. Linguists begin by observing the way in which people use language, on the basis of which they provide a description of language use, and finally, when all the data has been analysed, an explanation. Explanations of language use are the stage at which linguists endeavour to establish the underlying **rules** which speakers are following. It is a basic presupposition of modern linguistics that language is rule-governed – in other words, that speakers obey an internalised set of instructions in the way they construct and use SENTENCES. The word 'internalised' is important here, because these rules are derived not from any kind of external authority, like a dictionary or GRAMMAR, but from the speaker's own intuitive knowledge, or COMPETENCE. Once the rules for particular languages have been mapped in this empirical fashion the linguist hopes to provide a model which will explain how all languages work. The production of this model, or UNIVERSAL GRAMMAR, is the pinnacle of linguistic enquiry.

What I have been describing is the hard core of contemporary linguistic methodology. But, like all disciplines, linguistics has its highways and byways. There are very few subjects in which people agree about everything, and linguistics has its areas of dissent and dispute just like all the others. The 'bread and butter' of most linguistics, however, is the study of PHONOLOGY, SYNTAX and SEMANTICS: the central chapters of this book (Chapters 3–5) deal with each of these. The first, phonology, is concerned with the sounds of a language and the way in which these are structured into segments such as SYLLABLES and WORDS; the second, syntax, with the way we string words together in PHRASES, CLAUSES, and SENTENCES, to make WELL-FORMED sequences; and the third, semantics, with the way we assign meanings to the units of a language in order to communicate. Each of these has additional LEVELS; phonology is supplemented by PHONETICS, the study of the physical characteristics of sound; syntax by MORPHOLOGY, the study of the structure of words; and semantics by PRAGMATICS, the study of the situational constraints on meaning. Together all of these constitute the grammar of language, that is, the total set of rules which govern the production, construction and execution of utterances from their generation in the mind to their incarnation in sounds or letters. In addition to this staple diet, however, there are numerous sub-branches of the discipline, reflecting the diversity of contexts in which language is used. Chapter 6 discusses these and focuses in particular on three: SOCIOLINGUISTICS, the study of language and society, STYLISTICS, the study of various kinds of language style, and PSYCHOLINGUISTICS, the study of language and mind.

Whatever the particular branch of the subject, however, linguistics is always trying to answer the really basic questions about language: 'What is language?', 'How does language work?', 'What do all languages have in common?', 'Why do languages change?', 'How do we learn to speak?', and so on. It takes as its foundation, first, that language is uniquely human – it may share some characteristics with animal systems of communication but it is crucially different – and second, that language is the property of all. Linguists do not privilege any particular variety or form of language, or indeed any group of users. Their concern is with understanding language, rather than controlling it.

THE DEVELOPMENT OF LINGUISTICS

Early history

Linguistics, in the sense in which I have been describing it, first developed as a subject in its own right in the eighteenth century. Before then, language in the western world had been the interest largely of philosophers and prescriptive grammarians – people concerned to enforce particular language forms as 'correct'. But in the eighteenth century a number of scholars became interested in the relationship between European languages and those of the Orient. This came to prominence in 1786 when an Englishman, Sir William Jones, delivered a paper demonstrating that the ancient Indian language of Sanskrit bore striking structural similarities to Greek, Celtic, Latin and Germanic. The conclusion which he drew was that all of these languages must have sprung from a common source. So important was this discovery that for the next hundred years scholars became preoccupied with tracing the original ancestor from which all these languages were descended. **Comparative linguistics** became the dominant branch of linguistic enquiry. This entailed a detailed comparison of different languages in terms of their phonology, morphology, and lexis, or vocabulary, with the aim of internally reconstructing the lost original. As a result of these painstaking enquiries, we now have an evolutionary map of languages in the western world that shows their individual lineage and their relationship to the hypothetical ancestor, **Indo-European** (see Figure 1).

It was as a result of these comparative studies of language change that linguistics took a further step forward, when, towards the end of the nineteenth century, a group of German linguists began studying the effect of sound changes within a given language on other related sounds in the same language. They discovered that sound changes were regular: sounds do not change in isolation. Moreover, once a change takes place it tends to work its way productively through the language. So, for example, in English, the letters *ch* occurring initially before *e* or *i*, as in *chicken* and *cheese*, used to be pronounced as /k/, but then, sometime in the Old English period, a change took place in this environment, affecting the most commonly used words to begin with, and eventually spreading to all. Insights such as these have been important in the development of PHONOLOGICAL RULES, which attempt to express by formula the pronunciation rules of a language (see HISTORICAL LINGUISTICS, Chapter 6)

Ferdinand de Saussure
But if we were to award the credit for turning linguistics from the intensively narrow scholastic position it occupied in the nineteenth century into the broad-based intellectual discipline it is today, there would be little disagreement in awarding it to the Swiss linguist Ferdinand de Saussure, himself a nineteenth-century linguist, who had the vision to see a larger role for his subject. Saussure, sometimes called 'the father of modern linguistics', never actually published any major work on the subject. However, after his death, his students collected together his

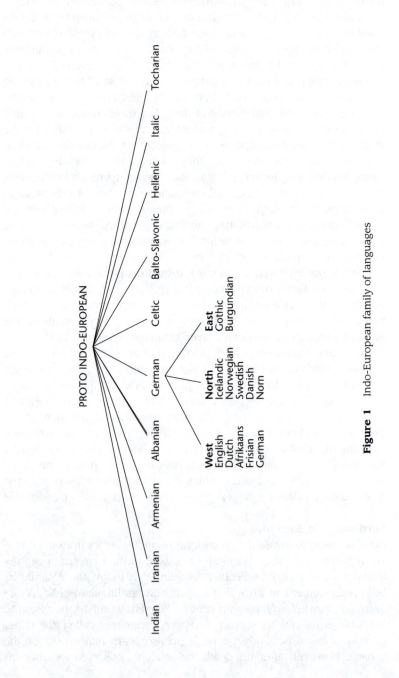

Figure 1 Indo-European family of languages

lecture notes and published them in a small volume entitled *Cours de linguistique générale*. Despite its slimness it had, and continues to have, a seminal influence on linguistics. Saussure was instrumental in the development of **structural linguistics**. He likened language to a game of chess in which each piece is defined by both its situation on the board and its relationship with the other pieces. Thus a bishop operating on the white squares has considerably more freedom of manoeuvre if its opposite number has been taken, and a pawn occupying a central square is more powerful if supported by other pawns. And just as games of chess, though all following the same rules, are all different, so languages can be said to vary in a similarly principled manner.

Saussure illustrated the relatedness of linguistic items by comparing the meaning of the English words *sheep* and *mutton* with that of the French term *mouton*. The French word can be used to refer both to the living animal and to the meat which is eaten, whereas in English these meanings are distributed over two words: *sheep* being used to refer to the animal in the field and *mutton* to the meat derived from it. The point is that in the French system *mouton* occupies more **semantic space** than *mutton* in English and, as a consequence, it has a larger meaning. If English did not have the term *sheep* then possibly *mutton* would expand in meaning to occupy that space as well. For Saussure, words define themselves against each other; they are continuously circulating, adjusting their **value** according to the state of play in the system as a whole.

This particular insight is intimately connected with Saussure's treatment of words as SIGNS. Signs have no natural relationship to the things they represent. The word *dog*, for instance, has no intrinsic connection with the animal it symbolises: any other word would do equally well to represent it. For Saussure the relationship is essentially **arbitrary**: it's a consequence of the way in which the language has evolved, but it could equally well have evolved differently. Since Saussure, the principle of arbitrariness has been much discussed and various refinements have been made to it, but it remains a foundation idea of modern linguistics. Indeed, it is one of the characteristics which distinguishes human language from much animal communication. In the wild there is often a recognisable link between the signal and the message being conveyed. But in language, with rare exceptions, this is not so. As Saussure himself pointed out, there is no reason why a castle in chess shouldn't be represented by any convenient object, providing it was sufficiently differentiated in some way from the other pieces.

Saussurean linguistics approaches language as a self-enclosed **system**. Words are related to each other as signs and can be strung together in various combinations to form sentences. The extent of a word's capacity to form sentences is seen as the sum of its potential to combine with, or substitute for, others. Saussure imagined sentences as having two axes on which items could be sorted in these ways. The axis of substitution he termed PARADIGMATIC, and that of combination he termed SYNTAGMATIC (see Figure 2).

If you try out any sentence, e.g. *The cat ate the mouse*, and substitute each of the items with others of the same WORD CLASS, you will see that it is possible to generate a considerable number of sentences; not all of them will make sense semantically, but they may none the less be WELL-FORMED syntactically. In general, Saussure did not have a great deal to say about syntax. Again, we can see here the foundation of an important and much discussed concept in modern linguistics: that of **autonomy**. Many contemporary linguists maintain that the various components of the linguistic system operate autonomously. Linguists following in the footsteps of the American Noam Chomsky, for example, commonly argue that the syntactic component (the one that generates sentences) operates separately from the one that assigns a meaning to them.

Basic to Saussure's view of language is the separation between language as substance and language as concept. The separation is there in the notion of the sign. A sign has two component parts: a physical token of some sort, such as a cross, a string of sounds (as in /tri/ – pronounced 'tree'), or the colour green; and a concept which is attached to it – the crucifixion, 'treeness', permission to go. The conceptual level of language, the abstract system of rules which comprises it, Saussure referred to as *LANGUE*; the substance side, the representation of those rules in actual sentences or utterances, he termed *PAROLE*. Saussure himself, concentrated on *langue* and had very little to say about *parole*, but in recent times the spotlight has moved more favourably to *parole*. Like much that is contained in Saussure's short book, these terms have been subject to considerable debate, but the distinction that he

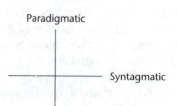

Figure 2 The axes of language (based on Saussure)

described between these two dimensions of language has been very influential. Most modern linguists accept a distinction between an abstract and a concrete side of language, although the boundary that separates them may be difficult to determine.

You will have noticed that Saussure's methodology typically involves working with two-term oppositions: paradigmatic/syntagmatic, *langue/parole*, and there are others – DIACHRONIC/SYNCHRONIC, SIGNI-FIER/SIGNIFIED. This **binary** model of language, in which two opposing terms interact dynamically, is distinctive of Saussure and has had wide-spread influence beyond linguistics. It has been particularly productive in related fields of enquiry, in the arts and social sciences, where it is possible to discern a similar set of sign-making features capable of being viewed as a system. This is sometimes known as **structuralism**, and while it has been somewhat overtaken by rival theoretical approaches, it remains a powerful influence in contemporary thinking about language.

Saussure's work came at a time when a number of scholars in Eastern European universities were turning their attention to the systematic study of language. At the Moscow Linguistic Circle and the Prague School of Linguistics, Saussure's ideas fell on fertile ground. Scholars such as Nicolai Trubetzkoy, Serge Karcevskij, Baudouin de Courtenay and, most famously of all, Roman Jakobson, were all deeply influenced by structuralist thinking. The concepts of MORPHEME, GRAPHEME, DISTINC-TIVE FEATURES, and MARKEDNESS, so influential in the development of linguistics, all emerged from these centres. When Jakobson emigrated to America in 1942 he took with him a generation of scholarly work on structuralist linguistics, work which ultimately had a strong impact on the development of GENERATIVE GRAMMAR through Jakobson's student Morris Halle, and subsequently through Noam Chomsky.

Mid-twentieth-century developments

It was in America that most of the important developments in mid-century linguistics took place. In many respects these owed much to the concern of American anthropologists to record the culture and languages of native American tribes, which were rapidly vanishing before the concerted power of the white races. Much of the credit for undertaking this work must go to Franz Boas, widely considered the founder of American linguistics and American anthropology. At the time that Boas commenced his work many erroneous ideas were in circula-tion about native American languages based on the belief that they were primitive in structure. So, for example, it was commonly thought that native Americans had to rely on gestures to communicate ideas such as 'here', 'there', 'yesterday', and 'tomorrow' as a consequence of the poverty of their vocabulary; and that native languages changed so fast and unpredictably that grandparents could not understand their grandchildren. Boas's innovation was to see that such languages were significantly different from European ones, with the result that categories such as time and location were represented differently. He argued that each language should be described in its own terms, something he called **linguistic relativity**. Not only that, he believed that each language should be analysed alongside the culture of which it was a part. A language represented the world view of its speakers. This idea was taken up, most famously, by one of Boas's students, Edward Sapir. Like Boas, Sapir did not accept the idea that native American languages were primitive, or that one could divide languages along some notional scale of linguistic development. Differences in languages represented differences in outlook and belief. Under the influence of one of Sapir's own students, Benjamin Whorf, this remarkably liberal idea hardened itself into the SAPIR–WHORF HYPOTHESIS, which holds that language structure determines thought, i.e the way we perceive the world is a product of our language, not the other way round. The hypothesis has been the subject of considerable debate over the years, with many linguists regarding it as too deterministic. It was fiercely attacked by Steven Pinker in the *Language Instinct* (1994). More popular nowadays is a weaker version of the hypothesis in which language is said to influence, rather than determine, thought.

In order to describe these non-European languages Boas and his followers had to construct an appropriate methodology. But it was left to the linguist Leonard Bloomfield to develop this into a methodology suitable for the description of any language. In 1933, he published a book called *Language* that attempted to do just this. Unlike Boas, Bloomfield had no interest in the cultural or psychological side of language. His principal concern was to develop linguistics as a science. As such, his approach was rigorously descriptive. It is sometimes referred to as **descriptive linguistics**, occasionally as 'structuralist' (in a slightly different sense than the Saussurean), and, despite the revolutions that have occurred in linguistic thought, it is still at the heart of much linguistic practice. For Bloomfield the task of linguists was to collect data from indigenous speakers of a language and then to analyse it by studying the phonological and syntactic patterns. The concept that all language is patterned was fundamental to these procedures.

Bloomfield argued that one of the principal ways in which items are ordered in a language is in terms of their **constituency**. Any sentence can be analysed in terms of what are called its **immediate**

constituents (see IMMEDIATE CONSTITUENCY ANALYSIS). These, in turn, can be analysed into further constituents, and so on, down to those at the ground level of words, which are the smallest constituents. A sentence is thus conceived of as a hierarchy of interlocking constituents, all of which can demonstrate their constituency, because they can be either substituted by similar constituents, or redistributed to form other sentences. Thus the sentence *The large Siamese cat jumped onto the table* can be represented hierarchically, in the form of a TREE DIAGRAM, to show the structural relationships of its constituent parts, as in Figure 3. This is an unlabelled **IC** (immediate constituency) diagram. A further refinement would be to attach a descriptive label – 'ADJECTIVE', 'NOUN', 'PHRASE', 'SENTENCE' – to each **node**, or intersection, of the tree. Bloomfield, and the descriptive linguists who followed in his wake, argued that any language could be analysed in this hierarchical manner. The important thing for the linguist to discover were the individual units, or constituents, of the language being observed. This was achieved through **discovery procedures**, a set of principles that covered the ordering, distribution, and substitutability of items.

Descriptive linguistics provided a powerful means of uncovering some of the surface structures of language, but it ignored two important aspects of language. First, it was not interested in meaning, or semantics, partly because it proved too difficult to analyse the meanings of constituents in the same descriptive fashion, and partly because it didn't seem immediately relevant to providing an account of syntactic structure. Second, it laboured under the illusion that description alone was sufficient for arriving at a set of language rules. It was Noam Chomsky, perhaps the most radical linguist of our time, who showed that more important than mere description for the linguist was **explanation**. To arrive at that meant penetrating beyond the output and understanding the system that produced it.

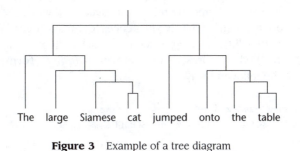

The   large   Siamese   cat   jumped   onto   the   table

Figure 3   Example of a tree diagram

Noam Chomsky

More than any other linguist Chomsky dominates contemporary linguistics. From his first important volume, *Syntactic Structures*, published in 1957, he has constantly challenged the orthodoxies of linguistic enquiry. In many cases his most searching ideas have developed from what, on the face of it, are fairly simple observations. In distinction from the descriptive linguists, for example, he claimed that it was not enough for a grammar simply to take account of existing sentences. It must also be able to account for sentences that have not yet been written or uttered. What struck him about language was its **creativity**, that is, its capacity to generate completely novel sentences, endlessly. This could only be possible if speakers had an internalised set of rules, or grammar, which specified which sequences of a language were possible, and thus grammatical, and which were not. This mental grammar comprised a speaker's COMPETENCE, and the task of the linguist, as he saw it, was to explain it and, in so doing, to penetrate the mysteries of the human mind.

The difficulty, of course, in such a task is that the mind is not open to immediate inspection. The linguist has to proceed indirectly, by examining actual language use and working backwards to the mental system responsible for its production. One thing that Chomsky saw immediately was that a description of the surface structure of sentences alone was not sufficient to achieve this. There were pairs of sentences, such as *John is eager to please* and *John is easy to please*, which had the same surface structure but which were entirely different sentences. In the first, *John* is the one doing the pleasing, whilst in the second, he is the one being pleased. Clearly there are different structural relationships here that are masked by a simple description of their surface forms. Observations such as this led Chomsky to posit two levels of structure: a **deep** structure and a **surface** structure. This meant that instead of one grammar there were two – the first consisting of rules for combining constituents and controlling the input into the deep structure, and the second specifying the rules by which the surface structure was derived; Chomsky referred to this as a TRANSFORMATIONAL GRAMMAR. Returning briefly, then, to our two sentences, Chomsky argued that they derived from two different deep structures, which (following the conventions of a method of representation known as **logical form**) we can express in the following way:

John is eager to please
BE (JOHN, EAGER) + PLEASE (JOHN, SOMEONE)

John is easy to please
BE {JOHN, EASY} + PLEASE {SOMEONE, JOHN}

We can see that the difference between the two sentences lies in the second CLAUSE of each. In the second instance *John* is the underlying object of *please* (this is indicated by its bracketed position after the comma), whereas in the first *John* is the underlying subject. The transformational rules of English allow the two clauses in each sentence to combine in ways that produce the same surface structure. None the less, our intuitive knowledge of their different deep structures allows us to interpret them correctly.

The deep/surface divide has proved useful in providing an explanation for a number of linguistic FEATURES that descriptive linguistics on its own could not. Ambiguity, for example, is a commonly recurring feature of language that the surface form alone does not reveal. In *The police caught Gus in their panda car*, the phrase *in their panda car* could be modifying (see PHRASE) either *the police* or *Gus*. Using a transformational approach we can see that there are two different deep structures possible here, again masked by a common surface structure. On the other hand, it's also possible for the reverse to be true, and that different surface structures can have the same deep structure. Sentences such as *The cat bit the dog* and *The dog was bitten by the cat* are **active** and **passive** (see VOICE) versions of the same basic structure.

Insights such as these into the relatedness of sentences were greatly advanced by the concept of transformation. At the same time it made SYNTAX into a highly elaborate study – arguably *too* elaborate, in that linguists began seeing transformations everywhere, with the consequence that the concept became troublesome. Nowadays, Chomsky has simplified the transformational approach and slimmed the processes down to just a few central operations. But it continues to be a fertile, if disputed, concept in modern linguistics. The terms 'deep' and 'surface' have also been refined so that Chomsky now refers to 'D' structure and 'S' structure. This is to avoid the possible suggestions of 'profound' or 'complex' in 'deep', and those of 'superficial' or 'obvious' in 'surface'.

Chomsky was responsible for initiating a new era in grammatical enquiry. Once it became possible to think of grammar as a mental construct, with language as the output of internalised mechanisms rather than as a set of skills that people simply acquire, it was not too great a step towards envisaging the possibility that language was somehow innate in human beings. In the last few years it has become almost axiomatic among linguists to argue that we are pre-programmed from birth with a basic knowledge of what languages are like; in other words, that language is genetic. Two developments, in particular, are important here. First, the growth of **psycholinguistics**, the study of language and mind, which has greatly advanced our understanding of the way in which we acquire language. It has been clear for some years that children do not learn their native language simply by imitating and copying. Indeed, Chomsky's first real target as a linguist was the behaviourist theory of language acquisition associated with B. F. Skinner that claimed just that. To Skinner, language consisted of a set of habits built up over years by a process of trial and error. Children learnt it in much the same way rats learnt how to find food pellets in laboratory experiments. In opposition to this, Chomsky argued that the conditioning process of approval and reward was counter-productive in language acquisition. Parents will tend to approve statements by their children that are true rather than grammatically correct. So, for example, an incorrect utterance such as 'Daddy home' will gain the mother's approval if it is true, whereas 'Daddy has come home' will not if Daddy is still at work. Moreover, the language that children hear about them which, according to Skinner they are copying, is full of unfinished sentences, mistakes, and slips of the tongue (so-called PERFORMANCE errors). Yet, despite this, children manage to learn the rules for correct CLAUSE construction. In the following sentences, for example, native speakers of English know that *he* in sentence 1 could refer to John, but not in sentence 2. And they know this without anyone having taught them:

1. John said that *he* was happy
2. *He* said that John was happy
        (Chomsky, 2002: 16)

With examples like these Chomsky was able to show that children are occupied, right from an early age, in formulating their own rules and sorting the data to which they are exposed, in a principled manner. They are able to do this because when they are born they already possess a grammar. The jury is still out on whether this is just part of the general cognitive functioning of the child's mind, or whether it forms part of what some linguists have called a language **module** (SEE MODULARITY). The second development has been the success of modern linguistics in discovering **linguistic universals**, that is, constructions and processes that all languages have in common. Clearly, when children are born, they do not come into the world with a knowledge of English, or Danish; their linguistic knowledge is not so highly particularised. Nevertheless, their knowledge must be of a kind that can develop into whatever language exists in the community around them. Language acquisition in this model becomes more like tuning in a television receiver than the old model of learning by imitation and reinforcement. Chomsky has argued that human beings have an inherited core of linguistic knowledge of the kind that is basic to all language. This he calls UNIVERSAL GRAMMAR, and the ultimate task of the linguist is in specifying what it consists of.

Linguistics today
It is a tribute to the combined influence of Saussure and Chomsky that the study of language became increasingly important in the late twentieth century to non-linguists as well as linguists, and that this interest has continued into the twenty-first century. The concern with the language potential of human beings has meant that a wide variety of disciplines, notably sociology, psychology, and literary criticism, have begun to take more interest in linguistics, and, in so doing, have left their own mark on the subject, whilst the emphasis of Saussure on the symbolic functioning of language has appealed to students of media and communication systems. At the same time, however, the last quarter of the twentieth century saw the development of alternative models of language. These are not necessarily at variance with existing models; as often as not, they prioritise aspects with which other models have not been primarily concerned.

A case in point is the **systemic grammar** (see FUNCTIONAL GRAMMAR) of the British linguist Michael Halliday. As opposed to the essentially 'formalist' approach of Chomsky, Halliday's is more 'functional'. He sees language as existing to fulfil certain human needs, such as our need to make sense of the world and to relate to others. The formal categories of language, he argues, derive as much from these as from any pre-programming. What Halliday draws our attention to is the importance of the 'world' and our relationship to it in the formation of the linguistic system. The three principal functions that he identifies, and which he uses as the basis of his grammar, are the **ideational** (the use of language to conceptualise the world), the **interpersonal** (the use of language as a personal medium), and the **textual** function (the use of language to form texts). In many respects Halliday's approach, which sees language as a symbolic signalling system, or, in his words, a **social semiotic**, reflects the influence of Saussure rather than Chomsky. Like Saussure he sees language as a social and cultural phenomenon as opposed to a biological one, like Chomsky,

Functional approaches are part of a general shift in some branches of linguistics towards a more socially situated account of language. There has traditionally been a problem here in that linguists have often found it difficult to describe the complex interplay between language and social/situational context, using formal linguistic procedures. As we noted earlier, the linguists of the Bloomfield school simply side-stepped the issue by ignoring the meaning of utterances altogether. And even though later grammars often incorporate meaning into their account of language, they frequently do so in a very restricted sense. The problem that linguists struggle with here is that language underspecifies meaning. There is no way that the full, context-rich, meaning of any utterance can be gleaned simply by a consideration of the words alone. Partly in recognition of this, recent years have seen the development within linguistics of PRAGMATICS (the study of language in its socially situated, or extra-linguistic, context). Pragmatics is a broad-based branch of linguistics concerned with placing linguistics within the domain of communication theory. Pragmatists explore the ways in which we interpret utterances using strategies of INFERENCE and PRESUPPOSITION. Language is seen as DISCOURSE, that is, as an interactive event occurring between participants; a form of 'doing' rather than simply 'speaking'. Such approaches have yielded many important insights into the nature of language, most especially in the field of SPEECH ACT THEORY, developed by the linguistic philosophers J. L. Austin and J. R. Searle. They have also led to the writing of what are called **communicative grammars**, which attempt to account for the more formal features of language in terms of the dynamics of interaction.

Recent years have also seen the development of what used to be considered as 'fringe' areas of linguistics into mainstream subjects. This is particularly so in the case of **sociolinguistics** – the study of language and society. The linguist who bears most responsibility for this is the American sociolinguist William Labov. Before Labov the study of regional and geographical varieties of English was largely restricted to vanishing rural DIALECTS. Labov focussed his attention on the language of the cities, and in particular New York. In so doing he gave status to forms of speech, such as that of New York blacks, which had been little regarded in traditional sociolinguistic accounts. Since Labov, studies of ACCENT and dialect have more routinely taken 'modern' dialects as their target and have assumed a more rigorous methodology in their analysis. In particular, Labov introduced the concept of the **linguistic variable** – a recognisable dialect feature the use of which varies in a community according to age, class and gender. By mapping the use of variables he was able to provide a more accurate picture of dialect features than hitherto.

In many respects sociolinguistics represented a reaction against the 'armchair' linguistics of formalists such as Chomsky. Whereas Chomsky's data consisted of **idealised** samples of speech, free from the localised influences of particular dialects, sociolinguists took as their material precisely those features which formalists left out. The utterances they considered were actually used by real informants rather than dreamt up in the study. As a consequence of this concern with speech in a social context, the net of topics that sociolinguistics grapples with has widened considerably over the years. Although the hard core is still geographical variation, sociolinguists also explore the importance of gender, ethnicity, and nationality in language, whilst a sub-branch, ETHNOGRAPHY, explores the social and cultural variables that influence language.

Linguistics today, then, is a subject whose boundaries are forever widening and which presents no single face to the world. Branches of the subject continue to proliferate. In addition to neuro-linguistics we now have clinical linguistics, corpus linguistics, critical linguistics, forensic linguistics, and so on. Meanwhile, in the intellectual heartland, it continues to grow in elegance in the current work of Chomsky and other GENERATIVE grammarians. Indeed, one of the strengths of Chomsky, and one of the principal reasons for his continued dominance, is his ability to challenge, not simply other people's orthodoxies, but his own. The account of transformational grammar that exists today differs considerably from that of its first heady outing. And yet, despite the inherent radicalism of linguistics, there is much that suggests continuity. The leading ideas of the subject are now in place and, after many years in which it was considered as something of an 'upstart' among academic disciplines, it has finally achieved the respect it deserves as a major humanistic discipline. Which is only what one would expect, since the final subject matter of linguistics is not so much language but ourselves, our human existence in time and space, and that will always be endlessly fascinating.

2 General Terms and Concepts

INTRODUCTION

The principal chapters of this book concern terms and concepts related to the specific domains of linguistics. But there are some terms and ideas which are so widely used across all the fields of the subject that it seems sensible to discuss them separately. Inevitably the choice of what is general and what is specific is an individual one, and it may well be that some items that you might be expecting in this chapter are to be found elsewhere. I toyed, for example, with including the term UNIVERSAL GRAMMAR before deciding to include it in the chapter on syntax. So if you are disappointed in searching for an item here, the index should direct you to the relevant chapter.

GLOSSARY

Acceptable/unacceptable.   A pair of terms introduced by Noam CHOMSKY in 1965 to describe native speakers' intuitions about the grammatical correctness, or otherwise, of sentences. Native speakers of English, for example, will automatically know that *Bought he the watch?* is not a WELL-FORMED question in contemporary English, even without knowing what the rules for forming a question are. Our knowledge of GRAMMAR, in other words, is largely unconscious. It is this submerged, intuitive sense of grammaticality – 'the judgement of native speakers', as Chomsky calls it – that linguists use as their primary source of evidence in their enquiries into linguistic COMPETENCE.

The problem with such evidence, however, is that acceptability judgements are not necessarily an accurate reflection of well-formedness. Some conservative English speakers would find the sentence *Who did you meet at the party?* unacceptable on the grounds that the 'correct' pronoun form should be *whom*. Linguistically, however, there is nothing ungrammatical, or ill-formed, about the use of *who* here. It is simply that, for many speakers, the overt distinction between **subject** and **object** has become redundant in this instance. So, whilst acceptability judgements are important in providing evidence for grammaticality, they have to be treated with caution. They are liable to be influenced by taste, fashion, and social prejudice. Because of this it is necessary for the linguist to compensate by filtering out factors that are perceived to interfere with natural competence. Most linguists, especially those working in the Chomskyan tradition, attempt to do this by assuming that they are working with ideal native speakers whose own use of the language directly mirrors their competence and who, therefore, make perfect well-formedness judgements. This, of course, is a fiction, but arguably a necessary one if we are to arrive at an understanding of the underlying grammatical structure of the language.

The most useful way to regard the notion of acceptability is to see it as a PERFORMANCE concept. Native speakers will comment on the way in which their language is performed, for example, saying something doesn't sound right or look correct, based on their own intuitions. It is up to the linguist, subsequently, to interpret this data and decide to what extent judgements are a reflection of native competence, and concerned with well-formedness, and how far they reflect personal or social factors.

Competence.   A term introduced by CHOMSKY to describe the knowledge possessed by native users of a language that enables them to speak and understand their language fluently. This knowledge is internalised within speakers and not necessarily something they are aware of possessing. All English speakers, for example, will know the rules for forming questions, statements, and commands, but, unless they have studied SYNTAX, will probably be unable to say what these rules are.

There are two main forms of competence: grammatical and communicative. The first is concerned with the linguistic abilities described in the previous paragraph, that is, with our knowledge of language as a grammatical system. Because of this we know how to pronounce words (phonological knowledge), how to arrange them in PHRASES, CLAUSES, and SENTENCES (syntactic knowledge), and how to assign meanings to them (semantic knowledge). Communicative competence is concerned with our use of this internalised knowledge to communicate effectively. For example, if you asked someone the way to the station and received the reply *It looks like rain today*, the fact that the reply was grammatically competent and a WELL-FORMED sentence would be of no use whatever in deciding which route to take. Communicative competence involves knowing what counts as an appropriate reply. Amongst other things, it means knowing when to abbreviate an utterance – saying simply *The pictures*, for example, in reply to the question *Where are you going?*

instead of producing the grammatically complete *I am going to the pictures*. Knowing how much information to give, how best to arrange it, and generally being considerate of our audience are all essential features of communicative competence.

Other kinds of competence have also been suggested by linguists. Chomsky differentiates between grammatical and PRAGMATIC competence, the latter being concerned with our ability to interpret sentences using non-linguistic information. His own example involves a fellow lecturer saying *Today was a disaster*, after giving a special lecture. Given this context it's possible for the listener to infer that the lecture went down badly. Nothing in the utterance itself would tell us this, and indeed the interpretation may be incorrect, but we clearly need more than grammatical competence to understand its meaning completely. It's possible also to distinguish a creative, or poetic, competence: that is, the ability to use language in a uniquely striking way of the kind we find in significant literature – poems, novels, plays, and so forth.

But, however many competencies we distinguish, the important point to grasp is that competence describes a **cognitive**, or mental, skill. We are talking here of what native speakers understand of the structure and use of their language. The practical execution of those abilities in terms of actual speaking and writing comes within the scope of the partner term to competence – PERFORMANCE.

Diachrony (diachronic). One of a pair of terms (the other is SYNCHRONY), introduced by the linguist SAUSSURE, which together describe the two basic perspectives for the study of language. Diachrony is the historical perspective for studying language, as opposed to synchrony, which is concerned with its present state at any particular time. Studying language diachronically involves analysing the changes that have taken place over time in sounds, SYNTAX, and vocabulary.

The great period of **diachronic linguistics** was the nineteenth century, especially in PHONOLOGY, when linguists were engaged in studying the sound changes which took place in the Indo-European languages and establishing a number of important PHONOLOGICAL RULES. Today, most innovatory work in linguistics is synchronic in character. The central linguists of our time tend to be preoccupied with the current state of the language rather than with its historical development. None the less, an awareness of diachronic variation is important for a complete picture of any language, and it is essential for any linguist working on aspects of earlier periods of a language. We should bear in mind that synchronic and diachronic variation are two sides of the same coin. Because language is a dynamic, continually evolving system, we can only arrive at a true understanding of how it operates by seeing it in three-dimensional, rather than two-dimensional, form.

Distribution.   The distribution of an item, i.e. a PHONEME, MORPHEME, or WORD, is the total set of linguistic contexts in which it can occur. Every unit has a characteristic distribution. So, for example, a verb such as *appear* has a range of SENTENCE contexts in which it can be found as a consequence of its grammatical and semantic properties. We can describe this range as its 'distribution' within the linguistic system. The notion of distribution was originally developed in PHONOLOGY and later extended to other linguistic LEVELS. The distribution of phonemes in the linguistic system is a major factor in their classification. It is used, in particular, by phonologists to distinguish variants of phonemes (ALLO-PHONES). Most allophones are said to be in **complementary distribution**, that is, they are found in mutually exclusive environments within SYLLABLES.

  'Distribution' is also sometimes used to describe the range of social, rather than linguistic, contexts in which items occur. Sociolinguists, for example, will talk about the distribution of certain DIALECT or ACCENT FEATURES within a community.

Duality of patterning/structure.   A term that describes one of the defining properties of language, namely, its ability to combine essentially meaningless units into meaningful sequences. So, for example, the sounds represented by the letters *p*, *t*, and *a* are not in themselves meaningful. However, arranged in the sequence *pat*, they are. In other words, they are patterned once as sounds, and twice as a grammatical unit, i.e. a word. Not only that, but they can be recombined to make another meaningful sequence: *apt*. Duality of patterning goes up through the linguistic system, with an increase in the range and complexity of meaning as an outcome. Sounds combine to form MORPHEMES, which combine to form WORDS, and so on, up to SENTENCES. This is a crucial design FEATURE of language that allows us to use the same units over and over again in a variety of meaningful patterns.

Feature.   A term that refers to any typical or noticeable property of spoken or written language. Like many such terms in linguistics it can be used in either a general or a precise sense. Using it generally, we could say, for example, that a feature of spoken language is the use of INTONATION because intonation is a typical property of speech, or that complete grammatical structures are a feature of written language, on similar grounds. Used more precisely, however, 'feature' refers not simply to typical but to **distinctive** linguistic properties. It is with this sense that phonologists use it in DISTINCTIVE FEATURE theory. In this approach sounds are classified according to the specific properties they possess: they are either VOICED or unvoiced, nasal or oral, VOWELS or CONSONANTS, and so on. In this way a distinctive profile is built up of each PHONEME. In a similar way, some grammarians build up **feature speci-fications** for WORDS in terms of their grammatical properties; they are either NOUNS or non-nouns, countable or non-countable, and so on. SEMANTIC features, likewise, can be handled in this manner, as in the specification for *spinster* as 'human', 'adult', 'never married', and 'female'. Most features of this kind are 'either/or', i.e. **binary**, and the usual way of indicating this is by the use of plus and minus signs. The specification for *spinster* would thus read [+ human], [+ adult], [+ never married], [+ female] (or, perhaps, [- male]).

Grammar.   The grammar of a language consists of a set of rules that native speakers intuitively follow in the production of WELL-FORMED constructions. So, for example, knowing that regular VERBS form their past tense by adding 'ed', is a rule of English MORPHOLOGY, and knowing that 'ed' may be pronounced as /t/, /ɪd/, or /d/, depending on the environment, is a rule of English PHONOLOGY. The term 'rule' has a special sense here: we tend to think of rules as externally imposed constraints which everyone has to obey, like *Don't walk on the grass*, but linguistic rules are not of this kind. They are internal, as opposed to external, constraints and, as such, unconsciously present in the minds of native speakers. They are better understood as principles by which the language operates.

Having said that, however, 'grammar' is a word that is open to a number of different uses and interpretations. Some linguists, particularly those of a more traditional bent, limit its application to the domains of SYNTAX and morphology, whilst others use it in the larger sense assigned to it in the previous paragraph, in which it is seen to encapsulate the entire set of rules possessed by speakers, phonological and semantic as well as syntactic and morphological. However, it is true to say that debates over different models of grammar tend to concentrate largely on syntax, and because of this I have reserved a fuller discussion of these models until Chapter 4. You will find in the introduction to that chapter discussion of **descriptive**, **prescriptive**, and **theoretical grammars**, and in the chapter itself there are entries on UNIVERSAL GRAMMAR, GENER-ATIVE GRAMMAR, TRANSFORMATIONAL GRAMMAR, and FUNCTIONAL GRAMMAR.

Despite the different approaches to grammar, it is worth noting that for the great majority of modern linguists, grammatical knowledge, even though it may be largely unconscious knowledge, is a mental property, that is, it represents the way in which our minds work. If this is the case, then understanding grammar is an important key to understanding the way in which we make sense of ourselves and the world around us.

Langue.   A term introduced by the Swiss linguist SAUSSURE to distinguish one of the senses of the word 'language' – the others being *langage* (the general faculty of language) and *PAROLE* (the individual use we make of language). It refers to the language system shared by native speakers of a language. In some respects it is similar to CHOMSKY's term COMPETENCE, with the difference, however, that competence is a term which relates to ability rather than to the linguistic system itself. We could say that part of our competence as native speakers of a language is a knowledge of its *langue*, that is, its communicative system. The concept of *langue* is inevitably tied up with Saussure's view of language as a SIGN system in which words are symbolically related to events, processes, and things, in the outside world. As users of a language we know that this relationship is not a natural one – in other words, there is no natural connection between the sound string /tri/ and the object growing in the garden. The knowledge that this particular set of sounds is able to represent the object is part of the *langue* of English, as is the knowledge that the word *tree* is related to similar words such as *bush*, *shrub*, and *plant*.

The concept of *langue* emphasises the systematic relationships between items in a language, when viewed as a vast signalling system. These operate at all LEVELS, semantic, syntactic, and phonological. Semantically, words are related through processes such as SYNONYMY, ANTONYMY, POLYSEMY, and HYPONYMY, and syntactically, through their classification into NOUNS, VERBS, ADJECTIVES and so on, each with distinctive PARADIGMATIC and SYNTAGMATIC properties. Similarly, the distinctive sounds of a language, its PHONEMES, are systematically related so that changing or rearranging them will create new words.

Inevitably, the notion of *langue* emphasises the importance of language as a social phenomenon. This again makes it somewhat different from Chomsky's 'competence', where the tendency is to see language as a biological and genetically inherited faculty. But in both, the view of language as an abstract system capable of being studied at a level divorced from individual usage, is held in common. Similarly, both approaches make some accommodation for individual usage. Chomsky refers to this as PERFORMANCE and Saussure as *PAROLE*. Again, these terms are similar, but not identical, and you should see the particular entries for further discussion.

Level (of analysis).   A language 'level' is a major dimension of structural organisation capable of being analysed separately from other dimensions, or levels. The most widely recognised levels are those of PHONOLOGY, SYNTAX, and SEMANTICS. Sometimes, however, PHONETICS is distinguished from phonology, as a separate level, and PRAGMATICS and LEXIS are also similarly distinguished from semantics, as is MORPHOLOGY from syntax. To a large extent the number of levels will depend on the linguistic model being used. Those which use the term GRAMMAR in a narrow rather than an expanded sense, for example, will see it as a distinct level incorporating the two sub-levels of syntax and morphology.

Older linguistic approaches viewed these levels as operating independently of each other. Analysis usually involved proceeding from the 'lower' levels of phonetics through the progressively 'higher' levels of phonology and syntax towards semantics. Modern linguistics, however, sees the relationship between them as more fluid and less determined by concepts of hierarchy.

Like many linguistic terms, 'level' is used in a number of different contexts. In TRANSFORMATIONAL GRAMMAR it is used to distinguish **deep** from **surface structure** (more recently, D structure and S structure), both of which are seen as 'levels of representation'. More commonly, the different structural layers within one of the established linguistic levels are also distinguished by the same term. So within syntax, for example, one might talk of the levels (sometimes RANKS) of SENTENCE, CLAUSE, PHRASE, WORD, and MORPHEME.

Marked/unmarked.   The concept of 'markedness' is variously interpreted in linguistics. In GENERATIVE GRAMMAR it refers to a distinction between sets of FEATURES, where one is considered to be neutral and the other non-neutral. So, for example, there is a formal feature, called an **inflection**, marking the plural in most English NOUNS, i.e. the addition of 's'; the plural is therefore 'marked', and the singular 'unmarked'. In describing the singular as 'unmarked' we are identifying it as the neutral form of the word, free from any modification, and the plural as derived from it by a process of marking. A similar case can be made for the inflection (see MORPHEME) 'ed', which formally marks the presence of the past TENSE. And in PHONOLOGY marking is important in distinguishing the DISTINCTIVE FEATURES of speech, e.g. ± VOICE. Here the symbol ± tells us that the presence of voicing is marked and its absence is unmarked.

Other interpretations of marking involve frequency of occurrence rather than presence *vs.* absence. In DISCOURSE ANALYSIS, for example, it is sometimes said that a falling INTONATION pattern is unmarked, because more common than a rising one, which is correspondingly marked. Yet another interpretation can be found in the SEMANTIC analysis of words, where pairs of items are seen as marked or unmarked, respectively, on the grounds that one has a wider DISTRIBUTION, or application, than another, e.g. *old/young* (*How old is John?* is more normal than *How young is John?*). A related SENSE has to do with specificity, where one term is more specific than another, e.g. *dog/bitch* (*dog* can be used to refer to animals of either sex, but *bitch* is limited to the female). And, finally, linguists interested in UNIVERSAL GRAMMAR use marking to distinguish properties that can be found in all languages as against those which are exceptional and which can only be found in a few.

The concept of markedness, therefore, can be used in a variety of contexts to distinguish what we can consider as the base, normative, or most common forms of items or features from those which are derived, non-normative, or less frequent.

Paradigmatic.   A term that describes the substitutional relationships that a linguistic unit has with other units. In the sentence *I like linguistics*, for example, each of the words can be exchanged with a number of others without changing the basic syntactic arrangement:

you	love	art
they	like	bread
I	**hate**	**linguistics**
we	despise	him
people	adore	treats

Substitutability is one of the criteria important in the classification of words into various categories such as NOUN, VERB, ADJECTIVE, PRONOUN and so on. Items which can substitute for *I* and *linguistics* will be pronouns, or nouns, whilst those which can substitute for *hate* will be verbs. Paradigmatic relations of this kind operate at all LEVELS of language. In the sound system, for instance, the PHONEMES /p/, /k/, and /t/, can all be substituted for /f/ in the context of /-ɪt/. Indeed, it is on the basis of such possible substitutions that phonologists are able to determine the phonemes of a language. Sets of paradigmatically related items are often referred to as **systems**, and so linguists talk about the 'CONSONANT system', or the 'pronoun system' of a language.

Most of us become aware of paradigmatic relations when we are searching for the right word to use in a particular context. We may know it's a verb with a stronger meaning than *frightens*, and a weaker than *terrifies*. We try various possibilities until we settle on *scares*. Some people have particular difficulty with the principle of substitution, and in severe cases may select a word from a totally different class. This is related to a special form of linguistic handicap known as **aphasia**, of which there are several varieties.

Paradigmatic relations are best visualised as the vertical dimension of language, but there is also the linear dimension, i.e. the arrangement of words sequentially. These relations are termed SYNTAGMATIC. Together with paradigmatic relations they constitute the identity of an item within the linguistic system as a whole. In other words, every linguistic item – phoneme, MORPHEME, GRAPHEME, WORD – can be characterised, or identified, by where it is able to occur sequentially with other units, i.e. its DISTRIBUTION, and by reference to the set of terms with which it can be interchanged. (See also SAUSSURE.)

Parole.   A term introduced by the Swiss linguist SAUSSURE to express one of the principal senses of the word 'language', the others being *langage* (the general faculty of language) and *LANGUE*   (the system of communication within a community). Whereas *langue* specifies the abstract code that users of a particular language all have access to, *parole* specifies their linguistic behaviour, i.e. what they do with language. Since the introduction of the term by Saussure, however, the precise extent of its application, and, more particularly, its relation with the co-term *langue*, have often been debated. In some respects *parole* is similar to CHOMSKY's term PERFORMANCE, which also specifies the individual use we make of language, but performance tends to be limited by most linguists to the actual way in which linguistic processes, such as speaking and writing, are carried out, whereas *parole* indicates the specific products of those processes.

The term is arguably of greatest use in PRAGMATICS, where it can be used to describe that area of meaning which is not recoverable from the system itself. So, for example, if we take the utterance *I love you*, a knowledge of the system of English, its *langue*, will yield a certain amount of intelligence: the fact that *love* has a specific SENSE, that the pronouns *I* and *you* relate to the speaker and listener, respectively. A full interpretation, however, involves knowing the context in which the utterance is made, whether it is said by a child or a lover, as a declaration, or in an attempt to escape the washing up.

Used in this way, *parole* signifies those FEATURES of language, some of them situational, which are additional to language as a CODE, but which are essential for the total realisation of any linguistic act. A second, related, use of the term is its application to the particular choices we make within the linguistic system. So, for example, the INTONATION and **stress** systems of a language operate in ways that can be abstractly described, but when we say something we have to choose from a range of options on offer. Our particular rendering of an utterance can thus be analysed at the LEVEL of *parole*, or individual instance, as well as at that of *langue*.

Historically, linguists have been more concerned about *langue* than about *parole*, but with developments in pragmatics and the revaluation of language in use, the interests of *parole* have been more widely promoted. More particularly, trends in disciplines such as SOCIOLINGUIS-TICS have tended to blur the distinction between *langue* and *parole*; so SPEECH ACTS, previously seen as examples of *parole*, are now frequently seen to work in a systematic way. As with the COMPETENCE/performance divide, which is similarly being questioned, the absolute separation between *parole* and *langue* is increasingly difficult to sustain, and it is safest to argue, along with the linguists Roman Jakobson and Mikhail Bakhtin, that the relationship is dialectical rather than oppositional.

Performance.   A term introduced by CHOMSKY to describe 'the actual use of language in concrete situations' (*Aspects*, 1965, p. 4). What Chomsky seems to mean by this is the physical execution of the linguistic system in terms of actual utterances and pieces of writing. So, for example, if we take the sentence *I hate linguistics*, it exists both as an abstract entity, something we are able to construct and understand because of our native COMPETENCE, and also as a physical entity, a sequence of sounds or letters capable of being reproduced, or performed, by as many speakers and writers as care to do so. And each performance of the sentence will be different, because no one speaks or writes in exactly the same way as anyone else. Being able to perform an utterance correctly is important in communicating successfully but, equally, we should bear in mind that **performance errors** do not necessarily reflect any lack of linguistic competence. Everyone makes slips of the tongue occasionally; sometimes these reflect grammatical uncertainty, but more often than not they are due to a variety of performance factors such as tiredness, boredom, drunkenness, drugs, external distractions, and so forth. Deciding whether a linguistic difficulty is due to performance or competence is often important in early language learning. A young child's inability to make a certain sound may be because s/he does not have that particular PHONEME in his/her arsenal of sounds, or it may be a motor difficulty to do with the movement of various speech organs.

The majority of linguists are more interested in competence than in performance, but for some, particularly PSYCHOLINGUISTS, performance is a very important concept. The study of performance errors has become increasingly significant in determining how we produce and comprehend utterances. Slips of the tongue invariably follow a pattern, and it is also the case that hesitations and repetitions are frequently DISCOURSE markers used in the management and planning of utterances. Indeed, the boundary between competence and performance becomes increasingly difficult to maintain the more closely we examine particular instances. Most linguistic phenomena can be studied both in terms of their conformity to an abstract system and as concrete realisations. In this sense it is useful to consider the notions of competence and performance as complementary rather than as opposites. (See also *LANGUE* and *PAROLE*.)

Productivity (productive). Productivity has both a general and a specific sense. In its general sense it refers to the creative capacity of language users to produce an endless number of new sentences, in contrast to the communication systems of animals, which are limited to set formulas and are thus 'unproductive'. Productivity is, therefore, one of the design FEATURES of human language. In its more restricted sense it refers to the use made by a language of a specific feature. Features are productive if they are currently used to produce further instances of the same type. For example, the plural affix 's' which is added onto the base form of NOUNS is productive because any new noun which is adopted into English will employ it, whereas the change from *foot* to *feet* is unproductive because it represents a fossilised plural form limited to a small set of nouns. Productivity is a useful concept for establishing the potentiality of particular linguistic patterns. Some, for example the prefix 'un', are **semi-productive**, because they are sometimes, but not always, attached to words to form their opposites, e.g. *lovely* > *unlovely*, but not *good* > **ungood*.

Rank. A term used in FUNCTIONAL GRAMMAR, particularly by the linguist **Michael Halliday** to describe the hierarchical arrangement of linguistic items within a linguistic level. So, for example, within the grammatical LEVEL we have the following ranks: SENTENCE–CLAUSE–GROUP (PHRASE in other models) -WORD-MORPHEME. The idea is that morphemes build into words, words into groups, and so on, up to the highest rank, sentences. The term **rank-shift** is used to describe a process whereby a particular unit is 'shifted' down the scale to operate within a lower rank. This is characteristically the case with **relative clauses**. In the sequence *the man* **who broke the bank at Monte Carlo**, the relative clause is contained within a NOUN group headed by *the man*. In other words, it has been rank-shifted to the rank of group.

Sign (signifier, signified). The term 'sign' is frequently used by people studying communication theory to characterise the way in which meaning is communicated, symbolically, via certain objects within individual cultures; thus the Cross operates as a sign within Christian cultures. The study of signs is termed **semiotics**. Not surprisingly, linguistics has been influenced by semiotics to the extent that words are sometimes described as **linguistic signs**. It's not difficult to see the connection here because it can be argued that words represent the world in a symbolic, rather than a literal, way, and that understanding these symbolic relationships is what distinguishes speakers from non-speakers of a language. The linguist most closely associated with the concept of linguistic signs is the Swiss linguist SAUSSURE. He argued that words comprised two elements: a sound image, that is, a pronunciation form (or **signifier**) and a meaning, or SENSE (termed the **signified**). So, to use the example Saussure himself used, the word 'tree' is made up of a sound image (or signifier), /tri/, and a sense (or signified), indicating 'treeness'. The relationship between them is a conventional, not a natural one: there is no reason why society shouldn't use any other sequence of sounds to represent 'treeness' if it so wished. The signifier, then, acts as a label, but for a concept, not an actual object. It is the signifier and signified together, the complete word, or sign, which is used by us as speakers of the language to refer to actual trees. This yields two types of meaning which words are capable of: **signification** or **sense**, and **reference**. Figure 4 illustrates the relationships on which these types of meaning depend.

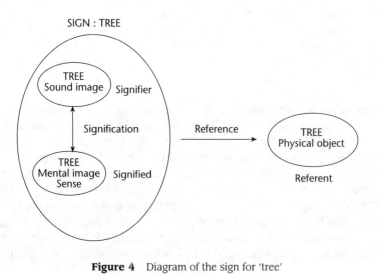

Figure 4   Diagram of the sign for 'tree'

The notion that words are internally structured as signs and represent the world symbolically has had an important influence on the study of language. Its effect has been most profoundly felt in SEMANTICS where the study of SENSE RELATIONSHIPS (that is, the relationships between signifieds) has led to some important insights into the ways in which words 'mean'. But beyond that, the splitting of the sign in this way between sound image and concept has become part of that movement of thought termed **structuralism**, which has had such a profound impact on interpretative procedures in literature and the arts generally.

Synchrony (synchronic).   A term introduced by the linguist SAUSSURE that refers to the state of a language as it exists at any given time. If we think of language as resembling a game of chess, then the linguist who is engaged in studying language synchronically is like an observer who comes in while the game is in play and analyses it from the present distribution of the pieces. The observer is not interested in how they came to be in their respective places on the board, being concerned only with the relationships between the pieces as they currently exist. Considerations of etymology and derivation are consequently irrelevant.

To a large extent, modern linguistics has been dominated by a synchronic perspective. Much work has been done on the systematic description of languages, and many grammatical theories, notably GENERATIVE GRAMMAR and TRANSFORMATIONAL GRAMMAR, have adopted a predominantly synchronic approach. This is not to say that synchronic grammarians ignore changes in the language, but, generally, they are only concerned with the more obvious ones and do not seek to account for them by appealing to historical factors.

Synchrony is one of a pair of terms; the other is DIACHRONY, and between them they capture the two basic perspectives for the study of language. Whereas synchrony is concerned with the present condition of a language, diachrony is concerned with its evolution over time.

Syntagmatic (syntagm).   A term that refers to the sequential characteristics of language. When we construct WORDS and SENTENCES we follow a certain order in arranging the individual items. To form the word /pɪt/, for example, we are obliged to utter the particular PHONEMES in that order; any other order would either make an entirely different word, or be nonsense. The phonemes, which in this instance are the constituents of the word, are referred to as **syntagms**, and the relationships that they enter into with the phonemes on either side are referred to as **syntagmatic relations**. If we identified all the syntagmatic relations which a phoneme was capable of entering into in a particular language it would provide us with a key to the range of possible words that could be formed using that phoneme. Establishing syntagmatic relations is important in the study of PHONOTACTICS, which is the study of the permitted or non-permitted arrangements or sequences of phonemes in a language. We know, for example, that English does not permit SYLLABLE endings in which /t/ is followed by /b/.

Syntagmatic relationships can be formed at all linguistic LEVELS. PHRASES and CLAUSES follow an implicit order in the arrangement of their constituents. These arrangements can often be altered as, for example, when a sentence is rearranged to make something thematically more important. But there is a limit to such rearranging: we can't move an item to any position. In the phrase *the table*, which consists of a DETERMINER and NOUN, we can put a variety of items between *the* and *table*, but we are not permitted to reverse them. Again, if we identified all the syntagmatic relations that a word was capable of entering into within the language it would provide us with a key to the range of possible constructions that could be formed using it. Syntagmatically related constituents, whether phonemes in a word, or words in a phrase, are referred to as **structures**.

Syntagmatic relations are one half of a pair of relationships, the other half of which is termed PARADIGMATIC relations, which together make up a constituent's function (see IMMEDIATE CONSTITUENCY ANALYSIS) within the language. Paradigmatic relations concern the ability of a constituent to substitute for another constituent in the same environment, or context; so /b/ could be exchanged for /p/ before the sequence /ɪt/ to form the word /bɪt/, and *a* could be exchanged for *the* in the sequence *the table*. Syntagmatic relations are best visualised as horizontal, or linear, as opposed to the vertical kind of paradigmatic relations. Figure 5 shows how the Swiss linguist SAUSSURE envisaged them.

We are most likely to become aware of syntagmatic relationships when we experience difficulties in sequencing sounds in pronunciation or when we don't know how to complete a phrase or clause. Severe

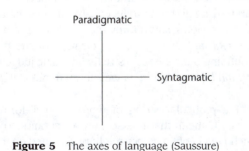

Figure 5   The axes of language (Saussure)

difficulties in forming correct sequences of sounds or words in a language may be an indication of some form of linguistic handicap.

Variety.   A term used, most commonly in SOCIOLINGUISTICS and STYLISTICS, to describe a particular form, or kind, of language. Geographical varieties of English, for example, would include regional DIALECTS, such as Cockney and Glaswegian, whereas American English could be described as an international variety of English. The term is also used in relation to different linguistic REGISTERS. So, religious English, or literary English, which have their own distinctive vocabulary and forms of expression, could be described as varieties of English. Many varieties are the product of a number of different ingredients, such as social class, occupation, age, gender, and context. Not surprisingly, the term has a fairly generous application and attempts to give it a precise definition have not been successful.

Well-formed/ill-formed.   Terms that linguists use to describe the grammatical status of an utterance or sentence. Many people popularly use the terms 'correct'/'incorrect' for this purpose, but the difficulty with the notion of correctness is that it blurs the distinction between social and linguistic judgements. A sentence like *I ain't got no money*, for example, might well be considered, by some, incorrect because it uses forms not recognised by standard GRAMMAR. But it is clearly not incorrect in the same way that *Got ain't money no I* is (the * is used by linguists to indicate an 'ill-formed' sentence). The first version, despite its use of the **double negative** and the colloquial term *ain't*, follows a distinct order in the sequencing of words, whilst the second one doesn't. The words in the second version are assembled randomly and, as a consequence, the string is uninterpretable. Describing both versions as 'incorrect', therefore, misses an important distinction between them. Despite its non-standard form, the first version has the regular construction pattern of an English SENTENCE – subject, VERB, object – and although there are two negatives they are in their rightful places. In other words, there is an underlying grammar to its construction – admittedly, not that of the standard version *I haven't any money*, but a grammar none the less, whereas *Got ain't money no I* is clearly not the product of any grammar. Confining ourselves to a strictly linguistic judgement then, we can say that *I ain't got no money* is well-formed, but *Got ain't money no I* isn't.

Saying that a particular string of words is well-formed, however, doesn't necessarily mean that it is socially ACCEPTABLE. There are occasions on which *I ain't got no money* might be frowned on, but that would be a social rather than a linguistic judgement, even though possibly disguised as a linguistic one. It's important not to confuse the two. It's also important to bear in mind that a sentence may be well-formed on one linguistic LEVEL but ill-formed on another. The sentence *My brother is a girl* is perfectly well-formed in terms of its SYNTAX – all the words are in the right places – but it is ill-formed semantically because it is manifestly a contradiction. Similarly, one might have the right word but an ill-formed pronunciation or spelling.

But a word of caution here: well-formedness, particularly semantic well-formedness, can only properly be judged contextually. Consider again the sentence *My brother is a girl*, which I called a contradiction; there are circumstances in which even this could make sense – if it were a comment on my brother's effeminacy, or perceived lack of manliness, for example, or if used ironically. In this case the observation would be exploiting the connotative (see ASSOCIATIVE MEANING) as opposed to the conceptual SENSE of the term *girl* and, as such, well formed.

3 Phonetics and Phonology

INTRODUCTION

Phonetics and phonology are concerned with the study of speech and, more particularly, with the dependence of speech on sound. In order to understand the distinction between these two terms it is important to grasp the fact that sound is both a physical and a mental phenomenon. Both speaking and hearing involve the performance of certain physical functions, either with the organs in our mouths or with those in our ears. At the same time, however, neither speaking nor hearing are simply mechanical, neutral processes. We endow the sounds we make and hear with meaning. They have a mental or cognitive existence as well as a physical one. Another way of putting this is to say that sounds are psychologically, as well as physically, real. Psychological reality is important in linguistics. Sometimes things can be psychologically real without having any real-world correlates. So, for example, most people will idealise their own speech and hear themselves speaking perfectly clearly and accent-neutral, when in fact the reverse is the case.

This division between the physical and mental dimensions of speech sounds is reflected in the terms 'phonetics' and 'phonology'. Precisely where the division comes has been, and still is, a matter of fierce debate between phoneticians and phonologists. No phonetician would say that s/he simply studies the way in which speech sounds are physically produced, transmitted or received, and phonologists would not restrict themselves to the way we construct mental shapes from sounds, but none the less there is a broad difference in their approach. Phonetics is really a technically based subject concerned with measuring sound, recording frequencies, and generally studying the physiology of speech. Phonology, on the other hand, is essentially preoccupied with sound as a system for carrying meaning. Its fundamental concern is with identifying PHONEMES. These are the small building blocks of the spoken language that provide the skeleton framework of speech. They are part of the mental blueprint that native users carry in their heads.

There are three main dimensions to phonetics: articulatory phonetics, acoustic phonetics, and auditory phonetics. These correspond to the production, transmission, and reception of sound.

(i)   Articulatory phonetics

This is concerned with studying the processes by which we actually make, or articulate, speech sounds. It's probably the aspect of phonetics that students of linguistics encounter first, and arguably the most accessible to non-specialists since it doesn't involve the use of complicated machines. The organs that are employed in the articulation of speech sounds – the tongue, teeth, lips, lungs and so on – all have more basic biological functions as they are part of the respiratory and digestive systems of our bodies. Humans are unique in using these biological organs for the purpose of articulating speech sounds. Speech is formed by a stream of air coming up from the lungs through the glottis into the mouth or nasal cavities and being expelled through the lips or nose. It's the modifications we make to this stream of air with organs normally used for breathing and eating that produce sounds. The principal organs used in the production of speech are shown in Figure 6.

Whereas acoustic phonetics describes speech sounds in terms of their relative frequencies, articulatory phonetics describes them in terms of the particular organs that are involved in their production. Sounds like /b/ and /p/ (*bit* and *pit*) that involve the lips are 'labial' sounds, and those which involve the teeth, such as /θ/ and /ð/ (*thigh* and *thy*) are described as 'dental'. (For more information on this, see PLACE OF ARTICULATION.) Not only do speech sounds differ from each other in their place of articulation but they also differ in the way, or manner, in which they are articulated. In producing /b/ and /p/, for example, the lips come together and air is released in a mini explosion – these sounds are 'plosives'; whilst in the case of /θ/ and /ð/ the tongue touches the top teeth and air is released continuously with friction – these sounds are 'fricatives' (for more information see MANNER OF ARTICULATION). Using articulation features to describe speech sounds has a number of advantages. To begin with it's very easy to distinguish between CONSONANT and VOWEL sounds, since consonants characteristically restrict the air flow in some way as a consequence of contact between the speech organs, whereas vowels do not. In addition, it's possible, by combining manner and place of articulation together with VOICE, to give a precise description of each distinctive speech sound. Articulatory phonetics has been particularly powerful in recent years in providing a descriptive framework for speech sounds that can be used by linguists across the discipline.

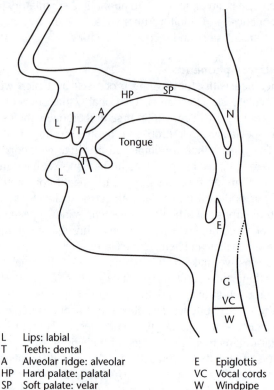

L   Lips: labial
T   Teeth: dental
A   Alveolar ridge: alveolar
HP   Hard palate: palatal   E   Epiglottis
SP   Soft palate: velar   VC   Vocal cords
U   Uvula: uvular   W   Windpipe
N   Nasal passage: nasal
G   Glottis: glottal

Figure 6   The organs of speech

(ii)   Acoustic phonetics

This is concerned with studying the properties of sound as a consequence of variations in air pressure. When we speak we disturb the
molecules in the air around us. These molecules **oscillate**, that is, they
move back and forth rather like the swing of a pendulum. Each complete
movement back and forward is called a **cycle**. Phoneticians plot these
cycles using instruments to arrive at the particular **frequency** of a
sound. The more cycles that occur in a second the higher the frequency.
Using this kind of measurement it is possible to show that on average
the frequency of a woman's voice is twice that of a man's.

Much more interestingly, however, it is also possible to measure the frequency of individual speech sounds, both vowels and consonants, and show that they have their own distinctive resonance. If you imagine that the vocal tract is a bit like an organ pipe, then what speech organs, such as the tongue, the lips and the teeth, do is to alter the length and shape of the pipe by interfering with the flow of sound, much after the manner of a musical instrument. As a consequence, the frequency of the sounds we make is continually changing. Phoneticians use a **spectograph**, a machine designed to analyse/decompose sound into its acoustic parameters, to capture the fluctuating frequency of speech. This produces a **spectogram**, a kind of chart that shows frequency in terms of relative degrees of light and dark. On the basis of these kinds of experiments phoneticians can establish the acoustic structure of speech and demonstrate the distinctiveness of particular segments.

(iii)   Auditory phonetics

This is the branch of phonetics that is concerned with the perception of speech sounds, i.e. how they are heard. Phoneticians working in this area study the physical ways in which the sound pressure waves we create by speaking are converted into meaningful units of speech. Part of this involves knowing something about the structure of the ear and the processes by which sound is carried along the nervous system to the brain. In simple terms, what happens is that the **outer ear** collects the sounds from the world around us, the **middle ear** amplifies them and passes them to the **inner ear** where the impulses are relayed to the **auditory nerve**, a kind of fibre optic cable, and onwards to the speech centres in the brain. At various stages the sounds are processed into linguistic units and ultimately into items of meaning. The areas of the brain considered to be most important in the processing of language are **Wernicke's area** and **Broca's area**, both of which are usually located in the left hemisphere in right-handed people.

Because of its link with perception, auditory phonetics has been very prominent in research into how the brain interprets sound linguistically. Phonetic units in a word are not strung together like beads on a string. When we hear the sounds in *cat*, for example, we don't process the sounds individually and add them together. We hear them as a meaningful sequence. The sounds are **smeared** across each other. The 'c' runs into the 'a', which runs into the 't'. This process is known as COAR-TICULATION. The question that phoneticians ask, then, is 'how is it, given this smearing, that we can reconstruct as hearers the underlying word?' A number of theories have been advanced to account for this but no single theory has been entirely successful in accounting for all aspects of speech perception. The following are among the most frequently cited theories:

(a) *Motor theory*. A theory developed in the 1960s that argued that listeners are able to reconstruct messages from the process of smearing by reference to their own speech production. In other words, because I also smear the sounds in *cat* when I pronounce them, I am able to use that knowledge, albeit subconsciously, in interpreting the same sounds when I hear them.

(b) *Analysis by synthesis theory*. A more complex theory, again developed in the 1960s. According to this, listeners analyse speech sounds for their DISTINCTIVE FEATURES. These features are the product of the articulation processes involved in speech production. As we have said, each sound has its own distinctive frequency and its own distinctive method of articulation. As native speakers we possess that knowledge and are able to use it in decoding incoming signals linguistically.

(c) *The associative store theory of speech perception*. A theory inspired by the development of computers in the 1970s and 1980s. Phoneticians using this model see the brain as a processor. An incoming sound wave is scanned by this processor, which automatically has access to a LEXICON of words stored in our memory banks. The information contained there includes phonetic detail about the sounds of words. The processor simply looks for a 'best fit' between the sound wave and items in the lexicon. When a match is found, sometimes on some kind of statistical basis ('it's most likely to be this one'), the item is pulled from the memory and handed on for further processing to other modules, whilst the original sound stimulus is discarded.

Auditory phoneticians are also interested in the issue of whether speech is special. In other words, is there something unique about speech that distinguishes it from other sound stimuli? This has implications for theories about the innateness of linguistic knowledge. Experiments with infants who are still in a prelinguistic stage have shown that they can perceive some of the properties of speech such as those involved in place and manner of articulation before being exposed to those sounds naturally. In addition, despite the fact that the frequencies of a child's speech production and those of an adult are quite dissimilar, children have no difficulty in perceiving sounds as representations of the same phonetic unit. For example, the frequencies that specify an /ɛ/ for a child are very different from those that specify an /ɛ/

produced by an adult male and yet they are perceived as the same unit. In other words, part of the processing of speech must involve **normalisation**. This is a process whereby listeners judge sounds to be equivalent even when acoustically they may be very different.

Not surprisingly, auditory phonetics has become increasingly important to those linguists interested in the mental processes of language acquisition (see CHILD LANGUAGE). It should also be apparent that, as we have said, although phonetics is concerned with the physical properties and processes of speaking and listening, these cannot, in practice, be completely separated from the cognitive or mental processes involved, nor should they be. Any account of speech sounds, whether of their production, transmission, or reception, must show some recognition of the dual dimension that constitutes their existence. It is here that phonology comes into its own.

Whilst phonetics is preoccupied with the technical dimension of speech, phonology is more concerned with its structural properties. Phonologists examine the systematic relationships between sounds within the grammar of the language. Of central importance here is the concept of the PHONEME. Phonemes are abstract units of sound that are part of the mental apparatus of native users of a language, and that constitute our essential competence as speakers and listeners. Having said that, however, not all linguists accept their existence. Some prefer to see the structural relationships between sounds in terms of their DISTINCTIVE FEATURES. These can be phonetically demonstrated to exist and, as a consequence, so the argument goes, make the phoneme concept unnecessary. However, most will accept that whilst the phoneme cannot be shown to have a physical existence, it none the less has a psychological reality in that native users find it operationally convenient. The best compromise is perhaps for us to regard the phoneme as a label, or cover term, for a bundle of smaller features rather like the way the concept of 'character' in literary theory can be broken down into smaller observable behavioural characteristics, such as 'arrogance', 'kindness', 'severity', and so on.

The ultimate goal of phonology is to describe the rules that we unconsciously obey in turning sounds into meaningful units. This involves more than simply studying the behaviour of phonemes, of course. The sound system also carries meaning through the patterns of stress we adopt in speaking, as well as through variations of pitch or tone. The study of this is termed **prosody** (see INTONATION). Prosody entails examining units larger than the phoneme, in particular the SYLLABLE, the **foot**, and the **tone** unit. These are termed **suprasegmentals**, meaning that they are units above the segmental level of phonemes. It is here that phonology becomes important to areas of linguistic study such as DISCOURSE ANALYSIS and PRAGMATICS.

Phonological rules are also important in the study of SYNTAX and, more particularly, MORPHOLOGY. Morphology is concerned with the structure of words and with the way in which we alter them, either by inflections or by the addition of various prefixes or suffixes. Such alterations have a phonological side to them in that they frequently involve pronunciation changes. For example, the plural morpheme 's' that we add to nouns such as *apricot*, *apple*, and *peach*, is pronounced in the following ways respectively: /s/ /z/ /ɪz/. The rules that determine pronunciation in these instances derive from the character of the final phoneme in the singular noun. The study of such rules is termed MORPHOPHONOLOGY.

The entries that follow provide a description of the principal aspects of phonetics and phonology in alphabetical order. Some of the detail is of a technical nature whilst other detail is more theoretical and speculative. This is in the nature of a subject which, as I have said, attempts to link physical and mental phenomena. Because of this you will also find some degree of overlapping in entries and a fair degree of instructions to 'see also'.

GLOSSARY

Allophone: see PHONEME.

Cardinal vowel system.   A reference system devised by the English phonetician Daniel Jones (1881–1967), for plotting the position of VOWELS in the mouth during their articulation. The principal difficulty with determining the precise articulation features of vowels is that, unlike CONSONANTS, they do not involve any interruption of, or interference with, the air flow. As a consequence, their precise location in the mouth cannot be described in the same way as for consonants. The cardinal vowel system gets round this problem by providing a set of reference points for the mapping of vowels. It does so by visualising the centre of the mouth as a grid diagram, the dimensions of which correspond to the 'vowel space', from where vowels are articulated (see Figure 7). This allows linguists to plot the movements of the tongue and the lips more precisely.

It's important to bear in mind that the vowels indicated on the system are 'idealised'. That is, they do not represent the actual vowels of any particular language. In other words they are phonetic symbols, not phonological ones. For example, the [i] of Figure 7 represents a vowel sound that comes from the highest and most forward part of the vowel space. But the articulation of this sound in English is not in such an ideal

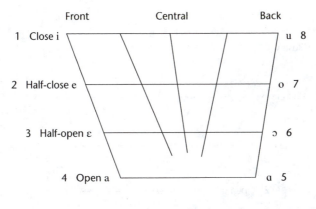

Figure 7 Primary cardinal vowels

position. The /i/ in *bee*, for example, although very near this point, is slightly lower. You can feel this if you compare it with French /i/, which is higher than its English counterpart, in the following words:

eels
ils

Similarly, English /u/, as in *sue*, is slightly lower than [u] in the cardinal vowel system. And again, English /ɛ/, as in *bet*, is mid-way between [e] and [ɛ] on the chart, whilst /ʌ/, as in *cup*, is much further forward than [ʌ]. You can compare the relative positions of these and other vowels if you compare Figures 7, 8, and 9.

The cardinal vowel system consists of eight **primary** vowels (Figure 7), and ten **secondary** vowels (Figure 8). The difference between the two sets is that the secondary vowels reverse the lip rounding of the primary set. That is, vowels that are rounded in one set are unrounded in the other and vice versa. English doesn't exploit differences in lip rounding much, but some languages do. You can feel the difference between the sets if you compare [i], the high unrounded vowel, which as I have said is found in *bee*, with its rounded equivalent [y] as in the French words *tu* and *lune*. In both sets, vowels from positions 1 and 9, [i] and [y], are articulated with the front of the tongue as high and as forward as possible, consistent with their being vowels (that is, without interfering with the flow of air and thus becoming consonants). Similarly, numbers 4 and 12, [a] and [œ], are articulated with the front of the tongue as low and as forward as possible, consistent with their being vowels. Correspondingly, the vowels 5 and 13, [ɑ], and [ɒ], are

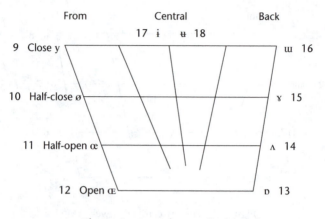

Figure 8   Secondary cardinal vowels

articulated with the back of the tongue as low and back as possible, and 8 and 16, [u] and [ɯ], with the back of the tongue as high and back as possible. Numbers 17 and 18, [ɨ] and [ʉ], are articulated with the central part of the tongue as high as possible. The remaining vowels are set out at equidistant points from these positions using a grid pattern.

This map of the vowel space enables linguists to specify any vowel using the three features of: (i) tongue height, (ii) part of tongue (front, centre, back), and (iii) lip posture. At the same time, however, because the cardinal vowel system is idealised it doesn't give us an inventory of all the vowels that are in use in a particular language. English has its own subset that we would need to include if we wanted to provide a diagram of English vowel positions, principally the short vowels, /æ/ (bad), /ɪ/ (sit), /ʊ/ (good), and /ə/ (banana). Similarly, there are many vowels in the cardinal system that do not occur in English, such as most of the secondary vowels. To include them in a vowel chart of English vowels would clearly be superfluous. To provide a chart specifically for English we have to provide a language-specific version of the system. Figure 9 shows this for the variety of English known as Received Pronunciation (see VOWELS for further information about this variety).

Coarticulation.   The effect of the influence of one articulatory segment on adjacent segments. In normal running speech it is usual to economise on the effort involved in articulation by relaxing motor control of the speech organs. This results in segments running into each other. Because speech segments contain a fair amount of redundant information this process doesn't usually harm communication. Most people strike a balance between ease of articulation and the need to

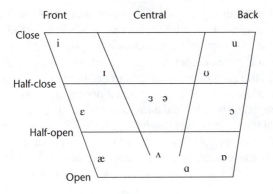

Figure 9 English vowels (southern British English)

prevent loss of communication. In the word *eighth*, for example, which phonologically we can transcribe as /eɪtθ/, the articulation of /t/ will tend, under the influence of the following phoneme /θ/, to move forward and become more dental – [t̪]. This process is sometimes called **assimilation**, because one sound moves in the direction of, or 'assimilates' to, another. Some linguists, however, restrict the term 'assimilation' to occurrences that are phonological rather than simply phonetic, that is, where the effect is to substitute one phoneme for another. Such substitutions frequently occur in running speech at word boundaries. In the sequence /ðæt bɔɪ/ (*that boy*), for example, the VOICELESS alveolar plosive /t/ is likely to move to the place of articulation of the following segment and become /p/ – [ðæp bɔɪ] (*thap boy*).

Consonants: *see* MANNER OF ARTICULATION, PLACE OF ARTICULATION. Consonant sounds are produced by obstructing the air flow as it comes up from the lungs. This distinguishes them from VOWELS, where the air flow is manipulated rather than obstructed. They are conventionally described in articulatory terms in respect of three main features: whether they are VOICED or not; where the obstruction occurs (place of articulation); and the type of sound made (manner of articulation). More subtle distinctions can be made between them, and this form is the basis of DISTINCTIVE FEATURE analysis. For a list of the consonants of British English represented phonetically, see 'A Note on Phonetics' at the front of this book (*see also* INTERNATIONAL PHONETIC ALPHABET and PHONEME).

Diacritic. A mark or symbol that indicates the pronunciation value of a speech segment. Diacritics are not pronounced themselves but serve simply to provide information about pronunciation. They are predominantly used in conjunction with the PHONEME symbols from the INTERNATIONAL PHONETIC ALPHABET (IPA), to indicate allophonic (*see* ALLOPHONE) variants. The voiced phonemes /d/, /b/ and /g/, for example, often lose their voicing at the ends of words. This can be shown by adding a small symbol, or diacritic, to the phoneme when it occurs; thus [d̥] indicates a devoiced pronunciation of /d/. Similarly, a wavy line through /l/, as in [ɫ], informs us that the sound is 'velarised'. In this case it indicates the difference between /l/ in *lip*, and /l/ in *milk*, where the back of the tongue is raised towards the velum, or soft palate. You will find details of the range of diacritics that are in common use in the IPA chart (see Figure 10, p. 47).

In addition to these made-up symbols, some letters of the conventional alphabet can also function diacritically. The letter (e), for example, often functions in this way at the end of monosyllables. In the case of *din* and *dine*, the silent (e) lets us know that the previous vowel is a diphthong, rather than a short vowel. As this is the only pronunciation difference between them the extra GRAPH performs a valuable service. Similarly, double consonants can also perform diacritically, usually in conjunction with (e), as in *diner* and *dinner*, where the second (n), although not pronounced, provides essential information about the length of the preceding vowel. An example without (e) is *halo* and *hallo*, where there is a similar difference in length between the initial vowels of both words.

Distinctive features.   The phonetic properties of speech sounds. Distinctive speech sounds, or PHONEMES, are said to differ from one another in terms of certain features such as VOICE, 'nasality', and so on. Many features derive from the process of articulation, so that, for example, the phoneme /p/, which in terms of PLACE OF ARTICULATION is 'bilabial', and in terms of MANNER OF ARTICULATION is a 'plosive', can be classed as a 'bilabial plosive'. And since it is also 'voiceless' we can add that to the description and term it a 'voiceless bilabial plosive'. These are all features of this particular phoneme. This kind of analysis provides the basis for a primitive mapping of speech sounds but it doesn't provide enough information for a complete specification of all phonemes. In the case of VOWEL sounds, for example, the terms 'bilabial' and 'plosive' are meaningless. We have to rely on a new set of terms here such as 'close' and 'front'. What we need, then, is a classification system that can capture the features of all sounds, both CONSONANTS and vowels, such that we can provide a unique description of any phoneme in the linguistic system.

The theory of distinctive features was elaborated by the linguist Roman Jakobson. His aim was to identify a universal set of features that might be drawn on by all languages, although not all would necessarily be found in every language. Since then, the set of features – twelve in all – that Jakobson identified have been revised by the linguists CHOMSKY and Halle. Here are the features that are most commonly in use today. A fundamental principle of these features is that the oppositions they describe are **binary**: they can have only two values, '+' or '-' , representing the presence or absence of the property:

Classificatory features
± *consonantal*
   (plosives, fricatives, affricates, nasals and liquids *vs.* vowels and glides)

± *vocalic*
   (vowels and liquids *vs.* plosives, fricatives, affricates, nasals and glides)

± *syllabic*
   sounds that can function as the peak of a syllable *vs.* sounds that cannot
   (vowels *vs.* consonants – with the exception of syllabic consonants)

± *obstruent* (*obstruent* vs. *sonorant*)
   sounds that involve a radical obstruction of the airflow *vs.* those which do not (plosives, fricatives and affricates *vs.* liquids, glides, nasals and vowels)

± *nasal* (*nasal* vs. *oral*)
   (nasal consonants *vs.* all other segments)

Articulatory features
± *high*
   sounds produced with the tongue raised above the rest position *vs.* those where it is not (palatal and velar consonants and high vowels *vs.* labial, dental consonants and non-high vowels)

± *low*
   sounds produced with the tongue lowered from the rest position *vs.* those where it is not (open vowels *vs.* all other segments)

± *back*
   sounds produced with the tongue retracted from the rest position *vs.* those where it is not (back vowels and velar consonants *vs.* all other segments)

± *round*
sounds produced with the lips rounded *vs.* those where they are not (rounded vowels and /w/ *vs.* all other segments)

± *anterior*
consonant sounds where the airflow is obstructed in the area of the post-alveolar region *vs.* those where it is not (labials, labio-dentals and alveolars *vs.* other consonants)

± *coronal*
consonant sounds articulated with the blade of the tongue raised from the neutral position *vs.* those where it is not (dentals, alveolars, post-alveolars and palatals *vs.* other consonants)

± *lateral*
this feature only relates to /l/, in the articulation of which the tip of the tongue closes with the alveolar ridge and air escapes over the sides. All other segments are – lateral

Manner features
± *continuant*
sounds that can be sustained without interruption *vs.* those which can't (fricatives, approximants and vowels *vs.* plosives and affricates)

± *delayed release*
sounds that are articulated with a complete closure, which is then gradually released (affricates *vs.* plosives)

Acoustic features
± *voice*
all voiced segments are + voice and all voiceless segments are – voice

± *strident* (*strident vs. mellow*)
sounds that are characterised by high-frequency noise *vs.* those which aren't (labio-dental, alveolar and palato-alveolar fricatives, and the affricates *vs.* all other segments)

Elision.   The omission of a PHONEME in speech. Words such as *hand-some* and *mostly* are frequently pronounced with the omission of /d/ in *handsome* and /t/ in *mostly*. Elision is common in casual speech styles, particularly at word boundaries. The most frequently elided consonants are /t/ and /d/:

last year: [lɑːs jɪə]
thousand points: [θaʊzn pɔɪnts]

Graph(eme).   A graph is the smallest discrete segment in a stretch of writing or print. In English these are usually called 'letters', but a moment's thought will show the inexactness of this term. If we take the letter (s), for example, this can be written in a number of different ways, lower case ('s'), upper case ('S'), archaic ('ʃ'). Clearly these forms are not separate letters but simply variants. 'Letters' exist both as concepts and as physical forms, rather like sounds. And as with sounds, we need a more technical vocabulary to describe the relationship between concept and physical substance. In the case of phonology we have PHONEMES, allophones, and phones. Similarly with written forms we have graphemes, allographs, and graphs. Using this vocabulary we can say that the grapheme (s) is realised by three different graphs: 's', 'S', and 'ʃ'. These graphs are allographs of (s). The relationships between them are these:

> grapheme = individual letter as concept
> allograph = physical representation of letter/concept
> graph = physical substance

Like phonemes, graphemes are minimal contrastive units. Changing a grapheme in a written word produces a different word whereas merely changing a graph doesn't. It makes no difference whether <soot> is written 'Soot' or 'soot', it is still the same word. This is not the case, however, if we substitute <l> for the first segment. Grapheme analysis is the main business of **graphemics** or **graphology**. The writing system of language is referred to as its **orthography**.

International Phonetic Alphabet (IPA).   An alphabet designed by the International Phonetic Association, as a means of symbolising the distinctive sound segments of any language or accent. The aim of the notation is that 'there should be a separate letter for each distinctive sound: that is for each sound which being used instead of another, in the same language, can change the meaning of a word' (Phonetic Teachers' Association, 1888). So, for example, the distinction in English between *sin* and *shin* can be shown by the use of /s/ and /ʃ/ for the initial segments in each word. The prime purpose of the alphabet is to handle the notation of phonemes in the 3000 or so languages that exist in the world.

   In addition, however, the alphabet has also developed a range of

DIACRITICS that allow it to be used for allophonic (see PHONEME) as well as phonemic transcriptions. But even without diacritics it can still handle many allophonic variants. This is because phonemes in one language may well be simply allophones in another. For example, the /m/ in *symphony* is often given a labio-dental articulation because of the influence of the following sound (*see* COARTICULATION), that is, the bottom lip, instead of touching the upper lip, touches the upper teeth. This allophone is symbolised as [ɱ] (note: allophones are conventionally enclosed in square brackets, as distinct from phonemes, which are enclosed in angled brackets). In a language such as Teke, however, [ɱ] is a separate phoneme, because Teke allows a phonemic distinction between that sound and [m]. The labio-dental nasal allophone occurs in a number of languages, principally English, Italian, and Spanish, and as a consequence [ɱ] tends to be used allophonically rather than for showing the phonemic contrast between /m/ and [ɱ]. Similarly, the glottal plosive [ʔ] which is used by many speakers of English as an allophone of /t/ (the 'glottal stop') exists in other languages as a separate phoneme.

Students sometimes think the IPA has the capacity to symbolise any human speech sound. It's important to recognise that it doesn't. As I have already said, its principal purpose is phonemic. The fact that the symbols (with or without diacritics) can also be used for an allophonic transcription is a valuable extra. Four versions of the IPA are in current use: 'revised to 1951', 'revised to 1979', revised to 1989', and 'revised to 1993'. There are a few differences between them in terminology – the 1951 version refers to 'frictionless continuants', for example, whereas subsequent ones use the term 'approximant' – and in notational symbols, but they all work on the same phonemic principle. Figure 10 shows the latest revision, to 1993. Notice that it draws a distinction between CONSONANTS and VOWELS and, in the case of consonants, between those that are 'pulmonic' (that is produced by exhaling air) and those which are 'non-pulmonic', (produced by inhaling air). A number of African languages use non-pulmonic sounds. There are also sections for 'other symbols', 'diacritics', and 'suprasegmentals'. This arrangement is intended to reflect the practical requirements of the user. Returning to the consonant chart, it's quite striking just how many empty 'boxes' there are. Three reasons exist for this. First, there are still some sounds that are made but for which, as yet, there are no IPA symbols (e.g. labio-dental plosives). In such cases scholars use their own *ad hoc* method for symbolising them. Second, there are some articulations that are judged to be physically impossible. It isn't possible, for example, to utter a pharyngeal nasal or velar trill. These are indicated by the shaded areas.

And, finally, other boxes are empty because a particular sound, even though it may be pronounceable is not thought to be used as a separate phoneme in any language.

CONSONANTS (PULMONIC)

	Bilabial	Labiodental	Dental	Alveolar	Postalveolar	Retroflex	Palatal	Velar	Uvular	Pharyngeal	Glottal
Plosive	p b			t d		ʈ ɖ	c ɟ	k g	q ɢ		ʔ
Nasal	m	ɱ		n		ɳ	ɲ	ŋ	N		
Trill	ʙ			r					R		
Tap or Flap				ɾ		ɽ					
Fricative	ɸ β	f v	θ ð	s z	ʃ ʒ	ʂ ʐ	ç ʝ	x ɣ	χ ʁ	ħ ʕ	h ɦ
Lateral fricative				ɬ ɮ							
Approximant		ʋ		ɹ		ɻ	j	ɰ			
Lateral approximant				l		ɭ	ʎ	ʟ			

Where symbols appear in pairs, the one to the right represents a voiced consonant. Shaded areas denote articulations judged impossible.

CONSONANTS (NON-PULMONIC)

Clicks	Voiced implosives	Ejectives
⊙ Bilabial	ɓ Bilabial	' as in:
ǀ Dental	ɗ Dental/alveolar	pʼ Bilabial
ǃ (Post)alveolar	ʄ Palatal	tʼ Dental/alveolar
ǂ Palatoalveolar	ɠ Velar	kʼ Velar
ǁ Alveolar lateral	ʛ Uvular	sʼ Alveolar fricative

VOWELS

Where symbols appear in pairs, the one to the right represents a rounded vowel.

OTHER SYMBOLS

ʍ Voiceless labial-velar fricative
w Voiced labial-velar approximant
ɥ Voiced labial-palatal approximant
ʜ Voiceless epiglottal fricative
ʢ Voice epiglottal fricative
ʡ Epiglottal plosive

ɕ ʑ Alveolo-palatal fricatives
ɺ Alveolar lateral flap
ɧ Simultaneous ʃ and x

Affricates and double articulations can be represented by two symbols joined by a tie bar if necessary

k͡p t͡s

SUPRASEGMENTALS

ˈ Primary stress	ˌfoʊnəˈtɪʃən
ˌ Secondary stress	
ː Long	eː
ˑ Half-long	eˑ
˘ Extra-short	ĕ
. Syllable break	ɹi.ækt
ǀ Minor (foot) group	
‖ Major (intonation) group	
‿ Linking (absence of a break)	
↓ Downstep	↗ Global rise
↑ Upstep	↘ Global fall

TONES & WORD ACCENTS

LEVEL		CONTOUR	
e̋ or ˥	Extra high	ě or ˩˥	Rising
é ˦	High	ê ˥˩	Falling
ē ˧	Mid	e᷄ ˧˥	High rising
è ˨	Low	e᷅ ˩˧	Low rising
ȅ ˩	Extra low	e᷈ ˧˩˧	Rising-falling etc.

DIACRITICS

Diacritics may be placed above a symbol with a descender, e.g. ŋ̊

̥ Voiceless	n̥ d̥	̤ Breathy voiced	b̤ a̤	̪ Dental	t̪ d̪
̬ Voiced	s̬ t̬	̰ Creaky voiced	b̰ a̰	̺ Apical	t̺ d̺
ʰ Aspirated	tʰ dʰ	̼ Linguolabial	t̼ d̼	̻ Laminal	t̻ d̻
̹ More rounded	ɔ̹	ʷ Labialized	tʷ dʷ	̃ Nasalized	ẽ
̜ Less rounded	ɔ̜	ʲ Palatalized	tʲ dʲ	ⁿ Nasal release	dⁿ
̟ Advanced	u̟	ˠ Velarized	tˠ dˠ	ˡ Lateral release	dˡ
̠ Retracted	i̠	ˤ Pharyngealized	tˤ dˤ	̚ No audible release	d̚
̈ Centralized	ë	̴ Velarized or pharyngealized	ɫ		
̽ Mid-centralized	ë̽	̝ Raised	e̝ (ɹ̝ = voiced alveolar fricative)		
̩ Syllabic	l̩	̞ Lowered	e̞ (β̞ = voiced bilabial approximant)		
̯ Non-syllabic	e̯	̘ Advanced Tongue Root	e̘		
˞ Rhoticity	ɚ	̙ Retracted Tongue Root	e̙		

Figure 10   The International Phonetic Alphabet (revised 1993)

The symbols are based as far as possible on the letters of the roman alphabet. If you look at the chart you will see that most of them are either roman, or modifications of roman characters: the velar nasal /ŋ/ is a modified /n/ whilst the vowel /ɔ/ is a turned around /c/. Only when the roman alphabet has been exhausted have other symbols been used. Some of these are from other languages, such as the voiceless dental fricative /θ/ from Greek, and its voiced partner /ð/ from early Irish writing. Others are specially made up, non-alphabetic characters.

Intonation.   A term commonly used to refer to variations in the **pitch** of a speaker's voice. Pitch is a mental phenomenon. Its physical basis is the sound **frequency** of speech. As the introduction to this chapter pointed out, speech disturbs the air around us. The rate of that disturbance, measured in cycles, is referred to as a sound's frequency. We interpret the changes in frequency that occur naturally in speaking as changes in pitch and, as a consequence, perceive our voices to be constantly rising and falling. **Tone** refers to the way in which pitch is used in language – 'the configuration of pitch', as it is sometimes called. In some languages around the world variations of pitch are used to create new words, or more properly, LEXEMES. Such languages are referred to as **tone languages**. An example of this is Chinese, in which saying a word with a rising or falling tone can completely alter its meaning, as in

ma	——	mother
ma	∨	horse
ma	＼	scold
ma	／	hemp

In English, however, and in other modern European languages, tone does not differentiate words in this way. Instead it has a **suprasegmental** function. That is to say, it operates above the level of individual segments, or words, and is perceived to influence the meaning of chunks of speech. These chunks are commonly called **tone units**, although some linguists also use terms such as **sense units**, **breath groups**, and **contours**, to describe them. Whatever term we use, they are word strings over which a particular tone pattern operates. When linguists use the term **intonation** it is usually this more specialised application that they have in mind.

Intonation is acknowledged by linguists to be crucially important in both the construction of speech and the determination of meaning. Not only do we make decisions about the words we are going to use and the syntactic pattern we are going to adopt, but we also choose from a range of possible intonation variants. Having said that, however, it's noticeable that attempts to provide a linguistic description of the intonation resources of English have been only partially successful. There are a number of reasons for this. A principal reason has to do with the comparative recency of serious analytic interest in speech compared with writing. Whereas writing has been studied systematically for centuries, speech has had to wait for the development of appropriate technology to receive similar attention. But apart from this, there are significant difficulties of a methodological kind in the way of would-be analysts.

To begin with, separating out pitch for detailed physical analysis from all the other variables that are possibly involved in intonation is not unproblematic. As well as variations in frequency, listeners are aware of **loudness** and **length** of utterances. These also contribute to meaning, but distinguishing the precise degree and nature of the contribution from that made by pitch is not easy. The distinction at a terminological level is usually made by grouping loudness and length within **stress**, usually acknowledged to be a separate phenomenon from pitch. But what this obscures is, first, that understanding of stress is itself limited and, secondly, that stress and pitch cooperate together in influencing meaning.

Another problem, related to all of this, is that of knowing precisely how intonation contributes to meaning. Some approaches have attempted to link intonation patterns with the attitude of the speaker, arguing that some tones indicate diffidence and uncertainty, and others positiveness and impatience. But the evidence here is not entirely stable because of the range of emotions that can be set against individual tones. Other approaches have tried to link intonation with grammatical structures such as phrase and clause, and with functions such as questions and statements. Again, there is a certain amount of evidence to support this but not enough for us to say that a particular grammatical form will always have a particular intonation pattern. And, more recently, linguists have tried to link intonation with discourse strategies, seeing it as a means of encouraging, or discouraging, certain kinds of response from listeners. The upshot of all this is the likelihood that intonation serves a number of related purposes rather than one exclusively.

And finally, a further complication is the lack of any agreed notation for representing these suprasegmental features. Some linguists adopt a musical notation, seeing the distribution of stresses as a kind of tune, whilst others rely on a variety of accent markers, capitalised syllables and underlined words. To some extent the form of notation depends on how much intonational detail is included in any analysis. Small variations of pitch are taking place all the time in any utterance, and if we are attempting to chart these we shall need to use a system that can indicate the contour of intonation, syllable by syllable. The contour method is the one most favoured by British phoneticians, such as O'Connor and Arnold (1961), Halliday (1967), and Crystal (1975). Many analysts, however, content themselves with indicating simply major pitch shifts. In any utterance there are syllables that are more prominent than others and which are responsible for carrying the tone of the speaker. An analysis that is concerned simply to show these prominences need not be so sophisticated.

Detecting movements of pitch is notoriously difficult without the aid of machines. People often think, for example, that their voices are rising when in fact they are falling. This is due in part to the influence of **key** on pitch variations. Key refers to the relative level of pitch within an utterance. If you think for a moment of the voice as a lift continually going up and down a tall building then a descent from level 10 to level 8 is different from that between levels 5 to 7. In our analogy, the descents are taking place within different keys. Linguists usually distinguish three levels of key: high-key, mid-key, and low-key. Speakers sometimes choose to jump to a high-key in which to initiate a fall, in order to contrast with a fall in a mid-key, as in the following example (taken from McCarthy, 1991, p. 112):

```
          SIS ter   NOT my
/she's my        /          COUsin
```

Here the speaker is expressing something contrary to the expectations of the listener and choosing to vary the key as part of the information structure of his/her utterance.

Variations of pitch are usually said to occur within what we earlier termed **tone units**. Not all linguists accept the existence of such units, but where they are accepted they are conventionally said to have the following structure:

(pre-head) – (head) – tonic/nuclear syllable – (tail)

The centre of the unit, around which everything else is constructed, is the **tonic syllable**, or nucleus. As the bracketing indicates, it is the only obligatory element in the tone unit, and indeed the simplest unit consists of one word: **NO**. The tonic syllable is the one on which the greatest movement of pitch occurs in an utterance:

There's no need to be so up**SET** about it

Occurring before the tonic syllable are the **head** and **pre-head**. The first of these, the head, starts with the first stressed syllable 'no' and continues up to the nucleus:

no need to be **so** up . . .

To distinguish the tonic syllable from the other stressed syllables it is sometimes referred to as a **prominence**. Tonic syllables are not only stressed, therefore, they are also made prominent by the movement of pitch that occurs on them. The pre-head consists of the unstressed syllables occurring before the head:

There's . . .

and the **tail** of the unstressed syllables after the nucleus:

. . . about it

The tail continues the pitch movement that occurs on the nucleus and in some cases the tone is thought to spread itself over the tail.

Linguists are not in complete agreement about the precise number of tones that are used by speakers of English. Some distinguish as many as eight, others work with four or five. The following tones are the ones most usually encountered in discussions of the topic:

1. Fall ╲
2. Rise–fall ╱╲
3. Fall–rise ╲╱
4. Rise ╱
5. Level →

As for the use speakers make of these tones, as we saw earlier, this is still the subject of debate. There is some evidence that they are linked with personal emotions or attitudes, and phonologists who pursue this approach have conventionally made the following connections:

1. Falling: assertive, positive – 'that's **MINE**', 'he's a **FOOL**'

2. Rising: polite, diffident, enquiring – '**COFF**ee?', 'it's not im**POR**tant'

3. Falling–rising: reservation, doubt, uncertainty – 'he **COULD**', 'I'm not **SURE**'

4. Rising–falling: emphatic, impatient, possibly sarcastic – 'it's up to **YOU**', 'how **NICE**'

5. Level: neutral, uninterested – 'I don't **MIND**', 'I'm **EAS**y'

The difficulty of linking tones with attitude with any degree of precision is that in many cases the interpretation of tone depends on context. The same intonation pattern can accompany very different emotions depending on the nature of the utterance and the context in which it is used. In the following example the rise–fall followed by the fall is first used to accompany exasperation and then to accompany delight (adapted from McCarthy, 1991, p. 108):

/if you opened your **EYES**/ you'd **SEE** it/
/i'm delighted to **SAY**/ you've **WON** it/

The consequence of this very loose association between tones and atti-tude is that we are forced to make the links as general as possible. In the instance above we could accommodate both emotions by describing them as 'emphatic' tones, for which the rise–fall is often said to be employed. But at that level of generality we have ceased to say anything very interesting.

We are perhaps on firmer ground in linking intonation with grammat-ical functions. Intonation can be used, for example, to distinguish gram-matical groupings with quite different meanings, as in the following case:

/i don't **KNOW**/ (one tone group)

/i **DON'T**/ **NO**/ (two tone groups)

And we can also point to the common use of rising tones for 'yes/no' questions, and falling ones for 'wh' questions:

/are you **GO**ing?/

/what's the **MATT**er?/

But here again there is not a one-to-one match. In the following example the 'yes/no' tag can be said with either a rising or a falling intonation depending on the mutual state of knowledge between speaker and listener (adapted from McCarthy, 1991, p. 106):

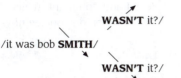

WASN'T it?/

/it was bob **SMITH**/

WASN'T it?/

More modern approaches to intonation see it as primarily fulfilling certain discourse roles rather than enforcing attitude or acting as a grammatical marker. The linguist Michael Halliday links it with information structure and sees intonation as a means speakers use to highlight 'new' information and background 'given'. In a similar vein Cruttenden (1986) and Brazil (1985) have argued that the function of intonation is principally interactive. According to this approach, falling tones have a **proclaiming** function (Brazil), and are used for **closed** meanings (Cruttenden), whilst rising tones have a **referring** function (Brazil), and are employed for **open** meanings (Cruttenden). The value of an interactive approach can be seen in the following examples from McCarthy (1991, pp. 108–11). Note that McCarthy, as is common in interactive approaches, does not limit the number of prominences in a tone unit to one. He distinguishes, however, between the nuclear prominence, in bold, and the non-nuclear, in capitals:

(i)   /IF you **LIKE**/ we can GO via **MAN**chester/

(ii) A: /are YOU mr **BLAKE?**/

    B: /**YES**/

In (i) the fall–rise has the function of referring the possibility of going via Manchester to the listener, whilst the fall indicates the extent of the offer with a closing tone. In the second example, 'Are you Mr Blake?' is an open-ended utterance that expects some completion, or closing.

A further refinement of the interactive choices is put forward by Brazil (1985), who distinguishes between the two closed tones in terms of speaker dominance, and similarly for the two open tones. He argues that in any exchange one speaker will exercise dominance and signal this by the appropriate tone. Of the two falling tones the rise–fall is more dominant than the simple fall, whilst of the rising tones the rise is more dominant than the fall–rise. Using these two parameters, open *vs.* close, and dominant *vs.* non-dominant, it is possible to assign intonation patterns more securely to utterances than is the case with grammatical or simple attitudinal approaches. In the following exchanges between a teacher and a pupil the rising–falling tones are closed and dominant, whilst the rising tone is open and dominant – with the force of 'do you see now?'

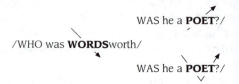

In the final example the two rising tones are both employed for the interrogative but the difference between them is that in the first instance the question is asked with more speaker dominance than in the second, which has the force of 'or might he have been something else?'

WAS he a **POET**?/

/WHO was **WORDS**worth/

WAS he a **POET**?/

Liaison.   The insertion of a sound in connected speech that is normally absent in citational form. This principally affects three speech sounds: /r/, /w/, and /j/, and occurs at word boundaries. Words such as <father>, <here>, and <far>, have an <r> in their orthography, but not in their pronunciation, in most varieties of British English. This is the consequence of a rule which deletes /r/ when it is not followed by a VOWEL. In phrases like *father and son*, *here and now*, and *far and away*, however, the rule no longer operates because the subsequent word begins with a vowel. The result is the reintroduction of /r/:

father and son: [fɑːðə r ən sʌn]
here and now: [hɪə r ən naʊ]
far and away: [fɑː r ən əweɪ]

Sometimes /r/ appears where it is not present in the orthography, for example, <India and Pakistan> – [ɪndɪə r ən pʰækɪstɑːn]. This is referred to as 'intrusive r'.

In the case of /w/ and /j/, these are commonly inserted in the following contexts: /j/ between words ending in /i/ and a following word beginning with a vowel, for example, <see it> – [siːjɪt]; and /w/ between words ending in /u/ and a following word beginning with a vowel, for example, <do at> – [duːwæt]. The CONSONANTS /w/ and /j/ are sometimes referred to as 'semi-vowels' and are related in terms of both PLACE and MANNER OF ARTICULATION to their respective vowels, /u/ and /i/. They serve as glides to smooth the passage from these vowels to another at a word boundary.

Manner of articulation.   The configuration adopted by the speech organs in articulating a sound. Together with PLACE OF ARTICULATION and VOICE this is a principal way in which speech sounds differ from each other. There are five principal types of manner which distinguish consonant phonemes:

Plosives: sounds in whose articulation the airstream is stopped by a brief closure of two speech organs and then released in a quick burst: /p/, /b/, /t/, /d/, /k/, /g/.

Fricatives: sounds in whose articulation two speech organs narrow the airstream, causing friction to occur as it passes through: /f/, /v/, /θ/, /ð/, /s/, /z/, /ʃ/, /ʒ/, /h/.

Affricates: sounds in whose articulation the airstream is stopped as for a plosive and then released slowly and partially with friction: /tʃ/, /dʒ/.

Nasals: sounds in whose articulation the airstream is diverted through the nasal cavity as a consequence of the passage through the oral cavity being blocked by the lowering of the soft palate, or velum: /m/, /n/, /ŋ/.

Approximants: sounds in whose articulation two speech organs approach each other and air flows continuously between them without friction. There are two main sub-groups:

(i) *Liquids*: (a)   the sides of the tongue and the sides of the teeth ridge approach each other whilst the tongue tip rests on the alveolar ridge and air flows over the sides of the tongue: /l/ (sometimes referred to as a *lateral*.

(b)   the tongue tip approaches the alveolar ridge and air flows down the middle of the tongue: /r/.

(ii) *Glides:*   two speech organs approach each other and then glide away: /w/, /j/.

In the case of vowel sounds, manner of articulation is less precise than for consonant sounds. There are two main indicators of manner:

(i) *Tongue height*.   This distinguishes sounds in relation to the height of that part of the tongue which is closest to the palate. When the tongue is high in the mouth, vowels are described as **close**, and when low, as **open**. Other reference points are **half-close** and **half-open**.

(ii) *Lip posture.* Vowels are produced with the lips in a rounded or spread posture. There are degrees of rounding but it is conventional to classify vowels as being either rounded or spread. Of the principal vowels of Southern English /ɑ/ /ɔ/ /ʊ/ /u/ are rounded, and the remainder, /i/ /ɪ/ /ɛ/ /æ/ /ʌ/ /ɜ/ /ə/ /a/, spread.

Morphophonology. The study of the phonological, i.e. sound, structure of MORPHEMES. There is a good deal of evidence to show that the way we pronounce words is affected by their morphological structure. As was pointed out in the introduction to this chapter, the plural morpheme 's' is pronounced in three different ways, (/s/ /z/ /ɪz/) depending on the final sound of the respective noun to which it is being added. It is pronounced /ɪz/ (*peaches*, *judges*) when attached to a sibilant sound (/tʃ/ /dʒ/); /z/ (*apples*, *pears*) when attached to other VOICED sounds; and /s/ (*apricots*, *maps*) when following a voiceless sound. The fact that these rules are morpheme-sensitive can be shown by considering environments other than the realisation of morpheme 's', in which /s/ can occur quite normally after a voiced sound, e.g.

/piːs/ *peace*

as opposed to:

/piːz/ *peas* (*pea+s*)

Similar constraints operate for the regular past tense morpheme 'ed', which can be /ɪd/, /d/, or /t/ depending on the final sound of the base form of the verb to which it is attached; /ɪd/ after alveolar plosives (*sorted*, *landed*); /d/ after other voiced sounds (*snowed*, *roamed*); /t/ after other voiceless sounds (*stamped*, *poked*).

Morphophonological rules also help to explain the different pronunciations of the two sets in Table 1. In the words of column A /ŋ/ is followed by /g/, whereas in column B it isn't. The difference between the two sets is in the way the words are constructed. The words of column B can be divided into two morphemes: 'sing + er', 'hang + er', whilst those in column A can't. They consist of a single morpheme each. From this evidence, then, we can construct a rule for the pronunciation of /g/ following /ŋ/ that states that within a word containing the letters 'ng', /n/ occurs without a following /g/ if it occurs at the end of a morpheme; if it occurs in the middle of a morpheme (as in *finger* and *anger*), it has a following /g/. This is not the full story since there are some exceptions to the rule, notably the pronunciation of comparative and superlative forms (*stronger*, *strongest*), where /g/ is pronounced despite occurring at the end of a morpheme, but these can be catered for by appending a further statement indicating that these forms are to be regarded as single morphemes for the purposes of this rule.

Table 1

A	B
finger /fɪŋgə/	*singer* /sɪŋə/
anger /æŋgə/	*hanger* /hæŋə/

Phone: *see* PHONEME.

Phoneme. The smallest unit of sound capable of distinguishing between two words. Phonemes are contrastive segments. This means that changing the phoneme will produce a change in the meaning of a word. So that, for example, exchanging /p/ for /b/, in the word *bin*, will result in the new word, *pin*. To establish a full phoneme inventory for a particular language, linguists work on the principle of **minimal pairs**. These consist of pairs of words that are distinguished from each other by a difference between two phonemes and by that difference alone.

Phonemes are never capitalised and always written between diagonal lines (or solidi). In many ways phonemes are rather abstract units. Indeed, many linguists see them simply as convenient labels, or cover terms, for more specific features of sound (see DISTINCTIVE FEATURES). This level of analysis is useful if we are investigating the phonetic properties of sound. For example, the phonemes /p/, /t/, and /k/ are all aspirated, when they are pronounced before a stressed syllable, that is, they are released with a small puff of air. You can test this by saying *pit*, *tin*, and *kiss*, with your hand in front of your mouth. Relying simply on a phonemic analysis we should need three rules to cover this occurrence. However, since all three have in common the fact that they are VOICEless plosives, we can use these features to capture it in one PHONOLOGICAL RULE:

[voiceless plosive] → [aspirated] / – V
[+ stress]

That is, all voiceless plosives are aspirated when they are the only CONSONANT before a stressed VOWEL. More complex rules allow linguists to use features such as 'syllabic' and 'sonorant' to describe whole classes of sounds without having to specify each individual phoneme.

A further indication of the abstractness of phonemes can be seen in the variety of ways in which they may be pronounced. The /p/ in pin, for instance, is different from the /p/ in *spin*, and the /l/ in *late* from the /l/ in *milk*. In the case of *spin*, /p/ is no longer aspirated – in fact the word may sound more like 'sbin' – and in the case of *milk*, /l/ is much weaker than in *late*, and for some people, particularly in the south of England, may resemble a vowel ('miook'). These different realisations are not new phonemes, because we are not talking here of a change of meaning – we have no words *sbin* or *miook* in English. They are simply different phonetic varieties of their respective phonemes. Linguists use the term **allophone** for these varieties. Allophones are always enclosed within square brackets. They are frequently accompanied by a small symbol, or DIACRITIC, which indicates the pronunciation form of the segment. So, from the above, we could say that /p/ has two allophones [p] and [pʰ], an unaspirated and an aspirated form, whilst /l/ also has two, [l] and [ɫ], a strong and a weak version, or as linguists prefer, a 'clear', and a 'dark' form. The number of allophones differs according to the phoneme in question. There are at least seven allophones of /t/, for example. Many are the result of COARTICULATION or **assimilation**, that is, the tendency of a sound to move to the PLACE OF ARTICULATION of the one following.

The question naturally arises from this concerning the method by which phonologists assign allophones to particular phonemes. Here, linguists need an even smaller unit – the **phone**. Phones are the smallest perceptible segments of speech sound. They represent the actual substance of our speech without any reference, as in the case of phonemes, to the meanings of the words that they compose. As such, they are not necessarily contrastive. There are three principal criteria that linguists use to group phones into phonemes:

(i) *Free variation*.   According to this, if two or more phones occur in the same environment, but without changing the word in which they occur, then they may belong to the same phoneme, that is, they may be allophones of that phoneme. For example, the articulation of the final consonant in *bid* may vary according to the degree of stress we give it. Because consonant sounds at the ends of words are often weakly articulated the 'd' may lose its voiced quality and become devoiced. The symbol for this devoiced /d/ is [d̥]. On another occasion, however, we may use the fully voiced form [d]. These two phones are in free variation with each other and substituting one for another would not change the meaning of any word in which they might occur. They are therefore allophones of the same phoneme.

(ii) *Complementary distribution*. According to this, if two or more phones occur in non-identical environments, then they may be members of the same phoneme. If we go back to the two allophones of /l/ which we distinguished just now, that is [l] and [ɫ], we can see that this criterion applies to them. [l] occurs before vowels, whereas [ɫ] occurs before consonants and at the ends of words. Unlike free variation they are not found in the same environments. From this evidence, there-fore, the likelihood is that they are allophones of the same phoneme.

These two criteria leave a loophole, however. If we take the phones [h] and [ŋ] it is evident that they fulfil the criterion of complementary distribution since [h] only occurs word-initially, whilst [ŋ] only occurs word-medially and word-finally. But it would be silly to argue from this that they were allophones of the same phoneme. These two sounds have nothing in common: as we can see from their descriptive features, one is a voiceless glottal fricative, and the other, a voiced velar nasal. However, this loophole is closed by the last criterion.

(iii) *Phonetic similarity*. According to this, if two or more phones are to be members of the same phoneme they must be phonetically similar. This effectively means that they must share at least two of the following features: voicing, place of articulation, and MANNER OF ARTICULATION.

Phonological rules. Rules that indicate the way in which an underly-ing, or 'phonemic', pronunciation is realised phonetically in actual speech. PHONEMES are abstract units of speech. They are realised in speech by their various allophones, the majority of which are predictable from the linguistic environments in which they occur. Phonological rules usually take the following forms:

(i) $X \rightarrow Y/A —$
(ii) $X \rightarrow Y/ — A$
(iii) $X \rightarrow Y/A — B$

The left-hand sides of these rules all say the same thing: 'X is pronounced as Y'. The diagonal slash has the meaning 'in the following circumstances'. To the right of the slash we have the circumstances in which this pronunciation rule operates. In (i), X is pronounced as Y when it occurs after A (where A represents the relevant conditioning factor); in (ii) the pronunciation rule operates when X occurs before the conditioning factor; and in (iii) it operates between two conditioning factors.

To see how this formula works in practice, consider the rules that apply to the pronunciation of /t/ when it follows, or is followed by, the dental fricative /θ/. In words such as *bathtap*, /t/ is pronounced with the tongue against the upper teeth instead of the alveolar ridge. This is the result of a backwards assimilation to the previous sound, which is dental. The process here is dentalisation. We can capture it with the following rule:

t → t̪ /θ —

This now tells us that the dental allophone of /t/ is produced following the voiceless dental fricative. However, the dental allophone also occurs before the fricative, as well as after it, in a word such as *eighth*, for example. We need another rule to capture this:

t → t̪ / — θ

This tells us that the dental allophone is produced before a voiceless fricative. In addition, however, dentalisation can also occur when /t/ is word-final and the following word begins with /θ/, as in *not thin*. Again we need another rule to capture this

t → t̪ / — #θ
(# = a word boundary)

Fortunately, as the process in the last two rules is the same, it is possible to achieve an economy of scale here by combining them together. This produces:

t → t̪ / — (#)θ

The brackets indicate a conditioning factor that is optional. The rule now states that /t/ has a dental pronunciation when it is followed by a voiceless dental fricative and also when it is followed by a word boundary and a word beginning with a voiceless dental fricative.

Phonological rules are part of every speaker's linguistic competence. They operate unconsciously, but systematically, as we speak. We can illustrate their function as in Figure 11. That is, the input to the P-Rules is the phonemic, or abstract representation; the P-Rules apply, or operate, on the phonemic strings and produce as output the phonetic representation. In the pronunciation of any given word there are likely to be several rules operating at the same time. To illustrate this we'll look briefly at the way three common pronunciation rules affect the pronunciation of the following words: *kill*, *skill*, *kin*, *skin*. The first rule to notice is the **aspiration** rule. This affects the voiceless plosives /p/, /t/, and /k/. When these sounds occur initially in a stressed SYLLABLE they are accompanied by the sudden release of air, whereas in other positions this does not occur. The rule states:

1. Voiceless plosives are aspirated at the beginning of a stressed syllable.

The second rule, the **nasalisation** rule, concerns the pronunciation of VOWELS before nasal CONSONANTS /n/, /ŋ/, and /m/. In these environments vowel sounds are usually nasalised, that is, some air is released through the nose. This rule states:

2. A vowel is nasalised when it occurs before a nasal consonant.

The third rule concerns the pronunciation of /l/. This has what is known as **clear** pronunciation when it occurs before a vowel but a **dark** one when it occurs after a vowel or before a consonant. In these environments the back of the tongue is raised towards the velum and produces a less clearly articulated sound. This rule of **velarisation** states:

3. Velarise an /l/ when it does not occur before a vowel.

input	PHONEMIC REPRESENTATION OF WORDS
	↓
	Phonological rules (P-Rules)
	↓
output	PHONETIC REPRESENTATION OF WORDS

Figure 11   How phonological rules operate

By applying these rules to the phonemic representation of the words we have selected we can derive their phonetic representation as in Table 2. (NA means 'not applicable'.)

Table 2

Phonemic representation	/kɪl/	/skɪl/	/kɪn/	/skɪn/
Rule 1 – aspiration	kʰɪl	NA	kʰɪn	NA
Rule 2 – nasalisation	NA	NA	kʰĩn	skĩn
Rule 3 – velarisation	kʰɪɫ	skɪɫ	NA	NA
Phonetic representation	[kʰɪɫ]	[skɪɫ]	[kʰĩn]	[skĩn]

Phonotactics.   The study of the permitted or non-permitted arrangements or sequences of PHONEMES in a language. In English, for
example, there are only eleven three-consonant combinations which
can occur in SYLLABLE-initial position:

/s/ + /p/ + /l/, /r/, /j/
/s/ + /t/ + /r/, /j/
/s/ + /k/ + /l/, /r/, /j/, /w/
/s/ + /m/ + /j/ (*smew*: a kind of duck)
/s/ + /f/ + /r/ (*sphragistics*: the study of seals or signet rings)

These restrictions are remarkable when one considers that arithmetically the number of possible combinations is 13,824. It is also interesting that the first phoneme is always /s/, the second, with the exceptions
of /smj/ and /sfr/, always a stop, and the third, always a non-nasal
sonorant (see DISTINCTIVE FEATURES). If we set aside /sfr/ and /smj/ as
exceptions, the general rule for initial CCC clusters in English is /s/ +
voiceless stop + approximant. This rule would also permit clusters that
do not exist in English at present, such as /spw/, /stl/ and /stw/, but
which are perfectly possible. Linguists call these 'potential' clusters, to
distinguish them from those like /bsn/ or /ftd/, which are impossible.

When it comes to two-consonant syllable-initial clusters there are a
total of 42 permissible combinations. Again, this is only a small propor-
tion of the arithmetically possible combinations – 576 in number. The
great majority of permissible combinations follow the rule plosive/frica-
tive + approximant. The exception to this is /s/, which may also be
followed by /m/, /n/, /f/, /t/, /k/, or /p/.

In addition to specifying permissible initial consonant clusters, the
phonotactic rules of a language also specify syllable-final clusters, and
which VOWELS can combine with which CONSONANTS. We never find syllables ending in /tb/ or /zv/, for example. And no word in English begins
with /ŋ/. As a consequence of these rules phonotactics is able to determine the range of permissible words in a language. These will include
potential words, such as /zvɔt/, and /spwæθ/, which do not exist at the
moment but which are possible, but exclude words such as /btæt/, and
/sbwigh/, which are not. These are sometimes termed 'illicit' words.

Place of articulation.   The point in the vocal tract where the speech
organs restrict the passage of air in some way so producing distinctive
speech sounds. Place of articulation is of particular importance in the
production of CONSONANT sounds. One of the principal distinctions
between consonant and VOWEL sounds is that the former restrict the air

flow to a much greater degree and have a more precise place of articulation. Consonant sounds are frequently referred to by their place of articulation. The following are the principal terms used in linguistics to describe these:

Bilabial: sounds formed by both lips coming together: /b/, /p/, /m/, /w/.

Labio-dental: sounds formed by the bottom lip touching the upper teeth: /f/, /v/.

Dental: sounds formed by the tongue touching the upper teeth: /θ/, /d/.

Alveolar: sounds formed by the tongue coming into contact with the hard, or alveolar, ridge immediately behind the upper teeth: /t/, /d/, /s/, /z/, /l/, /n/.

Post-alveolar: sounds formed by the tongue curled behind the alveolar ridge: /r/.

Palato-alveolar: sounds formed by the tongue in contact with both the roof of the mouth, or hard palate, and the alveolar ridge: /dʒ/, /tʃ/, /ʃ/, /ʒ/.

Palatal: sounds formed by the middle of the tongue up against the hard palate: /j/.

Velar: sounds formed by the back of the tongue against the soft palate (or velum): /k/, /g/, /ŋ/.

Glottal: sounds formed from the space between the vocal folds (or glottis): /h/.

It is also possible for sounds to be formed at the uvula by the uvula coming into contact with the back of the tongue, and also from the pharynx, by the root of the tongue against the pharyngeal wall. Some languages make use of these sounds, but English doesn't.

In the case of vowel sounds, the air is not so much restricted as manipulated by the shape of the oral cavity and the position of the speech organs. As a consequence the place of articulation is less precise. Linguists tend to rely on the part of the tongue on a front–back axis which is closest to the palate, or roof of the mouth (see VOWELS). This yields the following distinctions:

Front vowels: sounds produced from the front of the tongue in conjunction with the palate: /iː/ /ɪ/ /ɛ/ /æ/.

Middle vowels: sounds produced from the middle of the tongue in conjunction with the palate: /ʌ/ /ɜː/ /ə/.

Back vowels: sounds produced from the back of the tongue in conjunction with the palate: /ɑː/ /ɒ/ /ɔː/ /ʊ/ /uː/.

Reduction. This involves the substitution of a weaker vowel, usually SCHWA, /ə/, but sometimes /ɪ/ or /ʊ/, for a stronger one. This frequently happens in connected speech where many monosyllabic words, such as *to, for, and*, are lightly stressed, with the consequence that their vowel segments are reduced to schwa. Vowel reduction similarly occurs in polysyllabic words in those SYLLABLES that are unstressed. In *occurred*, for example, the initial syllable /ɒ/ is usually reduced to [ə] in running speech.

Schwa, *also* **shwa**. The name of the most frequent VOWEL PHONEME in English, the weak, and rather colourless unstressed vowel, in words such as *about*, and *banana* produced from the central area of the mouth. It frequently occurs in small function words like *the, and, for*, especially in running speech (SEE REDUCTION). Its phonemic representation in IPA is /ə/. The term 'schwa' comes from the German name of a vowel of this central quality found in Hebrew.

Syllable. The smallest linguistic unit of rhythm. Syllables are pure units of sound and as such are essentially meaningless. They serve to carry the stress patterns of English that are essential to the way in which speech is organised. The best way to determine how many syllables there are in a word is to say it slowly, tapping your hand at the same time. Doing this will accentuate the rhythmic structure. Because they are units of sound, not meaning, however, it is not always possible to decide from the written form of a word where syllable boundaries occur. For example, there are two syllables in *shovel* but are they *shov + el* or *sho + vel*? Both are possible, and in neither case do the units mean anything.

In structural terms syllables must contain a VOWEL or vowel-like sound. The simplest syllables, in fact, consist of just this, for example, *owe* /əʊ/. This forms the **nucleus** of the syllable. Occasionally a syllable can consist just of a consonant, as in the final syllable in *rhythm, bottle*, and *button*. In these cases the vowel that preceded the final consonant has been weakened to the point of elision, leaving us simply with the consonant. The consonants that act in this way, /l/, /r/, /m/, and /n/, are termed **syllabic consonants**. They all have a high degree of sonority (see DISTINCTIVE FEATURES), and as such are the most 'vowel-like' of the consonants.

In addition to the nucleus, syllables may have one, two, or three consonants preceding them. These make up the **onset**. Syllables that consist of an onset and a nucleus are traditionally termed 'open', e.g. *pray*, *spray*. Syllables can also have up to four consonants following the nucleus. These make up the **coda** and are termed 'closed', *cat*, *cats*, *bends*, *ankles*. We can represent the possible permutations in the manner shown in Figure 12.

Syllables are constructed according to the principle of **sonority**. Sonorant sounds involve little obstruction of the airflow and produce a greater degree of resonance than their converse – **obstruents**. The most sonorant sounds are vowels, after that come the nasals, glides and liquids. Permissible combinations in the onset and coda provide for the most sonorant consonant to be closest to the peak, or vowel. So, for example, we find monosyllabic words that begin with /k/ or /b/ followed by /l/, such as *club* and *blood*, but never the reverse combination. And similarly there are monosyllabic words that end with /l/ followed by /b/ or /k/, such as *bulb* and *talc*, but there are no words that end with the consonant sounds in reverse order (see PHONOTACTICS).

All monosyllabic, or single-syllable, words carry what is called 'primary stress' in their **citational** form – in other words, when they are pronounced singly. Having said that, however, it is not entirely clear what 'stress' actually consists of in physiological terms. To many people it seems as though a stressed syllable is being articulated more loudly or emphatically than a non-stressed one, but this is not necessarily the case. Other features such as duration (that is the time spent on a sylla-ble) and change in voice pitch also play a part. Many so-called 'struc-ture', or 'function', words (prepositions, articles, conjunctions, auxiliary verbs) will lose their stress in running speech and as a consequence their vowel will change to a weak variety, usually /ə/, /ɪ/ or /ʊ/. This is frequently the case with words such as *the*, *and*, *to*, *for*. On the other hand, words with a high lexical content (nouns, verbs, adjectives, adverbs) will tend to retain their stress. The succession of stressed and unstressed syllables that results from this produces a fairly regular rhythm, which is exploited in poetry and verse to produce **metre**. There is a tendency in ordinary speech for speakers to maintain an alternating pattern of stressed and unstressed syllables. It's a phenomenon known

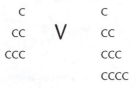

C		C
CC	V	CC
CCC		CCC
		CCCC

Figure 12 Consonant and vowel combinations in monosyllables

as **stress-timing** or **isochrony**. Speakers will subconsciously time when stresses occur to ensure that they fall at regular intervals. Disruptions of this pattern will normally signal to listeners some extra meaning that the speaker wishes to communicate. In the following examples the first utterance preserves an unmarked pattern of alternating stresses in which the main lexical words are stressed, whilst the second severely disrupts this in order to communicate the speaker's irritation more emphatically:

> IF i've TOLD you ONCE i've TOLD you TWICE
> IF I'VE TOLD YOU ONCE I'VE TOLD YOU TWICE

Polysyllabic words, those which consist of more than one syllable, all have one primary stressed syllable – just like monosyllabic words. But in addition they will also have a secondary stressed syllable and/or syllables with no stress. In the examples below, primary stressed syllables are marked with a superscript, secondary with a subscript:

Two syllables:	ˌan 'ti que, 'cot ton
Three syllables:	ˌmag a 'zine, 'inn o ˌcence
Four syllables:	re 'mar ka ble, ˌcir cu 'la tion

Unlike some languages, primary stress in polysyllabic words in English is not predictable. It may fall on the first, second or following syllables. Indeed, the lack of predictability is one of the significant hurdles that foreign learners of English have to master. Moreover, stress patterns of words are not immutable: the pronunciation of many words, like *controversy* and *formidable*, varies from speaker to speaker; and there are dialectal differences too. English and American stress patterns vary markedly in words such as *laboratory*. And, as with monosyllabic words, the stress pattern of polysyllabic words can change in running speech. Primary and secondary stress can both move under the influence of surrounding words in a phrase. In the following example, the primary stress moves from the second syllable in *thirteen* (which is its natural position) to the first. This is because of the relative awkwardness of having two stressed syllables together:

> Thir 'teen
> 'Thir teen 'wo men

Because of the way in which stresses move about in running speech many linguists argue that there are linguistic domains above the sylla-

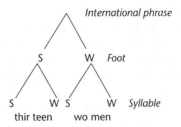

Figure 13 The distribution of stress in an intonational phase

ble, which account for the distribution of stress in utterances. Research into these domains is the concern of **metrical prosody**, one of the more recent fields of linguistics. A principal domain that prosodists in this field characteristically work with is that of the **foot**. A foot is a rhythmic unit immediately above that of the syllable, consisting of a stressed syllable plus any unstressed syllables which may be attached to it. Using such an intermediate level we could show the distribution of stress in the above phrase in the way shown in Figure 13. What this diagram tells us is that the string *thirteen women* consists of four syllables in a repeated strong/weak pattern. These in turn consist of two feet, which correspondingly make up the overall intonational phrase. And within that phrase one foot, the first, is stronger than the second. Two things are suggested by this analysis: first, that there are relative degrees of stress – something that is strong at one level can be weak at another, and, secondly, that stress flows down from the higher intonational units to the lower, rather than the other way round. If this is so, then possibly we can approach prosody in a similar way to that in which many linguists approach syntax. In other words, we can examine language in order to discover the underlying rules that govern stress and which generate the pronunciation pattern of utterances. This is the concern of **generative phonology**.

The fact that the stress pattern of *thirteen* changes when we put it together with another word to form a phrase alerts us to the significance of syntax in assigning stress within strings. Syntactic considerations also play a part in those words where a shift in stress results in a change of word class and meaning. This affects words such as the following:

| 'in sult (noun) | 'con duct (noun) | 'ab sent (adjective) |
| in 'sult (verb) | con 'duct (verb) | ab 'sent (verb) |

In these cases the rule seems to be that the verb form of the word requires the stress to fall on the final syllable in contrast to other forms that require it to fall on the first. This kind of **contrastive stress** often distinguishes compounds such as '*blackbird*, in which the stressed sylla-ble is '*black*, from *black* '*bird*, in which *bird* is the stressed syllable. In these instances semantic considerations also seem to play a part.

Voice. A DISTINCTIVE FEATURE in the articulation of VOWELS and some CONSONANTS. Voice, or voicing, occurs when the **vocal folds** vibrate as a consequence of air passing between them. The folds are situated in the larynx, commonly known as the 'Adam's apple'. They are sometimes called the **vocal lips**, **vocal bands**, or **vocal cords**, and their principal purpose, in evolutionary terms, is to prevent food from entering the windpipe (see Figure 6, p. 34). The folds are continually opening and closing to allow the passage of air into and out of the lungs. As they approach each other their inner edges lightly touch and are set into vibration by the airstream as it rushes between them. This produces **vocal vibration**, or **voice**. Speech sounds that are produced with vocal vibration are said to be **voiced** (e.g. [b], [z], [v]). When the vocal folds are wide apart so that air passes freely between them there is no vocal vibration. Speech sounds produced when the folds are in this position are said to be **voiceless** (e.g. [p], [s], [f]).

To experience voicing as a phenomenon the best method is to take a pair of sounds, one voiced and the other voiceless, e.g. [z] and [s], and say them alternately with your hands over your ears. The buzzing sound you hear when articulating the voiced sound is caused by the vibration of the vocal folds. All speech sounds can be classified into voiced or unvoiced sounds. In the case of consonants voicing serves as a major distinctive feature. This is not so with vowels, however, since all vowels are voiced. Despite our intuitions to the contrary, voiced sounds are articulated less 'energetically' than voiceless. This is because voiceless sounds do not have the support of voicing to amplify the sound wave: so [f], for example, is a more 'energetic' sound than [v]. This is suggested by the terms that are applied to them: **fortis** (= 'strong') and **lenis** ('weak'). Broadly speaking, 'fortis' and 'lenis' regularly correlate with 'voiceless' and 'voiced'.

There are two other positions that the vocal folds can adopt in addi-tion to those which produce voiced and unvoiced sounds. First, it is possible for the folds to approach each other in such a way that air passing through them causes friction without causing vocal vibration. This happens in the case of [h]. This particular sound is unique among consonants in that it doesn't involve any restriction in the mouth by the vocal organs. It is produced in similar fashion to a vowel but without voicing. Secondly, it is also possible for the vocal folds to be brought tightly together so that no air can pass through them, either inwards or outwards. This is the position they adopt when we are bracing ourselves for any muscular effort such as lifting a heavy weight. The only speech sound produced when this posture of the vocal folds is assumed and then released is the 'glottal plosive', also commonly known as the 'glottal stop'. It derives its name from the **glottis**, which is the term given to the gap between the vocal folds. Pressure builds up behind the closed folds and then is suddenly released in the manner of a 'plosive' (*see* MANNER OF ARTICULATION).

Variations in voicing are important in the generation of pronunciation variants, or **allophones** (*see* PHONEMES). All vowels, for example, are pronounced with a long allophone finally, and before a voiced sound. So that in words such as *bat* and *bad*, for instance, the vowel sound – [æ] – is slightly longer before the voiced consonant than before the voiceless. This is because the voicing of [æ] is allowed to continue uninterrupted in *bad*, whereas in *bat* the voiceless [t] effectively cuts it off. As a consequence we can say that the phoneme /æ/ has two allophones – [æ] before a voiceless sound and [æ·] elsewhere. The small · following the allophone is a DIACRITIC indicating that the sound is slightly longer. Since, as we have said, this is a phenomenon that is true of all vowels, we can formulate a rule to encapsulate it:

$$V \rightarrow [V] / \_ \, [- \text{voice}]$$
$$[V\cdot] \text{ elsewhere}$$

This rule states that vowels retain their quantity (or length) before a voiceless sound but lengthen in other environments (*see* PHONOLOGICAL RULES). Similarly, most voiced sounds can lose their voicing in certain environments and as a consequence have a voiced and a voiceless allophone. Sounds are then said to be **devoiced**. This happens to [w] in the word *twenty*. The voiceless consonant which precedes it serves to delay the onset of voicing, effectively devoicing [w]. We can say then that /w/ has two allophones – [w] and [w̥], the diacritic ̥ indicating the loss of voice.

Vowels: *see also* CARDINAL VOWEL SYSTEM, PLACE OF ARTICULATION, and MANNER OF ARTICULATION. Vowels are conventionally differentiated from CONSONANTS by reference to their articulation. Whereas with consonants the speech organs restrict the airflow in some manner, vowels are produced without any such restriction. The airflow is voiced as it comes through the glottis and then manipulated by the configuration of the vocal organs. If you open your mouth and make a sound it will be vowel-like in quality. Because of the ease with which they are made, they are the first sounds that babies produce. They are also more mobile than consonant sounds and, as a consequence, frequent indicators of variations in ACCENT.

Vowels are divided into single sounds (or **monophthongs**) and glides between vowel positions (known as **diphthongs**). For a description of monophthongs, see the entries listed at the beginning of this entry). The features that constitute the articulation of single vowel sounds – tongue height, position in the mouth, and lip posture – are collectively referred to as a sound's **quality**. Differences in **quality** are consequently distinctive, that is they serve to differentiate one vowel from another. Single vowels also differ from each other in length or **quantity** but, in modern English, differences in quantity are not distinctive (that is, they do not result in phonemic contrasts). The following are the short **monophthongs** of English (Southern Variety):

/ɪ/	bid	/ʊ/	put
/ɛ/	bed	/ʌ/	cup
/æ/	bad	/ə/	about
/ɒ/	box		

Short vowels are sometimes referred to as **lax** since they involve less tense articulation of the vocal organs. Another term for them is **checked** – this means that they can only occur in a closed SYLLABLE, in other words, those which have a **coda**, unless the syllable is unstressed. The remaining five single vowels are long:

/iː/	bead	/ɔː/	saw
/ɑː/	bard	/uː/	boot
/ɜː/	bird		

(ː is a DIACRITIC indicating length).

Although we have said that vowels are distinguished from consonants by reason of their different articulation, there are two consonants that are more vowel-like than their fellows. These are the consonants that occur at the beginning of such words as *yet* and *wet*. Many writers refer to them as **semi-vowels**. The most important thing to remember about these sounds is that they are phonetically like vowels, but phonologically like consonants. That is, the manner in which they are produced is vowel-like but the way in which we use them in the language is consonantal. The phonemes in question here are /j/, the initial sound of *yet*, and /w/, the initial sound of *wet*. In character the articulation of /j/ is practically the same as for the close front vowel /iː/, only shorter. Similarly, the articulation of /w/ closely resembles that for /uː/, but is shorter. If you make the initial sounds of *yet* and *wet* very long, you will be able to hear this. Despite this vowel-like character, however, we use them like consonants. Just as with other consonants, for example, they only occur before vowel phonemes. And they also behave like consonants in that they can only occur with the 'a' form of the indefinite article. The rule for the use of the indefinite article obliges us to use 'a' before a consonant (*a cat, a dog, a mouse*), and 'an' before a vowel (*an apple, an orange*). If a word beginning with /j/ or /w/ is preceded by the indefinite article it is the 'a' form that is used (as in *a wedding, a yacht*). Another example is that of the definite article, where the rule is that 'the' is pronounced /ðə/ before consonants: /ðə kæt/ (the cat) and /ðə dɒg/, but /ði/ before vowels: /ði æpl/ (the apple) and /ði ɒrɪndʒ/ (the orange). /j/ and /w/ behave like consonants in expecting the /ðə/ form; consequently, these sounds are invariably classed as consonants rather than vowels.

Diphthongs differ from monophthongs, or **pure vowels**, in that they involve a movement, usually referred to as a 'glide', from one vowel position to another. In southern British English there are eight diphthongs. Three glide towards the weak central vowel /ə/, or SCHWA, three towards the short front vowel /ɪ/, and two towards the short back vowel /ʊ/ (see Table 3).

In terms of length, diphthongs are very like long monophthongs. Indeed, there is frequently movement between them in certain accents. Long vowels can, over time, develop into diphthongs (a process known as **breaking**) and, conversely, diphthongs can become long monophthongs (a process called **smoothing**). The diphthong in *cure* – /ʊə/ – for example, has for many southern British speakers only a limited occurrence. In many words it has smoothed to /ɔː/, as in *poor* /pɔː/. On the other hand, the long monophthong /uː/ is frequently articulated as a diphthong, as, for example, in *cool*, producing a pronunciation with [uʊ]

Table 3

Towards /ə/		Towards /ɪ/		Towards /ʊ/	
/ɪə/	beer	/ɛɪ/	pay	/əʊ/	go
/ɛə/	bear	/aɪ/	pie	/aʊ/	mouth
/ʊə/	cure	/ɔɪ/	boy		

('coouhl'). Two other ways in which diphthongs can alter in quality relate to the first element of the phoneme. This can either widen, in which case it becomes more **open**, or it can narrow, in which case it becomes more **close** (*see* MANNER OF ARTICULATION). The diphthong in *face* – /ɛɪ/ – for example, has, for more conservative speakers of English, a closer starting point, more like /e/.

Finally, there is a group of vowel sounds that typically combine a diphthong and a monophthong together. These combinations occur systematically enough for us to identify them separately and to call them **triphthongs**. They are the most complex sounds of the vowel type, in English, and can be difficult to recognise. A triphthong is a glide from one vowel to another and then to a third. In each case the combination ends in SCHWA. This means that the diphthongs that already end in schwa do not extend to form triphthongs. The triphthongs that commonly occur in southern British English are as follows:

/ɛɪə/	**pl**ayer	/əʊə/	**lower**
/aɪə/	**fire**	/aʊə/	**power**
/ɔɪə/	**royal**		

4 Syntax

INTRODUCTION

Syntax is a term used for the study of the rules governing the way words are combined to form SENTENCES. If we take any sentence of English, it is clear that the words are arranged in a specific order. We are not at liberty to put them in any arrangement we like, that is, if we wish to be understood. Moreover, to change the word order is to alter the meaning. In the sentence *The cat chases the mouse*, we know that the individual items are related to each other in such a manner that it allows only one interpretation. Swap them around, *The mouse chases the cat*, and a totally different meaning is created. This is because the parts of the sentence are structurally related to each other, and this structure is reflected in the word order. In some languages the structure depends not on word order, but on the form of the words themselves. In such cases it's possible for sentences with a completely different word order to mean exactly the same. English used to be one of these, but it isn't any longer. The following examples are taken from **Old English**, or **Anglo-Saxon**. Although the items are arranged differently, in both cases the sentences have the same meaning:

Se cyning meteth thone biscop – The king meets the bishop
Thone biscop meteth se cyning – The king meets the bishop

The clue to interpreting these sequences is that *se* and *thone* are different forms of the same linguistic item: they are varying forms of our modern word *the*. The form changes according to whether it is attached to the person performing the action or the person to whom it is performed. Such changes are known as **inflexions/inflections**. Old English used to have a lot of them, similar to Latin, but over the centuries the majority have been lost and, as a consequence, word order is far more important to sentence meaning than it was in Anglo-Saxon times.

What we are talking about here is often described as GRAMMAR. Used in this sense, knowing the grammar of a language means knowing two basic things about it: first, what changes are required to individual words according to the way in which they are used – this is termed MORPHOLOGY; and second, the rules governing the combination of words into PHRASES, CLAUSES, and sentences. To go back to our sentence *The cat chases the mouse*: any native user of English would know that if there were more than one cat involved, the word would alter its form to *cats*, and, simultaneously, *chases* would alter to *chase*. The new inflectional form of *cat* is called the **plural** and its relationship with the VERB is termed **agreement**. In English, the **subject** of a verb has to agree with it. Subtleties of grammar such as this demonstrate that the form of a word, i.e. its MORPHOLOGY, interacts with syntactic arrangement (in English the subject normally precedes the verb). As a consequence of this interaction, morphology and syntax are normally studied together.

Fundamental to understanding both the morphology and the syntactic possibilities of words is a knowledge of the categories to which they belong. Words are conventionally sorted into classes, such as NOUN, verb, ADJECTIVE, ADVERB, PREPOSITION and so on (see WORD CLASSES), and it is on the basis of this sorting that higher units can be constructed. It isn't important that we know the label 'noun', or that we can define what a noun is, but it is important that we know which words can act as nouns. This knowledge enables us to rule out replacing the word *cat* with *up*, in our sample sentence. *The up chases the mouse* is not a well-formed sequence. This is because a preposition cannot follow a DETERMINER, only a noun can. All the syntactic rules of English, the rules that tell us how to construct phrases, clauses, and sentences, are **category-based**. That means they derive from the classes into which the vocabulary of English is sorted. Nouns, verbs, adjectives, adverbs, and prepositions can all act as the heads of phrases. These, in turn, combine into clauses, and finally sentences. Languages are hierarchically organised, and it is the structure of these hierarchies which syntacticians – people who study syntax – explore.

So far we have established that syntax (the study of word combination) and morphology (the study of word form) are twin aspects of the grammatical structure of language. We could represent this relationship as in Figure 14. This is a traditional way of dividing up the different levels, in which the term 'grammar' is understood as the system of rules specifying the forms of words and their combination into well-formed sequences. It's as well to remember that some linguists give 'grammar' a broader meaning and see it as relating to the entire system of structural relationships in a language. Used in this sense it subsumes PHONOLOGY and SEMANTICS and defines the total set of rules possessed by a speaker. The term 'grammar', then, can have both a narrow and a broad

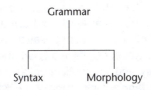

Figure 14 The scope of traditional grammar

meaning depending on the context in which it is being used. The pages that follow discuss various kinds of grammatical approaches which are current today. In each case there are wider implications for the phonological and semantic structure of the language, but given the specific focus of this chapter, I have chosen to concentrate on the narrower sense of the term.

The most straightforward treatment of syntax is that provided by **descriptive grammars**. These attempt to make precise, systematic statements about the morphology and syntax of a particular language. The examples of word structure and sentence formation that we have been considering are descriptive in nature. Descriptive grammars will outline the rules governing the way nouns inflect to form plurals, verbs to form the past tense, and adjectives to form comparatives and superlatives, as in *nice → nicer → nicest*. They will also tell us how each of the word categories behaves in the language; where nouns, for example, can occur in sentences, and what determiners can accompany them. Higher up the ladder they will specify the types of phrases to be found and the kinds of dependent words that can modify heads. And so on up to clauses and sentences. The basic methodology is simply to describe how the language works in practical terms. The most comprehensive of such grammars is Huddleston and Pullum's *The Cambridge Grammar of the English Language* (2002).

The procedure adopted by descriptive grammars is quite different from that used by **prescriptive grammars**, which attempt to lay down rules about how people ought to speak and write rather than how they actually do. Most of these rules, such as not splitting an infinitive (e.g., *to gently soothe away care*) are simply matters of social taste, and not linguistic issues *per se*. As a consequence most linguists are not interested in them except as an example of how not to approach linguistics. Prescriptive grammar is all that is left of **traditional grammar**. This is the form of grammar that, at one time, comprised the substance of school education in the English language. Much of the terminology of the descriptive approach is to be found in traditional grammar, which is similarly concerned with analysing phrases and clauses. But modern descriptive approaches have taken account of recent developments in linguistics at a more theoretical level, and are also not hampered by anxieties over matters of taste. It is fair to say that any modern course in linguistics requires the student to have a good understanding of current descriptive terminology and its application to language study. By the same token, most **pedagogic grammars**, i.e. grammars intended to teach people how to speak and write a particular language, are based on descriptive approaches

Descriptive grammars are necessarily language-specific; a description of English, for example, will not serve for one of French. **Theoretical grammars**, on the other hand, go beyond any individual language to try and establish what it is that all languages have in common. Most influential here is the concept of UNIVERSAL GRAMMAR. The assumption of grammarians working in this area is that linguistic knowledge is innate; in other words, that we are all 'wired' in some way, or programmed, to learn a language. What happens when a child encounters data from his or her native language, is that various switches are thrown in the brain to lock onto it, rather like tuning in a television set to receive a signal. The innateness hypothesis is well established now, and the search for what are termed **language universals** has yielded a number of insights into the way languages operate.

Underpinning these theoretical perspectives has been a set of **formal grammars**, which set out not simply to describe, but to explain, how language works. Most influential here has been the work that has developed from the initiatives of the American linguist Noam Chomsky. Chomsky set out to establish a grammar that would make explicit the mental framework which speakers have in their heads for the production, or generation, of sentences. GENERATIVE GRAMMAR, as it has come to be known, elaborates a set of rules, **phrase structure rules**, which encapsulate these formative processes. They are expressed in the form of **rewrite rules**, which are the basic blueprint for sentence formation. Generative grammar has become increasingly more sophisticated over the years, with the extension into X-BAR SYNTAX, the aim of which is to simplify all the rules for phrase, clause, and sentence structure, into a few overarching rules using X as a **category-variable**, that is, a symbol that can stand for any word category. X-bar theorists argue that all languages have a version of X-bar syntax, and as such, it is an essential component of universal grammar.

Another important component of the Chomskyan version of generative grammar has been TRANSFORMATIONAL GRAMMAR. From early on, Chomsky argued that sentences had two forms: a **deep structure** (which was the propositional core of the sentence) and a **surface form** (which was the way it appeared as an actual utterance). As such, two grammars were required. The first, a phrase structure kind, provided the underlying blueprint – telling us, for example, that an abstract sentence comprises a NP (noun phrase) plus a VP (verb phrase) – and the second, a transformational kind, specified all the transformations needed to turn it into an actual sentence of English. Some of these would be relatively minor, such as assigning **number** (singular/plural) to the noun, and TENSE (past/present) to the verb, and others would be major and result in the reordering of **constituents** (see IMMEDIATE CONSTITUENCY ANALYSIS) to form interrogatives, passives, and negations. Attitudes towards transformational grammar have been mixed over the years. Not all generative linguists are persuaded by the separation into deep and surface structure; Chomsky, though, has refined it considerably in recent times and it continues to be a potent influence in current work on syntax.

A different kind of syntactic analysis from the heady heights of generative grammar is that provided by FUNCTIONAL GRAMMAR. The concern of functional linguists is with language as a system of meanings, rather than as an abstract code. They pursue the interactive and communicative aspects of language. Arguably the most influential of these linguists is Michael Halliday, whose SYSTEMIC FUNCTIONAL model is widely used in STYLISTICS and DISCOURSE ANALYSIS. Halliday sees language as a sophisticated tool for accomplishing a number of central functions such as the need to represent the world to ourselves and others, and the need to interact with other humans. What he attempts to do is to map these functions onto language. Instead of simply analysing a sentence in terms of the phrases that comprise it, he is more concerned with the semantic role the phrases play in the communication of meaning. Sentences don't just contain **subjects** and **objects**, but **participants**, each of which can be assigned a specific role, such as **actor** or **goal**. And verbs can be distinguished in terms of the **processes** they encode, whether action ones such as running, and jumping, or mental ones such as thinking and feeling. In this way he establishes a link between language as a code and language as a human tool.

The great variety of approaches to syntax and the grammars on which they depend make this particular level of language probably the most complex and the most contentious in terms of linguistic criticism. If there are 'hard men' in linguistics, they inhabit the rarified world of syntax. The entries that follow attempt to say more about some of the principal kinds of grammar that students need to be conversant with, but, equally important, the Glossary tries to provide a convincing and intelligible description of the common terms and topics that are in everyday use by linguists. It recognises, a point made earlier, that in order to engage with the more theoretical aspects of syntax the student needs a good descriptive model of his, or her, own.

GLOSSARY

Adjective. Adjectives are words that specify the attributes of NOUNS. Typically, they give information about the size, colour, shape, and appearance of entities. In formal terms adjectives are usually defined by their distribution, that is, where they can occur in word strings. We characteristically find them in two places: first, in an **attributive** position within a noun PHRASE, as in *the **lovely** book*; and secondly, in a post-verbal, or **predicative** position, as in *The book is **lovely***. Adjectives that can occur in both of these positions are termed **central**. We can think of these as prototypical adjectives.

Not all adjectives are prototypical, however. Some, such as *outright*, *utter*, *chief*, and *former*, will only occur attributively. So whilst we are able to say *an outright lie*, for example, we cannot say **The lie was outright*. Other adjectives will only be found predicatively. These include *unwell*, *loath*, and *asleep*. *The boy was asleep* is fine but not **the asleep boy*. These, more restricted, adjectives are termed **peripheral**. The difference between the two positions available for adjectives seems to correlate with a difference in meaning. Attributive adjectives tend to indicate qualities of the noun that are felt to be permanent, like size or colour, whereas predicative adjectives specify features that are considered to be non-permanent, such as being asleep or unwell.

There are two other criteria also used to distinguish adjectives. First, many adjectives are **gradable**. That is, they can be modified by ADVERBS, such as *very* and *quite*, indicating intensity (e.g. *very beautiful*, *quite short*). And, second, they can also be used in a **comparative** and **superlative** form (*lovely, lovelier, loveliest*, or alternatively, *more lovely, most lovely*). But again, not all adjectives can do this. Adjectives such as *previous, inherent, former* and *mere* are not normally gradable and do not form the comparative or superlative. Having said that, however, the instinct to grade is perennial and we sometimes find **intensifiers** in novel combinations with non-gradable adjectives, e.g. *He's very dead*.

As with other WORD CLASSES, once we start to examine the criteria for membership of the adjective class we tend to find degrees of 'adjectiveness', with some items, notably the central ones, fulfilling all the criteria, and others fulfilling only some. As a consequence, the sub-classification of adjectives is not without its problems. Some grammars, for instance, would label everything in attributive position between the DETERMINER and the noun in the following phrase as an adjective: *my uncle's large old country barn.* But including other nouns such as *country* and *uncle's* within the adjective class is not very helpful since it blurs any distinction between them and adjectives proper, like *large* and *old.* A more satisfactory solution to the difficulty is to recognise a form and function distinction here. In other words, that whilst such peripheral items are formally members of another class, nevertheless, when they occur in environments such as the one above, they are functioning like adjectives. This allows us to term them **adjectivals**, i.e. words that are fulfilling an adjectival function, as distinct from items that are formally adjectives.

The order in which adjectives occur in attributive position suggests an underlying semantic pattern in which colour terms come before indications of size in proximity to the noun, followed by evaluative terms, as in *his beautiful small black cat.* Where adjectivals are present, they normally occur immediately before, or immediately after the adjectives, e.g. *his **father's** beautiful small black **Manx** cat.*

Adverb(ial).   Adverbs are the most mixed of all the major WORD CLASSES. Typically, an adverb modifies a VERB by giving circumstantial information about the time, place, or manner in which an action, event, or process takes place. Many adverbs, although not all, are formed by adding the **suffix** 'ly' onto an ADJECTIVE, e.g. *beautiful**ly**, quick**ly**, sad**ly**.* Beware of *friendly*, however, where the suffix is not an adverb signal, since this is an adjective formed from the NOUN *friend*. In non-standard grammar the 'ly' suffix is frequently dropped from adverbs altogether, as in *She talked very clever.* Indeed, the interconnection of adjectives and adverbs has led some linguists to suggest a super-class called **advectives**. Interestingly, 'ly' (or **manner adverbs**, as they are loosely called) can also occur in comparative and superlative form with *more* and *most*, just like many adjectives, and they can usually be graded by **intensifiers** such as *very* and *quite*.

But not all adverbs are of this form. Into the adverb class also come *here, there, now,* and *tomorrow*, words that indicate the time and place of some occurrence but which are not gradable and cannot occur as comparatives or superlatives. Also placed here are **degree adverbs** – in addition to *very* and *quite* we have *extremely* and *awfully*. These serve to intensify adjectives and other adverbs, e.g. *quite bad(ly)*. And lastly, there are adverbs that, instead of modifying a verb, an adjective, or another adverb, seem to modify a whole sentence. These include *maybe, perhaps, however, frankly,* and *hopefully*. Their function as **sentence adverbs** is often signalled by their frequent occurrence in initial position within a sentence. At the same time, however, they are extremely mobile and can occur almost anywhere. The adverb *occasionally* can be inserted into any position, for example in the sentence *I go home*. The heterogeneous nature of adverbs as a class is perhaps their most distinctive characteristic and it is difficult to avoid feeling that to some extent this very looseness operates as a convenient way of labelling words that do not have an obvious home elsewhere.

The CLAUSAL function that adverbs perform is termed **adverbial**. However, this is also a function that can be performed by other categories above word level. PREPOSITIONAL PHRASES, noun phrases, and also adverb phrases can all be used in sentences to give circumstantial information about time, place, and manner, e.g. *I am going* **in five minutes/next week/very soon**. The term 'adverbial', as a consequence, is much larger than simply 'adverb'. Along with terms like **subject**, **object**, and **complement** it denotes an element of clause structure, as opposed to a word class.

Argument.   A term used by linguists to describe the role played by particular entities in the semantic structure of sentences. All VERBS are said to have arguments. Indeed, it is the number and nature of the arguments they require which distinguishes them grammatically. A verb like *fall*, which is typically **intransitive** (*see* TRANSITIVITY), requires only one argument, as in ***The man*** *fell*, whereas a mono-transitive verb, such as *kick*, needs two, ***The boy*** *kicked* ***the ball***, and a di-transitive verb needs three, ***I*** *gave* ***her some flowers***. Expressions that do not function as arguments are described as 'non arguments'. For example, if we added *yesterday* onto the last sentence, *I gave her some flowers yesterday*, we would be adding on a wholly optional element that is not part of the sentence's argument structure. Information about the arguments required by verbs is contained in our mental LEXICON and plays a vital part in the construction of well-formed sentences.

The term 'argument' itself comes from philosophy, more particularly from predicate calculus. Sentences are regarded as propositions in which something is predicated, i.e. claimed, about another entity or entities. The argument structure of verbs is particularly important in THETA THEORY, which seeks to describe the thematic role arguments fulfil in individual sentences.

Aspect.   A category used in the description of VERBS that refers to the duration of the activity indicated by the verb. It's important to distinguish it from *tense*, which is primarily concerned with location in time, i.e. when something occurred, rather than how long it occurred for. There are two types of aspectual contrast: the **progressive** and the **perfect/perfective.**

The progressive aspect is the one most people know as the 'ing' form of the verb (*walking/throwing/seeing*). It is used to indicate continuous activity. Indeed, you may find that some grammars refer to it as the **continuous** aspect. In order to form the progressive we have to use the **auxiliary** verb *be* together with a main, or **lexical**, verb, as in the following:

(i)   *I am walking the dog*
(ii) *I was walking the dog*

In both cases the progressive indicates an activity which is continuous or on-going, whether in the present, as in (i), or the past, as in (ii). This differentiates it from the **simple** form of the verb, which stresses the unity, or completeness of the activity:

(i)   *I walk the dog*
(ii) *I walked the dog*

Here, the focus is on the completed event rather than its continuous nature. The distinction between progressive and simple forms can be used to express subtle distinctions of duration. Most people will tend to rely more heavily on progressive than on simple forms in situations where the action being described is co-extensive with the time of utterance. We would say *I'm reading a book* rather than *I read a book*. One of the few occasions where the reverse is the case is in sports commentaries, which frequently employ simple forms, e.g. *Keegan gathers the ball*, *passes to Robson*, *Robson shoots*, in order to convey the immediacy of the action with clarity and economy.

Not all verbs can readily occur in the progressive. Those that do are characteristically action verbs of some kind, e.g. *kick*, *eat*, *throw*. These are traditionally referred to as **dynamic** verbs. Other verbs, such as *seem* and *be*, termed **stative** verbs, which identify states of being, are not usually found in the progressive:

He seems nice	* *He is seeming nice*
He is a footballer	**He is being a footballer*

However, there are special contexts in which the progressive is possible with many stative verbs:

Q: *What game is Tommy playing?*
A: *He's **being** a footballer today.*

As with other grammatical distinctions, such as **mass/count** in the case of nouns (*see* NOUN), and **transitive** and **intransitive** in the case of verbs (*see* TRANSITIVITY), it is better to think of stative and dynamic as terms describing **uses** rather than exact categories.

The perfect aspect is also concerned with duration but in a rather different way than the progressive. Despite its label, the perfect is used to indicate indeterminate time, most usually in respect to an activity or condition in the past that has continuing or present relevance. Some grammars describe the perfect aspect as a **secondary tense**. Under this model the simple past is called the **preterite**, and regarded as a **primary tense**. Whatever model we use, however, the perfect is formed by using the auxiliary *have* together with a main verb. And whereas the progressive uses the 'ing', or **present participle**, the perfect uses the 'ed' (sometimes called 'en'), or **past participle**:

> *I am living in London (progressive)*
> *I have lived in London (perfect)*

The sense of present relevance conveyed by the perfect (or perfective) is evident if we compare it with the simple past tense:

> *I lived in London for ten years (I no longer do)*
> *I have lived in London for ten years (I still do)*

The second sentence gives a sense of the past continuing up to and including the present. This is the **present perfective**. The perfective can also be used, however, to express a sense of relevance in respect of some activity firmly in the past:

> *He was angry that he had missed the bus*

In this case both being angry and missing the bus occurred in the past and are completed events, but we can clearly see that missing the bus happened first, or was **anterior** to being angry, and moreover, that it was of current relevance to the anger, i.e. he was still in the state of having missed the bus whilst he was angry. This is the **past perfective** – the clue here is the use of the past form *had* in conjunction with the main verb.

Verb phrases can combine both the progressive and the perfect in their construction to convey a sense of continuous activity which is of current relevance either to the present or to some time in the past. In these cases the ordering of the verbs is always the same:

HAVE + BE + MAIN VERB

In other words we indicate perfect aspect before the progressive, as in the following examples:

He has been doing the washing up
*He been has doing the washing up
He had been doing the washing up
*He been had doing the washing up

Clause.   A term used in some grammars to refer to a grammatical unit intermediate between PHRASE and SENTENCE. The distinctive feature of clauses is that they have a **subject-predicate** structure. A predicate is typically a claim or assertion made about a thing or person. Its formation requires a **predicator**, or verb, with which to make the claim:

subject	**predicate**
The boy	*kicked the ball over the fence*
The tall masted schooner	*sank*
She	*slept*

All of these clauses are also complete sentences in their own right. This enables us to say that a **simple sentence** consists of a single clause. **Multiple sentences** will consist of more than one clause.

Clauses are made out of **elements**. We've already mentioned two of them, i.e. subject and predicator (or verb). The remaining elements are **object**, **complement**, and **adverbial** (or **adjunct**). This structure is sometimes referred to as **SPOCA** (alternatively, **SVOCA**). The subject usually identifies the theme or topic of the clause, that is, the item about which the remainder of the clause is informing us. The verb, or predicator, is its heart – a good rule of thumb in identifying clauses is to look for the presence of a verb. The third element, the object, identifies who or what has been directly affected by the activity of the verb. There are two sorts of object, direct and indirect. In the following example, *the girl* and *some flowers* both qualify as objects of the action of giving. The first, however, is direct and the second, indirect. A good test in cases of uncertainty is to rephrase the clause with a *to*, or sometimes a *for*, phrase which causes the indirectness to appear more clearly:

I gave the girl some flowers
I gave some flowers to the girl

The fourth element, the complement, gives further information about either the subject or object of the verb and shares its area of reference. Some verbs, particularly **copula** types, will not take objects. These are 'linking' verbs such as *be*, *appear*, *seem*, and *become*. In clauses such as *The boy seems **nice*** and *He is **Peter***, neither *nice* nor *Peter* can be considered objects of their respective verbs. They 'complement' their subjects by referring back directly to them. In such cases subject and complement are said to be in an intensive relationship. Similarly, an object can also be complemented by a phrase which gives further information about it. In the clause *I consider you much nicer*, the ADJECTIVE phrase *much nicer* is acting as a complement of the object *you* and refers directly back to it. It gives us important information about *you*, in the opinion of the speaker.

The fifth element, the adverbial/adjunct, is grammatically optional in clauses. In other words, you could leave it out and still have a complete structure. It's the element that provides circumstantial information about when, where, or how, something took place. In the following clause, the NOUN phrase, *last night*, is a time adverbial: *Mave went to the dance **last night***. Similarly, in *Jim passed the salt **down the table***, the PREPOSITIONAL phrase *down the table* is a place adverbial. In both instances the omission of the adverbial would not damage the clause structurally.

The optional character of the adverbial brings us to an important point about clause elements, which is that the requirement for a particular element to be present or not depends on the type of clause we are constructing. This, in turn, is largely determined by the character of the verb, or predicator. We have already said that some verbs take complements rather than objects. There are others that don't require either. And there are some that require not one, but two objects. Verbs tend to select the elements that accompany them. It's on the basis of these SELECTION RESTRICTIONS that they are said to be **sub-categorised**. There are five major types of clause structure that result from the possible permutation of elements:

(i)   S + V: *The man died*
(ii) S + V + O: *I love you*
(iii) S + V + O + O: *She gave him some chocolates*
(iv) S + V + C: *The milk went sour*
(v)   S + V + O + C: *He thought the exam much harder*

The first type, S + V, is an **intransitive** construction (*see* TRANSITIVITY). This construction is complete on its own. Numbers (ii) and (iii) are both **transitive** in that they require objects: (ii) is **monotransitive**, requiring a single object, whilst (iii) is **ditransitive**, needing both, a direct and an indirect object. The verb *give* is typical of such predicators – one gives something to someone. Example (iv) is the **intensive** type where the subject and complement are linked intransitively together. And finally, (v) is a **complex-transitive** type. The object *the exam* needs a complement to complete the sense of the clause – *He thought the exam* is not sufficient on its own. Notice that none of the clauses requires an adverbial. There are no predicators that are sub-categorised by an adverbial. However, what about a sentence like *My mother was in the kitchen*, where the prepositional phrase *in the kitchen* is clearly not omissible? Using the proposed model of analysis, *in the kitchen* is functioning here as a complement not an adverbial, as opposed to the sentence *My mother is sleeping in the kitchen*, where its function is clearly adverbial.

The clauses we have been considering as exemplars of construction types are all **kernel clauses**. In other words, they are complete, not elliptical, and **declarative**, not **imperative**, **interrogative**, or **exclamative** (*see* SENTENCES). They are also positive, not negative, and UNMARKED in terms of word order. This is not how we always encounter clauses, since they are subject to various discourse transformations in the production of actual sentences, but it's useful to take idealised examples like these in order to establish basic grammatical syntagms. One such transformation is the reduced or **verbless** clause, as in *When ripe these oranges are delicious*. Here, the omitted elements indicate *when ripe* to be a reduced type (iv) structure. Similarly, whilst all main clauses are FINITE, subordinate ones need not necessarily be (*see* SENTENCE). In the sentence *Eating people is wrong*, the clause *eating people* is non-finite and, as such, incomplete on its own. However, it is contained within the main clause which has the finite verb *is* as its predicator.

Finally, we might just consider how necessary the term 'clause' is. At the outset we established that a simple sentence consists of one clause. If the terms are identical at this level the question arises as to whether both of them are really necessary. Grammars tend to take different positions over this. The traditional view has been to keep the distinction since once we get beyond the simple sentence into the territory of **compound** and **complex** sentences the terms are no longer the same. These grammars will discuss such structures in terms of **main clause**, **coordinate clause** and **subordinate clause** (*see* SENTENCE). More commonly nowadays, however, you will find that many grammars, particularly, of the GENERATIVE kind, avoid the term 'clause' and describe all clauses as sentences. Where there are more than one in a construction they are differentiated in terms of their hierarchical importance as **S1**, **S2**, and so on, or alternatively, using the notation of X-BAR THEORY, as S' and S". There is no 'correct' answer here, just different descriptive frameworks.

Conjunction (conjunct).   A conjunction is a linking word whose main function is to connect words or other constructions together. Conjunctions typically serve as hinges to combine together two units, a NOUN and a NOUN, as in *Jack **and** Jill*, or two CLAUSES, as in *Jack went up the hill **and** Jill came after*. There are two main kinds of conjunction: **coordinating**, and **subordinating**. The first sort link together units that are of equal status. The examples already given are of this kind. *And* is the most frequent **coordinator**, followed by *but* and *yet*. Subordinating conjunctions, or **subordinators**, involve a more complex relationship between the units being joined, where one is thought to be subordinate to, i.e. dependent on, the other. These conjunctions typically occur between two clauses, e.g. *I will do it **if** I can*; *He will come **when** he is ready*. In each of these SENTENCES the clause following the conjunction elaborates a requirement that has to be fulfilled for the action in the main clause to be accomplished. Other subordinating conjunctions are *while*, *whether*, *because*, and *since*. In GENERATIVE GRAMMAR these conjunctions are more usually called complementisers

A third kind of linking can be achieved by using what are termed **conjuncts**. These are words like *however*, *meanwhile*, *moreover*, *so*, *nevertheless*, and *now*, which have a form of ADVERBIAL function in that they serve to provide, or introduce, circumstantial information. Conjuncts are principally used as textual devices in developing and staging an argument or narrative.

> **Now** *I was intending to go home.* **However**, *it was raining as usual.*
> **Meanwhile**, *we played monopoly.*

A useful term to describe conjunctions and conjuncts is **connectives.**

Determiner.   Determiners are a class of words that always occur with a NOUN and serve to specify, or 'determine', its number and definiteness. The most frequently occurring determiners are the **indefinite article** *a(n)*, and the **definite article** *the*. Other words which can have a determiner function include **possessives** (*my*, *your*, *his*), **demonstratives** (*this*, *that*, *these*, *those*), and **quantifiers** (*some*, *many*, *several*).

Many grammars distinguish between **central determiners**, **prede-terminers**, and **postdeterminers**. **Central determiners**, which include the items listed above, can only ever occur singly. We can't say *the my book* or *his a dog* (*his many books* is possible, but see below). **Predeterminers** are a small set of words that occur before central determiners and which characteristically express notions of quantity. They include items such as *all*, *both*, and *half*, as in **all** the cats, **both** my brothers, **half** the loaf. Correspondingly, **postdeterminers** occur after the central variety. As with predeterminers, they also usually express quantity. Included here are **numerals**, both **cardinals** (*the **three** boys*), and **ordinals** (*the **first** time*), as well as quantifiers (*the **many** cats, a **few** people*). Notice that these can also occur as central determiners, e.g. **many** *cats*, **few** *people*, and also as predeterminers, **many of** the cats, **few of** the people.

The most recent version of X-BAR THEORY has raised the status of determiners and sees them as forming the heads of the PHRASES in which they occur. According to this view, which remains controversial, rather than premodifying nouns, determiners are complemented by nouns or noun phrases.

Ellipsis.   A term used to describe the omission of a word or words from a SENTENCE, where they are recoverable from the context. So, in the exchange **A**: *How are you feeling?* **B**: *Fine*, the full form of B's answer (*I am feeling fine*) is predictable from the context. Ellipsis is a frequent feature of speech. It is generally used for the sake of economy, but also sometimes for emphasis, as in **A**: *Can I go out?* **B**: *No!* Linguists would not normally use the term, however, to apply in the case of abbreviated utterances where the full sense was not predictable, for example, saying *Sorry* after bumping into someone which could mean *Sorry, I didn't see you* or *Sorry for bumping into you*, or something else.

Finite.   A term used in the grammatical description of verbs. Finite verbal forms are those which can show formal contrasts of:

TENSE:	*past* and *present*
NUMBER:	*singular* and *plural*
PERSON:	*first*, *second* and *third*
MOOD:	*indicative*, *imperative* and *subjunctive*

Those which can't show these contrasts are termed **non-finite**. This means that **participle** forms – the present participle, or 'ing' form, and the past participle, or 'en' form – are always non-finite, because they are not able to indicate them. As a consequence, when they occur in an independent SENTENCE or main CLAUSE they must always be preceded by one or more **auxiliary** verbs. It is these that carry the burden of indicating tense, number, person, and mood, not the participle, as in the following:

> I am/was ***walking***
> They are/***were walking***
> I have/had ***walked***
> They have/had ***walked***

These are all finite clauses, but the participles *walking* and *walked* remain the same whoever is being talked about – *I* or *they* – and whether or not the action is past or present. There is one more non-finite form: the **infinitive** (or the 'to' form). This uses the **base** form of the VERB, as in *I/they want/wanted **to see** you*, where again *to see* remains the same whatever grammatical variation precedes it.

The only occasion on which non-finite verb forms can occur on their own is in **subordinate**, or dependent, clauses, for example, ***Breaking windows*** *is against the law* or *It is against the law **to break windows***. In these cases the finiteness of the sentence is the property of the main clause to which the subordinate unit is attached.

Functional/systemic grammar.   A functional grammar is one that seeks to derive syntactic structures from the functions which language is said to perform. All syntactic analyses take some account of functional categories. Terms such as **subject** and **object**, for example, are of this type. Functional grammar, however, attempts to discriminate, with a greater degree of delicacy, between different types of subjects and objects and relate these to semantic possibilities within the language. In essence, the development of this kind of grammar was a reaction to the more abstract approaches associated with Chomskyan TRANSFORMA-TIONAL GRAMMAR.

Functional approaches vary somewhat in the terminology and procedures they adopt. One of the most influential of such approaches is that of the British linguist Michael Halliday. His model of the language is sometimes called **systemic grammar**. In simple terms, this means that he sees language as a semantic system, i.e. a system for expressing meanings. At every point of the system a user is offered a series of choices that are both syntactic and semantic. The context within which these choices are made consists of three overarching functions which language is said to fulfil:

(i)   the **ideational** function: the use we make of language to conceptualise the world. This function emphasises language as an instrument of thought, a symbolic code, with which we represent the world to ourselves.

(ii) the **interpersonal** function: the use we make of language as a personal medium. This function emphasises language as an instrument of trans-action by which we represent ourselves to others.

(iii) the **textual** function: the use we make of language to form texts, whether spoken or written. This function emphasises language as an instrument of communication with which we construct cohesive and coherent sequences.

According to Halliday, these functions relate to three central purposes that govern the form that CLAUSES take. Clauses act as a repre-sentation (ideational function), an exchange (interpersonal function), and a message (textual function). Halliday's procedure is to take each of these in turn and describe the choices open to native users of the language.

The clause as representation
This sees the clause as a means of representing the experiential world. As such, it is composed of three functional components: **participant**, **process**, and **circumstance**. The 'participant' function incorporates subjects and objects; 'process' incorporates the VERB element; and 'circumstance' incorporates **adjuncts/adverbials** (*see* CLAUSE). So, in the sentence *She gave me a book yesterday/with a smile/in the garden*, there are three participants (*she*, *me*, *a book*), one process (*gave*), and a variety of circumstances. Centrally important in Halliday's model is the process component. It is this that largely determines the types of participants that are possible. Halliday refers to this as 'the system of TRANSITIVITY' and distinguishes six main processes:

(i) *Material processes.*   These are expressed by verbs of action, *run*, *kick*, *climb*, *spring*, and so on. Material verbs have as their principal participants an **actor** (i.e. someone who performs the action) and a **goal** (the thing, or person, which is acted on). So in *The boy kicked the post*, *the boy* is the actor and *the post*, the goal. Other functional approaches use the term **agent** instead of actor, and **patient** instead of goal, although these are not always synonymous.

An important gain in functional descriptions is that sentence roles stay the same even when the form of the clause is altered. Thus, in *The post was kicked by the boy*, *the boy* remains the actor even though it is no longer the grammatical subject. We can consider the actor as the logical subject, and the goal as the logical object of the clause.

(ii) *Mental processes*   These are expressed by verbs to do with feeling and thinking. Verbs such as *like*, *hate*, *love*, *know*, *think*, and *understand*, fall into this group. The participants in mental processes are different from those in material ones. In *He likes toffee*, the participant *he* can't be said to perform the act of liking. Halliday refers to this subject as the **sensor** (other approaches use the term **experiencer**), and the object *toffee* as the **phenomenon** (or **experienced**). There are quite a number of verbs, however, which can have both a mental and a material meaning. The verb *to see* can be used in this way, e.g.

The man can see a tree (material: actor/goal)
The man can see your argument (mental: sensor/phenomenon)

(iii) *Relational processes.*   These are characteristically expressed by **copula**, or 'linking', verbs. The purpose of these verbs is to relate two participants together. The fundamental process here is one of 'being', i.e. asserting that something is, e.g. *John is nice*; *Joanna is a teacher*. However, there are a number of different ways of 'being'. Halliday distinguishes six. First of all there are three main forms:

(i)   intensive: 'x is *a*'
(ii)   circumstantial: 'x is at *a*'
(iii) possessive: 'x has *a*'

each of which can exist in two modes:

(i)   attributive: '*a* is an attribute of x'
(ii)   identifying: '*a* is the identity of x'.

This gives six possible permutations (as shown in Table 4).

Notice that the identifying types are reversible whereas the attributive aren't. Notice also that although there are six relational types, there are only two sets of participant roles. In the attributive mode an attribute is being ascribed to an entity, as either a quality, a circumstance, or a possession. This defines two elements, an **attribute** and a **carrier**. In the identifying mode, however, one entity is being used to identify another, within the same parameters. The structural functions in this mode are **identifier** and **identified**.

Table 4

Type	Attributive mode	Identifying mode
Intensive	*John is nice*	*John is the leader* *The leader is John*
Circumstantial	*The fair is on Tuesday*	*Tomorrow is the 10th* *The 10th is tomorrow*
Possessive	*Peter has a piano*	*The piano is Peter's* *Peter's is the piano*

(iv) *Behavioural processes.* These are processes of physiological and psychological behaviour, expressed by verbs such as *cough, yawn,* and *smile.* They have some similarity to material verbs in that they describe physical actions, but they differ in that the action is not performed on anything – **A girl laughed a boy* is meaningless, whereas *A girl kicked a boy,* isn't. Moreover, behavioural verbs need a subject that is animate, i.e. living. People and animals smile, yawn, and cough, but not trees or rocks (except figuratively). Material verbs, on the other hand, can have trees or rocks for subjects, e.g. *The tree swayed in the wind.* In this respect, behavioural verbs are like mental ones, which also require animate subjects. As distinct from other groups, however, they only require one participant – the person doing the laughing, coughing, or yawning. This participant is termed the **behaver**.

(v) *Verbal processes.* This is a large category that includes verbs such as *say, report, claim, question,* and *explain.* As with mental and material processes, the participant performing the activity is normally animate, although, in a figurative sense, we can often include inanimate participants (as in *My watch says . . .*). Halliday terms the first participant the **sayer**. Unlike previous processes, however, there are two object participants: first, what is said, and secondly, the person it is said to. These are, respectively, the **verbiage** and the **target**.

(vi) *Existential processes.* These consist of clauses in which *there* acts as a grammatical subject: for example, *There was a cat; There seemed to be a problem,* and so on. In these cases, what we are doing is affirming the existence of something, or someone. As with behavioural verbs there is only one participant here. Although *there* is the subject in existential clauses, it doesn't fulfil any function outside of its grammatical role. The only significant element is the thing, or person, being affirmed as existing. This is termed the **existent**.

There are other participant functions that Halliday, and others, have described, principally **beneficiary** and **range**, but the main ones are those listed above.

The clause as exchange

In addition to acting as representations of the world, clauses also function as an interpersonal medium. Principally important here is MOOD, that is, the relationship speakers forge with listeners through the form of the language. Traditionally, sentences are classified as **declarative**, **interrogative**, **imperative**, and **subjunctive**. These forms correspond to some of the SPEECH ACTS which we use language to accomplish. We can, of course, use these forms to carry out a number of different activities. We frequently employ declaratives, for example, to ask questions and, on occasion, to issue instructions (*see* MOOD). Halliday also includes within the exchange function of grammar the issue of finiteness (*see* FINITE). Finiteness is seen as a semantic property and, more particularly, as the means by which we give something a point of reference in the here and now. This is done partly through mood, but also through the assignment of TENSE. For Halliday, tense is a way of relating an event to the moment of speaking. As such it can indicate more than simply time. The analysis of this dimension is complex and concentrates on viewing different elements of the clause as vehicles for the speaker's presentation of his/her particular orientation to the world.

The clause as message

The message function of clauses is connected very much with their information structure. Functional linguists characteristically distinguish between **theme** and **rheme**, or alternatively, **topic** and **comment**, although these pairs are not always used in the same manner. The theme of a clause is its first major constituent. This may be simply a word, ***John*** *has done his homework*, a phrase, ***Our garden gate*** *needs mending*, or a clause, ***Going home***, *we saw a badger*. The theme is the starting point of the clause – what it is principally going to be about. It is sometimes referred to as the 'psychological subject'. Halliday points out that a clause can have a multiple theme. Of necessity it must have an ideational theme – clauses have to be about something. But, additionally, they may have textual, and/or interpersonal, themes as well. Textual themes include conjunctive items, such as *on the other hand*, *however*, and *now*, and interpersonal ones, including *frankly* and *maybe*.

In the following sentence we can find all three: *But* (textual) *surely* (inter-personal) *Sunday* (ideational) *would be better*. The rheme, or comment, is simply the remainder of the clause after the theme (*would be better*). Its typical use is to expand on the theme and provide more information.

Theme and rheme overlap with another pair of terms, **given** and **new**. These relate specifically to the information structure of the clause. Any text/utterance is necessarily delivered in a linear fashion, and as such, we are forced, as listeners/readers, to process it in a similar fashion. Because of this it is easier for us to process sequences in which the burden of new information comes towards the end of the clause. We expect the starting point of the clause to present us with information that is largely given (i.e. assumed to be known). This gives us time to prepare ourselves for the new, which comes later. We are much more likely to say *There's a bird on the lawn* than *A bird is on the lawn*. In this case, the existential sentence, with *there* as an empty subject, prepares us for the receipt of the infor-mation. In many instances the theme is also the grammatical subject, but there are frequently cases where another element may be promoted to theme, as in *Down came the rain*, where the **complement** *down* is given extra prominence by being placed first. Linguists refer to such themes as MARKED. We can see also here that this clause is unusual in that the given element – the fact that it's raining – comes in final position.

Just as clauses have a theme so they also have a **focus**. The focus is the new information being conveyed by the clause. In unmarked clauses it will therefore come at the end. Linguists refer to this as **end-focus**. But its position is not so fixed as that for theme. Indeed, the focus of a clause is often picked out by intonation rather than word position, as in the following:

MAry did it

Here 'Mary' functions as theme, but it is also the focal point of the sentence because it's new information – the stress pattern signals this. The given information here is contained in the rheme, *did it*. The theme/rheme distinction, therefore, whilst overlapping with new/given, does not exactly cross-reference. Theme and rheme are more formally descriptive terms than new, given, and focus, which essentially derive from communication theory.

Generative grammar.   A generative grammar is one that sets out to specify, i.e. establish rules for, the formation of grammatical structures. You might think that all grammars do this, but the key word here is 'formation'. Generative linguists are interested in how PHRASES, CLAUSES, and SENTENCES are created. They aim to provide a rigorous and explicit framework that can produce (or **generate**) from a small number of general principles, or rules, all the well-formed sentences of a language. The term 'generate' was introduced by Noam CHOMSKY, and much of the development of this grammatical approach bears the hallmark of his influence. TRANSFORMATIONAL GRAMMAR has been one of the principal types of grammar to have emerged from the generative stable and in many ways it is characteristic of the generative approach. Sentences are seen as being formed according to an initial mental blueprint, or **deep structure** (now **D structure**), and then transformed by various grammatical processes, involving the assignment of TENSE and ordering of **constituents** (*see* IMMEDIATE CONSTITUENCY ANALYSIS), into a **surface structure** (now **S structure**). Since Chomsky, generative grammar has grown into a sizeable mammoth, incorporating a number of different theoretical approaches and developments, which vary considerably in their friendliness towards transformational methods of analysis. It's probably better to think of generative grammarians as constituting a school within which there are different departments, as well as particular variations in methodology. What they all have in common, however, is a rigorously empirical and formalist approach to language.

The ultimate concern of generative linguists is with the way in which the structure of language mirrors that of the human mind. Language is viewed as a mental property, the understanding of which can lead to unlocking some of the secrets of the mind. In this respect, the most ambitious offshoot of generative grammar is UNIVERSAL GRAMMAR. This is the term used to describe the grammatical principles that are held to be innately present in everyone's brain, regardless of what language they speak. For generative linguists the discovery of these principles, and the way in which they operate in particular languages, is the main goal of linguistic theory.

Immediate constituency analysis. A form of analysing word strings, beginning with the smallest linguistic unit, and showing how this combines with others to form larger ones. The term **constituent** is a basic term in linguistics for a unit that is a component of a larger one. So a SENTENCE can be analysed into a series of constituents, such as NP (noun phrase) plus VP (verb phrase). These constituents can be analysed into further constituents, e.g. a NP might consist of a DETERMINER plus a NOUN, and such analysis can continue until no further subdivision is possible. In the case of individual words it can continue down to the level of particular MORPHEMES. The major divisions that can be made within a construction are known as the **immediate constituents** and the irreducible elements are known as the **ultimate constituents**. So, for example, in the sentence *The boy loves the animals*, the immediate constituents of the noun PHRASE *the boy* are *the* and *boy*, which in turn are the ultimate constituents of the SENTENCE as a whole.

Constituents are always represented hierarchically but the precise form in which they are shown varies among linguists. The most popular representation is in the form of a TREE DIAGRAM. However, they may be represented in rectangular boxes as in Figure 15, or in a 'Chinese box' arrangement as in Figure 16.

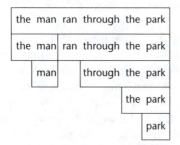

Figure 15   One way of representing constituents in a sentence

Figure 16   A second way of representing constituents in a sentence

Alternatively, parentheses can be used:

(((the) (man)) ((ran) ((through) ((the) (park)))))

Constituent analysis is an important feature of most grammatical accounts, but it is particularly significant in **constituent-structure grammar**, which analyses sentences wholly in terms of a hierarchy of structural layers.

Lexeme.   A term frequently used in linguistics as an alternative to the term WORD. This is because individual words can have different forms whilst still, in one sense, remaining the 'same word'. So, for example, a word such as *nose* has a written form (nose) and a phonological form /nəʊz/. Most people would not want to call these two different words.

Neither would they if we put *nose* into the plural – *noses* – since all we have done is grammatically inflect it. The term 'lexeme' helps to solve these difficulties by specifying an abstract unit which underlies the physical form. The lexeme *nose* has a number of different word forms depending on whether it is transmitted by morse code, semaphore, speech, or writing. Moreover, as a NOUN lexeme it has a singular and a plural form. It is these abstract units, or lexemes, that are listed in dictionaries. You won't, for example, find words such as *walks, walking* and *walked* in the dictionary, but you will find *walk*. This is because they are simply grammatical variants of the root lexeme, *walk*.

Part of the usefulness of the lexeme/word distinction is that it enables us to deal with items that change their grammatical category through **conversion** (*see* MORPHEME). If we change *nose* from a noun into a verb, as in *I'll nose around for a bit*, we have clearly altered it quite substantially even though it looks the same. It can now be inflected for tense (*nosed*) and aspect (*nosing*). In this case, it's the abstract unit that has changed. In other words, whilst we still have the same word, in the sense of word form, we have a new lexeme.

All of this makes clear the inexactness of the term 'word'. Most of us don't have to worry very much about the elasticity of it until we come to study linguistics. It's only then that the need for a more precise vocabulary becomes apparent.

Lexicon/lexis.   The 'lexis' of a language is its vocabulary or word hoard. You will usually come across the term in its adjectival form, **lexical**. A **lexical item**, for example, is a vocabulary unit, or LEXEME; in other words, something you will find in a dictionary. The complete inventory of all the lexical items possessed by native speakers is referred to as a 'lexicon'. 'Why not simply use the term "dictionary"?' you might ask. The reason is that dictionaries are actually existing repositories of information about lexical items whereas lexicons exist in our minds. Most linguists argue that we all possess a **mental lexicon**, in which is stored the mental representation of all that we know about the lexical items of our language; information about how to pronounce them, what their meaning is, and what WORD CLASS they belong to. In GENERATIVE GRAMMAR these properties are formalised into FEATURES and put in square brackets. So, for example, an entry for the word 'child' would assign it to its appropriate word class with the feature [+ N], and indicate its SEMANTIC features as [+ human], [- adult]. Lexicons are not open to direct viewing by linguists – we can't open our minds for them to see inside. Therefore, linguists have to work backwards from samples of actual language use and deduce from these what the lexicon of native speakers consists of.

Over the years linguists have tended to extend considerably the amount of information stored in the mental lexicon. In the early days of generative grammar it was supposed that practically all of the work done in composing SENTENCES was undertaken by the syntactic component, i.e. that part of our linguistic knowledge that stores information about the grammatical rules of language. The lexicon was thought to be little more than a word hoard with fairly basic information about individual entries. But recent approaches have been concerned to distribute the load more evenly. Entries for VERBS, for example, are regularly thought to contain information about their TRANSITIVITY, their ARGUMENT structure, and their THETA marking. The relationship between the syntactic component and the lexicon remains the same, however. In simple terms, the syntactic bit of our knowledge allows us to construct WELL-FORMED blueprints for sentences, with slots for words from the various word classes to be assigned to them. These are then filled with items drawn from our internal lexicon.

Minimalism/minimalist programme. The theory of grammar (outlined by Chomsky, 1995) that requires grammatical descriptions to be as simple and economical as possible. The minimalist programme is associated predominantly with GENERATIVE GRAMMAR. During the 1980s generative grammar became increasingly complex, particularly with the advent of X-BAR THEORY, and the growing interest in UNIVERSAL GRAMMAR. As a consequence, linguists were postulating ever more complex structures and principles. In reaction to this proliferation of descriptive apparatus, Chomsky advanced the **economy principle**, which eventually became the cornerstone of minimalism. This states that 'Derivations and representations . . . are required to be minimal . . . with no superfluous steps in derivations and no superfluous symbols in representations' (Chomsky, 1989, p. 69). What this effectively means is that diagrammatic representations of sentences, for example in TREE DIAGRAMS, should avoid representing categories that are contentless (referred to as the **no-contentless-projections constraint**). This particularly affects empty categories, which have become an important feature of modern generative descriptions of sentences. The minimalism programme requires that, where such categories have no phonetic, semantic, or grammatical properties, they should not feature in grammatical descriptions. Indeed, if you compare modern representations of sentence structures, for example in Radford (1997), they are considerably more economical than earlier diagrams, despite the increased theoretical sophistication that underlies them.

Mood (modality).   Mood, or modality, is a feature displayed by VERB phrases. It refers specifically to the way in which the VERB expresses the attitude of the ADDRESSER towards the factual content of what is being communicated, i.e. whether it is being asserted, questioned, demanded, or wished for. There are three broad types of mood: **indicative**, **imperative**, and **subjunctive**. The indicative is used for expressing, or 'indicating', factual meaning. This incorporates two sub-types: **declarative** and **interrogative**. Declarative SENTENCES are used to state things, and interrogative sentences used to question them:

> We're going to the pictures this evening (declarative)
> Are we going to the pictures this evening? (interrogative)

These two sub-types are formally related in that the interrogative is created by inverting the **subject** and **auxiliary verb** of the declarative sentence.

The imperative mood is used to express **directive** utterances, that is, those that direct someone to do something. This may be a simple command (*Shut the window*) or a request (*Please shut the window*). In both cases it typically involves the omission of the subject – in this case *you*. The last mood, the subjunctive, is probably the least used in contemporary English. Where it is, it expresses wishes, or conditions, of a non-factual kind, as in *If I were you I wouldn't go*. The use of the plural form *were*, instead of the indicative *was*, marks this out as subjunctive – as does the base form of the verb *stay*, as opposed to *stays*, in *I insist that he stay*.

It's worth remembering that the formal, i.e. grammatical, mood of a sentence may differ from its functional use. It's possible for someone to question something using a declarative, as in *We're going out?*, said with a rising INTONATION, or to issue an order using an interrogative, *Will you sit down!* This is another example of the way in which form and function in English usage don't always coincide. The best way to handle this is to use terms such as **statement**, **question**, and **command** to describe functions, and reserve declarative, interrogative, imperative, and subjunctive, for formal categories. Mood functions have been extensively described by SPEECH ACT theorists such as John Searle and John Austin.

In addition to these sentence paradigms, however, English can also signal mood through its use of **modal auxiliaries** (see VERB). These are verbs like *can*, *may*, *shall*, and *must*, which indicate a wide range of moods, such as permission, possibility, intention, and necessity. Where they occur in a verb PHRASE they must always be in initial position – *He can have a bike*; **He have can a bike*. Mood distinctions involving auxiliaries have been much discussed by logicians in an attempt to categorise the principal contrasts. The most frequently observed ones are **alethic**, **epistemic**, and **deontic**. The distinctions can best be seen if we consider an example using the auxiliary *must*:

> He must be on the plane

This can have one of three principal meanings:

(i) *He must be on the plane* (as a logical conclusion, e.g. because he's not in the departure lounge) – **alethic**

(ii) *He must be on the plane* (as an affirmation of belief: 'surely he must be on the plane') – **epistemic**

(iii) *He must be on the plane* (as a statement of obligation: 'I order him to be on the plane') – **deontic**

Morpheme/morphology.   A morpheme is the smallest grammatical unit. Words such as *lucky*, *management* and *attacked* can all be divided up into smaller units, *luck + y*, *manage + ment*, *attack + ed*. These units are termed 'morphemes'. There are two types of morphemes here: **free** morphemes (those that can occur on their own as separate words, *luck*, *manage*, and *attack*; and **bound** morphemes (those that cannot – *y*, *ment*, and *ed*). Words that consist of just one morpheme are termed **monomorphemic**, and those that are made up of more than one are termed **polymorphemic.**

Morphology is the study of the processes whereby morphemes combine to form words. There are two main kinds of morphology: **inflectional** and **derivational**. The first is concerned with the grammatical processes by which we form such things as past TENSE, plural, and present participle. The inflectional system of modern English is much diminished from its Old English parent. The few inflections that do remain are signalled by a comparatively small number of regular morphemes:

VERB inflections

(i)   past tense: **ed** (*attack* + **ed**)

(ii)   past participle: **ed** (*attack* + **ed**)

(iii)   present participle: **ing** (*attack* + **ing**)

(iv)   3rd person singular present tense: **s** (*attack* + **s**)

NOUN inflections

(v)   plural: **s** (*dog* + **s**)

(vi)   possessive: **'s**, **s'** (*dog* + **'s**, *dog* + **s'**)

ADJECTIVE/ADVERB inflections

(vii) comparative: **er** (*large* + **er**)

(viii) superlative: **est** (*large* + *est*)

In addition to these there are some PRONOUN inflections indicating **number** and **case.**

The sorts of morphemes that signal the inflectional processes we describe are **grammatical** morphemes. Their purpose is to indicate relationships demanded by the grammar. As such they don't create new LEXEMES, or new dictionary items. Derivational or **lexical** morphemes, however, do. There are a variety of derivational processes that are productive in this respect:

(i) **Affixation**: adding a **prefix** or **suffix** to a word (**in** + *sincere*, *soft* + **en**)

(ii) **blending**: fusing two words (*smoke* + *fog* → *smog*)

(iii) **compounding**: combining two words (*day* + *dream* → *daydream*)

(iv) **clipping**: shortening a word (*refrigerator* → *fridge*)

(v) **conversion**: changing the form class of a word (*table* [noun] > *to table* [verb])

Like most classificatory systems in linguistics, the morpheme/word distinction is not without its problems. To begin with, there are difficulties over segmentation. The usual rule in segmenting a word is to continue until you reach the **root** morpheme, i.e. the free morpheme to which the bound ones are attached. In this respect, the words we have taken so far have been fairly easy to segment. The identification of free and bound morphemes in *attacked*, for example, is unproblematic. But what of a word such as *receive*? The first item *re* is found elsewhere, in combination with other words, to mean 'do again' (e.g. *re* + *negotiate*). Similarly, *ceive* also occurs with other prefixes (*deceive*, *conceive*). But neither, of course, is a free morpheme. Should we, therefore, analyse this as *re* + *ceive*, and say that in this instance the word is the product of two bound morphemes? Some grammars take this route, with the consequence that words like *concur* and *conduct*, *reduce* and *deduce* are so divided. The problem here is largely the consequence of etymology, or word derivation. All of these words are derived from Latin originals, formed in their native language from the combination of a free with a bound morpheme, but borrowed whole into English. The difficulty, however, with continuing to recognise what is really a historical, and no longer productive part of the linguistic system, is that it could lead us into analyses that are unrealistic. *Caterpillar*, for instance, is said to derive from Old French *chate* + *piller*, but to present-day users of English it is a single, indivisible, item. Arguably, the best solution here is to judge all such items in terms of the rules of word formation that are productive in English. Following these it makes little sense to analyse words such as *conduct* and *conceive* into two morphemes. We can regard them as single, free, morphemes, or root stems, in their own right.

A more serious problem with segmentation, however, arises from the invisibility of some morphemes. In the case of regular paradigms, such as past tense 'ed' and plural 's', identification is straightforward since these morphemes are simply added to the root. This is not the case, however, with irregular forms like *ate* or *mice*, where the inflections are signalled by a sound change in the root. These difficulties are, again, the consequence of morphological processes that are no longer productive in English. Most native speakers are completely ignorant of the rules by which such regular forms are constructed, and which lie hidden in the past. As a consequence, we could argue that they are fossilised forms that fall outside the scope of any useful grammatical description. This is not an entirely comfortable position, however, since there are a considerable number of irregular forms in the language and part of the competence of native users is a knowledge of their morphological relatedness. We know, for example, that *mice* is not a free morpheme because its root is *mouse*; the inflected form results from the combination of the root with a plural morpheme. The issue, then, is how to absorb irregularities within our descriptive framework.

A basic point to take note of here is that morphemes are abstract units. In this respect they are similar to other categories in linguistics with an 'emic' status, e.g. 'phoneme', 'grapheme', 'lexeme', in not having any substantial form. Beginners in linguistics sometimes find this confusing and wish to identify a particular form with a grammatical category. Separating the two, however, does enable us to cope with irregularities in a more principled manner. Earlier, we described the inflectional suffixes 'ed' and 's' as past tense and plural morphemes, respectively. This is not strictly true. A more correct description would be to describe them as **morphs**. Morphs are the physical, or substantive, shape which morphemes take in order to be realised in word form. In the case of a regular past tense paradigm such as *attacked* we can identify two morphs, *attack* + *ed*, which in turn realise two morphemes, {ATTACK} + {past}. Similarly, in the case of *dogs*, the morphs *dog* + *s* realise the morphemes {DOG} + {plural}. In the same way, at the morphemic level, the irregular forms *ate* and *mice* have an identical abstract structure to their regular counterparts, i.e. {EAT} + {past}, and {MOUSE} + {PLURAL}. The differences lie in the way the morphemes are mapped onto words, or realised. In the case of *ate* and *mice* there is no separate realisation of the inflectional morphemes. We have to consider these forms as single morphs that realise their respective morpheme strings as a whole. Describing their formation in this way enables us to give a similar account for both regular and irregular formations and at the same time avoid resurrecting historic realisation processes that are no longer productive. We can call the rules that generate them **fusional** as opposed to the **agglutinative** (linear sequencing) rules responsible for regular formations.

A related difficulty that linguists have in describing the morpheme/morph relationship is that a morpheme may be realised by more than one morph. In the case of the regular plural morpheme, for example (marked orthographically by 's'), there are three different pronunciation forms:

judges:	/ɪz/
proofs:	/s/
bags:	/z/

When a morpheme is realised by a series of different morphs in this way the alternative realisations are called **allomorphs**. These particular allomorphs are determined by the phonological characteristics of the final segment of the stem, thus:

Allomorphs of English {plural}
/ɪz/ occurs after stems ending in a voiced or voiceless sibilant,
/s/ occurs after stems ending in a voiceless segment other than a sibilant,
/z/ occurs after stems ending in a voiced segment other than a sibilant.

A similar kind of phonological conditioning occurs in the case of the regular past tense morpheme, which also has three allomorphs:

saved:	/d/
missed:	/t/
landed:	/ɪd/

Again, it is the phonological characteristics of the final stem segment that are determinative here:

Allomorphs of English {past tense}
/ɪd/   occurs after stems ending in alveolar plosives (/t/ and /d/),
/t/   occurs after stems ending in a voiceless segment other than an alveolar plosive,

/d/   occurs after stems ending in a voiced segment other than an alveolar
      plosive.

The examples above are all of allomorphs selected by phonological
circumstances. Many allomorphs, however, are the product of grammatical, rather than phonological, conditioning. This is most particularly
the case with stem allomorphs. The morpheme {CHILD}, for example,
has two allomorphs. In singular form it is realised by the morph /tʃaɪld/
but in the plural it is realised by /tʃɪld/. Variation of form in this way is
frequent in lexical morphology: the morpheme {SIGN} has a different
realisation in *sign* from *signature*, and {REGISTER} in *register* from *regis-
tration*. Sometimes the grammar may have a morphemic distinction
where there is no overt marker in the form of the word. This is so with
the plurals of words such as *sheep*, *deer*, *salmon*, and *grouse*, which are
exactly the same as their singular form. In such cases most linguists
postulate a zero morph.

From this brief overview of morphology it should be evident that
much of the difficulty in providing a principled account of it lies in the
problem of relating morphemes to morphs in any consistent fashion.
Over the years, linguists have suggested a number of different solu-
tions, including 'replacive morphs' and 'empty morphs', to deal with
changes that do not follow a regular pattern, but modern approaches
suggest that the simpler we keep our explanation the better. The key
point to remember is that morphemes have no concrete existence. They
are purely mental items that are realised, substantively, by morphs. The
second point to remember is that morphs and allomorphs are sound
units. Their presence in written form is a consequence of the conventions of the alphabet. Although, for convenience sake, we talk of 's' as
the regular plural morpheme, strictly speaking it is only its formal
marker.

Noun.   A term used in the grammatical classification of words.
Traditional grammars define it as the 'name of a person, place or thing'.
In modern linguistics, however, this definition is regarded as too loose
since there are many nouns – for example, 'advice' and 'consequence' –
that it is difficult to think of as names. The criteria for sorting words into
WORD CLASSES now depend on word behaviour. According to these criteria a noun is a type of word that behaves in a particular manner. Crucial
here are morphological and syntactic behaviour. A useful account of
these is given by David Crystal (1988, p. 92). He lists three basic criteria.
'A word is a noun,' he says, 'if some of these factors apply':

(i)   its meaning and use are decided by one of the DETERMINERS, e.g. *a*, *the*, *some*;

(ii)   it acts as the head of the noun phrase;

(iii)   it changes form to express singular and plural, or the genitive case.

Some nouns, particularly those which we think of as characteristically nouns (for example, *chair* and *table*), will fulfil all of these criteria, but there are many that will only fulfil one or two. Some nouns, such as *music*, do not have a singular and a plural form, whilst others, so-called **proper nouns**, cannot occur with a determiner. We are not able to say *a/the/some London*, for example, except in very special circumstances. And neither can they be put into the plural. Proper nouns are really rather peculiar in their limited 'noun-ness', and some linguists prefer to regard them as **names**. They tend to function as labels with little semantic content. If we ask 'What does *London* mean?' it is very difficult to give a meaningful answer. On the other hand, they can perform other functions that are typical of nouns – serving as the **subject** of a SENTENCE (*London is the capital city of England*), for example, and occasionally they can convert to more ordinary or **common nouns**, as in *The London that I grew up in has vanished*.

Common nouns comprise the vast majority of nouns. But even within this large sub-class, there are further divisions to be made. The most important concerns the division into **count** and **mass** (or **non-count**) **nouns**. This is an interesting distinction in that it seems to correlate with the way in which we semantically conceive the world. We tend to think of 'things' either as individual (i.e. **countable**), items, such as *tables*, *chairs* and so on, or as some indefinable mass or substance which is essentially (**non-countable**, for example, *music*, *sincerity*, *butter*). This difference is reflected in the way such nouns behave. First, count nouns must occur with a determiner in their singular form, e.g. *The book is red*, **Book is red*, but mass nouns are not required to, e.g. *Music is fun*. Secondly, mass nouns don't have a plural form – **musics*, **butters*, **sincerities*. And thirdly, mass nouns can't usually be used with an **indefinite article** – **a butter*, **a music*, **a sincerity*. However, the messy thing about this distinction is that some nouns can belong to both camps depending on how we use them. So in a supermarket we purchase *coffee*, not **a coffee*, or **coffees*, because 'coffee' is a mass noun, but in a restaurant we might very well ask for *a coffee*, or *two coffees*, because here it is a count noun. Indeed, even *music* has recently developed a plural form, albeit of a restricted kind, in the phrase *new musics* to describe the range of contemporary styles available in modern music. What we find, in fact, is that individual nouns vary in the extent to which they are mass and count. And occasionally distinct varieties of English classify the same noun differently. In American English, for example, *accommodation* is a count noun and can occur in the plural (*accommodations*), whereas in British English it is always mass. It's not surprising that foreign learners of English often find it difficult to know whether a particular noun has a plural form or not and whether it can be used without a determiner.

Mass and count are formal, classificatory, categories. Cutting across them are the more widely known semantic categories, of which the most significant is the division into **concrete** and **abstract**. Concrete nouns tend to be those that are most prototypically nouns, such as *table*, *chair*, *desk* (i.e. objects of some kind). They are characteristically count but can sometimes be mass, e.g. *butter*, *tea*, *wine*, although even these have count versions. Abstract nouns, as the name implies, indicate non-tangible entities, usually qualities, such as *sincerity* and *honesty*, or mental and aesthetic ones, such as *advice* and *music*. They are characteristically mass but can have count forms. *Beauty*, for instance, is a mass, abstract noun, but in the sentence *What a beauty*, it is behaving in a count manner. In addition to concrete and abstract, there are smaller, splinter groups composed of **collective nouns** (e.g. *jury*, *team*, *committee*) and **general nouns** (e.g. *people*, *folk*, *livestock*), all of which have their particular idiosyncrasies. We can represent these subgroups as in Figure 17.

A final broad classification that is sometimes used to categorise nouns is the distinction between **variable** and **non-variable** nouns. Variable nouns are those that have a singular and a plural form, whereas invariable nouns don't. So count nouns are variable but mass nouns aren't. However, there are some irregularities dotted throughout the system. A few count nouns, such as *sheep* and *deer*, have no actual

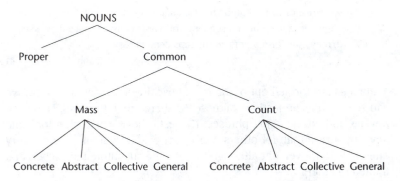

Figure 17   The subgroups of nouns

marker of plurality and can be used with both a singular and a plural sense. These are said to have **zero plurals**, a manoeuvre which enables us to continue classifying them as variable. Correspondingly, there are some mass nouns that, unlike their compatriots, are inherently plural instead of singular and lack a singular form. Collective nouns, like *police*, *cattle*, and *poultry*, for example, and nouns that seem to derive from 'a pair of', such as *jeans* and *scissors*, can only be used in the plural. In such cases the mass/count division is no longer very helpful.

From this brief overview of noun sub-classifications it should be evident that arriving at a descriptive account of 'noun-ness' is not without its problems. As with most descriptive phenomena we are forced to rely on a fairly broad range of criteria. Fortunately, however, the classificatory system is sufficiently flexible to cope with the vast majority of nouns.

Phrase.   A phrase is a syntactic unit that typically consists of more than one word, and is intermediate between WORD and CLAUSE level in SENTENCES. In most modern grammars it is regarded as the cornerstone of syntactic theory. In a phrase the individual words cohere together to form a single syntactic entity, capable of being moved around and also of being substituted by another word. In the following sentence, for example, the words in bold are capable of both of these:

> **The man** *went* **down the hill**
> **Down the hill** *went* **the man** (movement)
> **He** *went* **there** (substitution)

The two tests that are being applied here are described by Nigel Fabb in the following way:

> (i) if a sequence of words can be moved as a group, they may form a phrase (the movement test); (ii) if a sequence of words can be replaced by a single word, they may form a phrase (the replacement test).
>
> (Fabb, 1994, pp. 3–4)

Phrases are formed out of the main lexical WORD CLASSES. Indeed, we can see them as projections of these. So there are NOUN, VERB, ADJECTIVE, ADVERB, and PREPOSITIONAL phrases. The tests above work better for some types of phrase than for others. Verb phrases, for example, are not very amenable to movement although they can be substituted for, albeit in a limited manner:

*The man **went down the hill** and the dog **did** too.*

In this example, *did* is substituting for the string *went down the hill*, and as a consequence is evidence for identifying it as a phrase.

You will have noticed from the previous example that phrases can contain other phrases within them. The verb phrase *went down the hill* has the smaller phrase *down the hill* embedded in it. And indeed we can break this down even further since *the hill* is also capable of being moved and substituted for and is therefore a phrase. The principle of embedding is crucial to the way in which phrases link together to form sentences. In fact, some complex phrases often contain other sentences embedded within them.

Each phrase has a **head word**, taken from the word class that forms its basis. A noun phrase will have a noun as its head, a verb phrase a verb, and so on. In very simple phrases the phrase may just consist of this head word. In the following sentence *John* is acting as a noun phrase:

John *went home*

But in a sentence like:

John, **who is an actor**, *went home*

it is being significantly modified by *who is an actor*. Modification is a process that allows phrases to expand and incorporate a variety of subordinate material. It can occur either before or after the head word and consists of words, phrases, and sentences that are dependent in some way on it. Where modification occurs before the head it is termed **pre-modification**, and where after, **post-modification**. The kinds of words that can fulfil this function depend largely on the type of phrase itself. This is because phrases take their character from the head word. Noun phrases, for example, can be extensively modified both before and afterwards by a range of items, whereas prepositional phrases are subject to much more limited modification. With the development of X-BAR THEORY, however, it has become possible to see how all phrases have a common structure. Apart from having heads, their modifiers can be separated in functional terms into **specifiers**, **adjuncts**, and **complements**. In addition, it has also become possible to describe more accurately stages intermediate between the full phrase and the items that compose it. So, for example, *the hungry dog* is a noun phrase (although see the entry on X-bar theory for a more recent analysis), but what of just *hungry dog*? It isn't the final phrase but it is a unit of some sort. Using X-bar vocabulary we can describe it as a **noun bar**. And so on for other types of phrase.

Because of the versatility and power of the phrase syntactically, it is common nowadays to describe sentences in terms of the phrases that comprise them. **Phrase structure grammar** provides us with rules for sentence formation that utilise this form of analysis. The simple formula S → NP + VP is a **rewrite rule** which captures the generalisation that a basic sentence consists of a noun phrase plus a verb phrase. It is sufficient to express the rule that generates the sentence with which we started:

(*The man*) (*went down the hill*)
S → NP + VP

Phrase-marker.   A term used to refer to the structural representation of sentences in terms of their particular **constituents**. Phrase-markers specify the hierarchical structure of sentences and analyse them into a linear sequence of phrases, words, and sometimes MORPHEMES. They are usually represented in the form of a TREE DIAGRAM but may also employ bracketing or boxing (*see* IMMEDIATE CONSTITUENCY ANALYSIS).

Preposition.   Prepositions are words that relate two parts of a SENTENCE together where the relationship is typically one of time, place, or logic, as in the following examples:

(i)   Time: *He went home **after/during/before** the lecture*
(ii) Place: *She went **in/to/by/from** the house*
(iii) Logic: *She went **because of/in spite of** you*

Simple prepositions consist of one word (*e.g. about, from, at, across*), and complex prepositions of more than one word (*e.g. apart from, ahead of, in front of*).

You will usually encounter prepositions in prepositional PHRASES. These consist of a preposition plus a **complement**, most often a NOUN phrase, but it can also be a CLAUSE:

*I saw him **at the bus stop*** (preposition + noun phrase)
*I stay **with whoever I can*** (preposition + clause)

Pronoun.   A word that can be used to substitute for a single NOUN or a complete noun PHRASE.

*He's got a blue **jacket** and I've got a red **one*** (replacing a noun)
Your brother Jack's *here.* **He's** *over there* (replacing a noun phrase)

There are many types of pronoun. The following are the ones most usually recognised by linguists:

Personal pronouns
I/me, you, he/him, she/her, it, we/us, they/them

Possessive pronouns
mine, yours, his, hers, ours, theirs

Reflexive pronouns
myself, yourself, himself, herself, ourselves, themselves

Demonstrative pronouns
this/that, these/those

Interrogative pronouns
why, which, when, where, who, how

Relative pronouns (substitute for nouns in relative CLAUSES)
who, which, whose, that

Indefinite pronouns
anybody, somebody, anything, something

Sentence. Traditional definitions of sentences tend to describe them as grammatically complete units capable of standing on their own and semantically independent. This is true of many sentences, including the previous one. But it is clearly not so for all sentences. In actual speech we often abbreviate utterances and elide elements in order to maintain fluency and avoid pointless repetition, as in the following exchange:

Q. *Where are you going?*
A. *To the pictures*

Here the sequence *To the pictures* can only function as a reply because the full meaning is recoverable from the context. **Sentence fragments** of this kind are frequent in speech and increasingly common in writing, too. They have always been a feature of novels or short stories, where the aim is to reproduce the utterance flavour of language, but they can also be found in advertisements and even public announcements. The linguist Geoffrey Leech has called this style **public colloquial** and has observed its growing frequency in written English as a phenomenon of late twentieth-century culture.

Sentences, then, are units of style as well as grammar. This raises the problem of how we can formally describe them in grammatical terms. How can we arrive at a description that takes account of both the fully independent kind and the sentence fragments? We can make a start by distinguishing, as some grammars do, between **minor** and **major** sentences. Minor ones are incomplete in some way whilst major ones are complete. This is a useful terminological distinction that enables us to focus our attention, for purposes of grammatical description, on the major variety. It also allows us to discern two sets of rules here; first, the grammatical rules which govern sentence formation, and second, **text formation rules**, which operate on sentences when they become part of connected discourse. Having said that, however, there are clearly degrees of incompleteness possible in sentences which make the distinction between major and minor occasionally tricky. Consider the following:

(i)   *And a half of lager*
(ii) *Mary denied letting the cat out*
(iii) *She denied it*

We would have no problem in identifying the first sequence as incomplete since it lacks both a **subject** and a VERB. By contrast, (ii) is clearly complete and could stand as an independent unit. But what of (iii)? As an utterance it is dependent on something preceding it since we have no way of knowing what *she* or *it* refer to. The use of what are termed **proforms**, such as these, is only allowable when the sense is recoverable from the rest of the discourse. On the other hand, to call it a minor sentence would seem odd since it is grammatically complete. Subject, verb, and object are all present and correct. It is a reduced, rather than abbreviated, major type. A useful solution to the classification dilemma here is to distinguish between *grammatical* and *semantic* completeness, reserving the term 'minor' for sentences that fail the former rather than the latter. This is a significant distinction because there are some minor sentences such as aphorisms (e.g. *Easy come easy go*) and formulas (e.g. *Goodbye*), which although lacking all the elements for major status are, arguably, semantically complete.

Linguists working within the formal methodology associated with Chomsky usually confine their attention to major sentences, considering the formation of minor ones as the province of discourse, or text analysts. More particularly, they normally take, as their sentence paradigms, idealised forms that exhibit the rules of sentence construction free from the distractions one finds in natural sentences, such as repetition, hesitation, abbreviation, or variations in REGISTER and DIALECT. Major sentences are those that consist of all the **elements** to be found in a main clause (**subject**, **verb/predicator**, **object**, **complement**, and adjunct/**adverbial**), for example:

> *The girl* (subject) *hit* (verb) *the ball* (object)
> *The woman* (subject) is (verb) *a pilot* (complement)
> *The dog* (subject) *died* (verb)

Sentences that consist of a single clause, such as those above, are called **simple sentences**, and those with more than one clause are termed **multiple sentences**. There are two principal ways by which the latter are formed. The first is through **coordination**. This involves adding on another clause using a coordinating CONJUNCTION, for example,

> *Jack went up the hill and Jill followed him.*

Here the two clauses have equal status within the sentence, although quite frequently the second may be reduced because of elements which are understood from the first, as in

> *Jack went up the hill and Jill followed.*

Sentences which are joined in this manner, with or without any reduction, are called **coordinated**, or **compound**, sentences.

The second form of combination is through **subordination**. In this case the two clauses are not equal. One is clearly the main clause in the sentence, and the other subordinate to it. One of the most frequent ways of indicating this relationship is by using a subordinating conjunction such as *if*, *while*, *since*, or *because:*

> *I sang* **while he played the piano**
> **If you sing** *I will play the piano*
> **Since he sang** *I played the piano*

In each case the subordinate clause is the one introduced by the conjunction. Sentences such as these are described as **complex**. This is because subordination works by **embedding** one clause in another rather than merely attaching the two together. In the examples above, the subordinate clauses are sentence elements, more particularly, adverbials (*see* CLAUSE), within their respective main clauses. The principle to remember here, then, is that subordinate clauses normally expand an element of main-clause structure. In the following examples the subordinate clauses (in bold) are respectively the complement and the subject of their main-clause hosts:

> *He said I* **could come**
> **Honesty is the best policy** *is my favourite proverb*

There are a few instances where subordinate clauses expand only part of an element rather than the whole, the most common being the relative clause:

> *I saw the man* **who robbed the bank at Monte Carlo**

Here, the clause in bold is subordinate to the NOUN PHRASE *the man* (the object of *saw*), and not to the sentence.

Multiple sentences may contain several layers of either subordination and/or coordination. Multiple coordination is fairly easy to describe since it simply involves the addition of more clauses:

> ((*Jack went up the hill*) *and* (*Jill followed*) *but* (*she fell over*))

In the case of multiple subordination, however, it's important to keep the hierarchical arrangement clear:

> (*Jack said* (*he would go home* (*if Jill followed him*)))

Where sentences combine both coordination and subordination they are described as **compound-complex**:

> (*Jack said* (*he would go home*) *and* (*have a good sleep*))

Sentences are normally classified in terms of their form and function. Formally, most grammars recognise **declarative**, **interrogative**, **imperative**, and **exclamative** types (see MOOD). These relate to the functions of **statement**, **question**, **command**, and **exclamation**. But it's important to bear in mind that form and function do not always coincide in English usage. It's quite possible, for instance, to ask a question using the declarative form, e.g. *You're going out?*

Tense.   A category used in the description of VERBS that refers to the location of an action in time (as distinct from ASPECT, which is concerned with its duration). Many linguists make a distinction between **form** and **function** in analysing tense. By this analysis 'tense' refers to the grammatical changes made to the form of a verb, as opposed to 'time', which refers to the semantic function such changes signal. The corollary of this is that there are only two tenses in English – **past** and **present**. In other words, there are only two ways in which tense is grammaticalised. If we wish to indicate the present tense we use the base form of the verb, whilst the past involves adding 'ed' (in the case of regular verbs). There is no separate **inflection** for the future, however. To indicate that, we use either the present tense, *I am going home tomorrow*, or the **modal** verbs *shall* and *will* in conjunction with a main verb, *I shall/will go home tomorrow*.

The distinction between form and function is a useful one in dealing with the complicated relationship between tense and time. Tensed forms (i.e. variations in the structure, or MORPHOLOGY, of the verb) can be used to signal a wide variety of meanings other than temporal ones. We can, for example, use the past tense to indicate some kind of hypothetical meaning, as in *I wish I had your money* (i.e. have it now). And in the case of modal verbs it is quite common for tense difference to signal degrees of politeness: *Can I see you now?* is more likely to be said by an employer to an employee, as opposed to *Could I see you now?* where the reverse is the case. Here, the distinction seems to be between near vs. remote, with remoteness indicating a greater degree of deference. This distinction helps to explain the use of the present tense to refer to past events – the so-called **historic present** – where the present is used to make the past seem as if it were happening now, e.g. *I hear you've got married*. This usage is very common in story-telling to promote dramatic immediacy – *I'm walking down the road and who should I bump into but Fred*.

What is clear from studies of tense and time is that there is no easily stateable relationship between them. We use the two formal grammatical distinctions, past and present, to perform a number of functions, some of which are purely temporal, and some which are modal, or interpersonal in some way. It's another indication of the way in which the human meanings we have to convey exceed the strictly grammatical means at our disposal.

Theta/θ-theory.   Theta theory is concerned with assigning thematic roles to the ARGUMENTS of verbs. 'Theta' is the name of the Greek letter θ, which corresponds to *th* in English, and since *thematic* begins with *th* it has become standard to abbreviate the expression 'thematic role' to 'θ-role'. It's important to recognise that 'theme' is being used differently here from its use in functional grammar, where it has largely a DISCOURSE meaning as the first item in a clause. In theta theory 'theme' indicates one of a number of semantic roles that arguments fulfil. CLAUSES are seen as consisting of propositions, or logical statements, which require certain types of arguments in order to be acceptable sentences of English. The approach is similar in some respects to Halliday's 'participant, process, circumstance' model (*see* FUNCTIONAL GRAMMAR), and indeed some of the terms overlap, but whereas Halliday is principally concerned with TRANSITIVITY, theta theory is more concerned with 'agency': who does what to whom. The essential elements of the theory differ somewhat from linguist to linguist, but the following are the commonly assumed theta-roles:

(i)   **Theme** (or **patient**) = entity undergoing the effect of some action
(**The cat** *died*)

(ii)   **Agent** (or **actor**) = instigator of some action
(**John** *threw the ball*)

(iii)   **Experiencer** = entity experiencing some psychological state
(**John** *was happy*)

(iv)   **Benefactive** = entity benefiting from some action
(*Mary bought some chocolate* **for John**)

(v)   **Instrument** = means by which something comes about
(*Joanna dug the garden* **with a spade**)

(vi)   **Locative** = place in which something is situated
(*John put the washing* **in the bin**)

(vii)   **Goal** = entity towards which something moves
(*Mary passed the plate* **to John**)

(viii)   **Source** = entity from which something moves
(*John returned* **from London**)

The value of incorporating thematic roles into a model of syntax is that it allows us to give a more principled account of the way in which linguistic items behave than relying simply on formal grammatical criteria. In the following pair of SENTENCES, the phrase *the vase* fulfils the same grammatical role, that of subject, but two distinct thematic roles:

(i)   *The vase shattered the glass*
(ii)   *The vase shattered*

In (i) the vase is the cause of the shattering, hence it performs the role of instrument, whereas in (ii) it is the entity which undergoes the effect of shattering, hence it acts as the theme, or patient. The difference of thematic status is reflected in a difference of SELECTION RESTRICTIONS. In (i) we can replace *the vase* with *the noise*, or *a hidden flaw*, but not in (ii). Analysing the thematic structure of these two sentences enables us to reveal differences that are not reflected in their **constituent** structure (*see* IMMEDIATE CONSTITUENCY ANALYSIS).

Transformational grammar.   Transformational grammar is largely the product of the pioneering work of the American linguist Noam CHOMSKY. He was interested in the way in which sentences with apparently identical surface forms could express completely different meanings. The classic case, frequently cited, is the pair:

> *John is eager to please*
> *John is easy to please*

A conventional TREE DIAGRAM of these SENTENCES would miss completely the difference between their logical and surface forms. The solution to this dilemma, suggested by Chomsky, was that underlying both sentences was a more basic level of structure, called **deep structure**. This was the primary grammatical level at which the sentences were formed, and represented their propositional core. The subsequent surface structures were seen as the consequence of a series of transformations that moved items into various syntactic slots.

The descriptive appeal of Chomsky's approach is evident if we think of the way in which sentences are sometimes related:

(i)   *The man kicked the ball*
(ii)   *Has the man kicked the ball?*
(iii) *The ball has been kicked by the man*
(iv)   *Which ball has the man kicked?*

There is clearly a semantic relatedness between these sentences. The person doing the kicking is always the same as is the thing being kicked. We could say then that all of these sentences derive from a common original, or deep structure, represented most nearly in the sentence *The man kicked the ball*. Linguists usually express the logical form of this in the following way:

> *kick (man, ball)*

This representation means that there is a verb *kick* that has as its subject *man*, and as its object, *ball*. To get from this abstract mental proposition to our starting sentence we have to imagine a minor transformation involving the addition of tense to *kick* and determiners to *man* and *ball*, plus some reordering. To derive the passives, negatives and interrogatives, above, however, would involve more complex transformations.

The consequence of Chomsky's approach, then, is to suggest that we all possess two grammars as part of our linguistic competence. First, a phrase structure grammar, which consists of the rules governing basic sentence formation, and secondly, a transformational one that enables us to manipulate sentences to produce the full range of sentence types. Transformational grammar has been enormously influential in recent years and has effectively changed the way in which most linguists approach syntax. But it has also been the subject of a great deal of debate and revision. In the beginning, linguists tended to treat every sentence variation as a transformation with the result that anyone studying it encountered a plethora of complicated movement rules. It soon became clear, however, that there were so many exceptions to the rules that their power had to be constrained in some way.

An example of one such constraint is the rule for **dative movement**: this was supposed to relate pairs of sentences, like *Tom gave a sandwich to Jane* and *Tom gave Jane a sandwich*. The transformation here was said to involve deleting *to* and moving the NOUN PHRASE following it – *Jane* – to a position immediately after the VERB. The problem for this as a general transformation is that it is severely limited. There are some verbs, such as *transmit*, which will allow the first form but not the second:

> They transmitted propaganda to the enemy
> *They transmitted the enemy propaganda

and others, like *ask*, which will permit the second but not the first:

> *John asked a question to Mary
> John asked Mary a question

The constraints on this movement appear to be lexical rather than grammatical. As a consequence, any rule that we might formulate here would have to be verb-specific. Arguably, the place for this information is in the LEXICON, rather than in a separate set of syntactic transformational rules.

Because of problems such as this, transformational grammar has, over the years, been streamlined to a few central operations. Not only that, but the terminology has changed. 'Deep' and 'surface' structure have become 'D' and 'S' structure, principally because the original terms seemed to imply some sort of qualitative evaluation; 'deep' suggested 'profound', whilst 'surface' was too close to 'superficial'. Nevertheless, the principles of transformational grammar still remain very much alive in contemporary linguistics. Chomsky himself has simplified the rules down to one general transformation: **move alpha**. In essence this means 'move anything'. This may seem extraordinarily liberal but its operation is strictly controlled by a range of constraints that take into account a number of things, including the behaviour of individual lexical items. Some of these constraints take the form of additional theories that define the kinds of relationships possible within a grammar. Two of the most important of these are X-BAR THEORY and THETA THEORY. Others include **government theory**, **binding theory**, **bounding theory**, and **control theory**. Fundamentally, what has happened is that the responsibility for transformations has been distributed around the linguistic system rather than being located in one particular corner of it.

Inevitably, one consequence of this redistribution has been increasing pressure on transformational grammar to provide evidence for the remaining operations. Probably the most important of such evidence has to do with **trace theory**. According to this, constituents that are moved leave behind a trace, or echo, of themselves in the surface structure. To see how this works in practice consider (iv) above: *Which ball has the man kicked?* Transformational grammarians would argue that this derives from the sentence *The man has kicked the ball*. First of all there has to be a rule that allows us to use *which* as an interrogative determiner replacing *the*. This may seem a bit odd to begin with, but it isn't impossible to encounter it in ordinary conversation: *The man has kicked which ball did you say?* Then there are two major transformations. First, the interrogative, which switches round the auxiliary verb *has* and the subject *the man* (known as 'I' [inflection] movement) and secondly, a 'wh' transformation (or 'wh' movement) – that moves the noun phrase *which ball* to the front of the sentence (see Figure 18). Now, the verb *kick* is one of those verbs that require an **object** – you have to *kick* something – and we know that objects in English normally follow the verb. But in our transformed sentence **Which ball has the man kicked*, there is nothing following the verb at all. According to transformational grammarians this is because the object which was generated in the deep structure has been moved out of its normal slot. We can test this by trying to insert an object there – *Which ball has the woman kicked the dog* – which results in nonsense. Other items could be put there, e.g. an **adverbial**, as in *Which ball has the man kicked through the window*, but

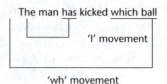

Figure 18 An example of transformational movement

not an object. The reason for this is that the moved constituent has left behind an invisible mental trace of itself to indicate that the object slot has already been taken, rather like leaving a reserved notice on a table whilst we make our way to the food counter.

Transitivity. A category used in the grammatical analysis of CLAUSE/SENTENCE constructions to describe the relationship between the VERB and the other units that are dependent on it. **Transitive** verbs are those that can take a **direct object**. In the case of some verbs this is obligatory, for example, *enjoy: *The man enjoyed* is clearly incomplete as a sentence and needs an object to complete it – *The man enjoyed his meal*. Correspondingly, verbs that can't take an object are referred to as **intransitive**. Into this category come *die, fall*, and *digress*. All of these verbs can appear simply with a **subject**, e.g. *He died/fell/digressed*, but are not able to occur with an object: we can't die, fall, or digress something or somebody. However, the situation is more complicated than that because many verbs have both a transitive and an intransitive use. Where this occurs there is usually a different meaning being expressed, as in the following:

intransitive	transitive
He's washing (i.e. washing himself)	*He's washing the car*
She's expecting (i.e. pregnant)	*She's expecting a letter*
She's working (i.e. busy)	*She's working miracles*

With some verbs, however, such as *read* and *eat*, the change from transitive to intransitive does not involve any change in meaning: compare *I'm reading/eating*, as opposed to *I'm reading a book/eating a cake*. Indeed, even the verb *enjoy* has recently acquired an intransitive form in the waiter's instruction to diners to *Enjoy*. As a consequence of this dual capacity it's probably more useful to distinguish between transitive and intransitive *uses* of verbs rather than rely on an inflexible classification.

Transitivity is treated in a more substantial way than this, however, in

FUNCTIONAL GRAMMAR, where it is regarded as lying at the heart of clause construction. The linguist most associated with this approach is Michael HALLIDAY, for whom the relationships that verbs allow between their dependent parts reflect the way in which we conceptualise the world.

Tree diagram.　A diagram widely used in linguistics as a way of showing the internal hierarchical structure of SENTENCES. The 'root' of the tree is at the top of the diagram, indicated by the symbol S ('sentence'). From this topmost point branches descend that correspond to the categories specified by the rules. First in order of descent will come PHRASES (e.g. VERB phrase, NOUN phrase), then WORD CLASSES (e.g. verb, noun), and finally the individual words drawn from the LEXICON that comprise the individual sentence. The diagram in Figure 19, for example, tells us that the root of the sentence (S) has produced two large, forking branches, a noun phrase (NP) and a verb phrase (VP), which have each produced in turn two more branches, leading, in the case of the noun phrase, to a DETERMINER and a noun, and in the case of the verb phrase, to another noun phrase and a verb. This second noun phrase has produced a determiner and an ADJECTIVE, plus a noun. Finally, each of the word-level categories has taken words from the lexicon to fill their respective places.

In a tree diagram power is seen to flow from the top down and the entire tree is held together by the principle of **dominance**. Each point of intersection in it is called a **node**, and each node dominates those below it. S, for example, dominates all the items below it. But, because it is closer to the nodes NP and VP, it is said to 'immediately' dominate them. Similarly, VP dominates everything below it, but immediately dominates Verb and NP, and so on. In addition to this, linguists frequently use 'family tree' terminology to describe the system of internal relationships produced by the diagram. If two categories derive from a single node

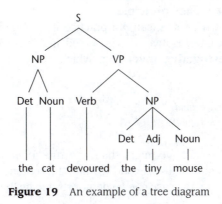

Figure 19　An example of a tree diagram

they are said to be 'sisters' and 'daughters' of the 'mother node' from which they derive. So in Figure 19, the NP 'the tiny mouse' is a sister of the verb 'devoured', and both are daughters of the complete VP 'devoured the tiny mouse'. This VP is in turn the sister of the first NP 'the cat', and both are daughters of S, the complete sentence. Interestingly, the terminology is always female; there are no fathers, brothers and sons (although in Italian, however, the corresponding tree relations are male).

The great advantage of tree diagrams is that they enable us to see at a glance the syntactic relationships between sentence units and also to describe these more exactly. The diagram in Figure 19, for example, captures certain basic facts about what is termed **constituency**. Constituents are the categories (i.e. words and phrases) from which sentences are constructed (*see* IMMEDIATE CONSTITUENCY ANALYSIS). So a string like 'the cat' is a **proper constituent** of the sentence 'the cat devoured the tiny mouse', whereas the string 'devoured the' is not. Similarly, facts about **functional relations** can be described more accurately using 'tree' terminology. The **subject** of the sentence can now be identified as the NP daughter of the sentence node, and the **object** as the NP daughter of the VP and sister of the main verb.

Universal Grammar. The grammatical properties common to all languages and innately present in human beings. For many linguists, the discovery and description of these properties is the ultimate pinnacle of linguistic enquiry. Such properties as have been identified are called **language universals**. There are two types of these: **formal universals** and **substantive universals**. The formal kind have to do with the general design features of languages. We might say, for example, that all the operations that languages allow, involving the movement and order-ing of items, are **structure dependent** and, consequently, follow a **structure dependency principle**.

We can see what this means in practice if we briefly consider the formation of the interrogative. This is formed, in English, by a movement known as **interrogative inversion**, which operates in the manner below:

(i)   *John will stay behind*
(ii) *Will John stay behind?*

From an initial glance we might think the rule for forming questions simply involved moving the second word in the sentence in front of the first. That this is not the case can be demonstrated by the following pair:

(iii)   *John and Mary will stay behind*
(iv)   **And John Mary will stay behind*

The correct form of the interrogative here, of course, is

(v)   *Will John and Mary stay behind?*

To form a question of this type correctly requires an inversion of the **subject**, *John and Mary*, with the **auxiliary** VERB, *will*. This means that we must possess, in our minds, concepts such as 'subject of a sentence', and 'auxiliary verb'. Without this elementary structure we would never be able to understand how questions were formed. And we must also implicitly be aware of another formal universal: that all languages are **category-based**. Every language has NOUNS, verbs, ADJECTIVES, and ADVERBS, although the individual items that count as such may vary from one language to another. Formal universals, then, are very general principles which all languages obey, although they don't all obey them in the same sort of way (not every language forms questions in the manner English chooses to). Substantive universals, on the other hand, are the particular structural features that all languages have in common. In a sense, they are part of their linguistic 'content'. All languages, for example, have structures such as 'noun PHRASE' and 'verb phrase', etc. And it is argued that they also have versions of X-BAR THEORY and THETA THEORY, which collectively determine how phrases combine into sentences.

As well as these universal principles, which serve to determine the broad grammatical structure of languages, there are also, as I have already intimated, language-particular aspects of grammatical structure. Languages vary in the way they perform certain operations, but the interesting thing is that they do so in a principled manner. They vary according to certain **parameters**. If we accept that children are born with a knowledge of Universal Grammar, then the grammatical learning required of them is limited to learning which particular parameters their language conforms to. One such parameter, for example, accounts for a distinction between those languages that allow sentences to be formed without a subject, and those that do not. In Italian, *Parla Francese*, is a well-formed sentence, but the equivalent in English, *Speaks French*, isn't. The difference is that Italian allows for an understood subject, *he/she*, whereas English doesn't. Languages such as Italian, which have subjectless sentences of this type, are called **pro-drop** languages because main verbs are allowed to omit their subjects. It has also been found that they share a number of other characteristics, such as the ability to change the order of subject and verb – in Italian, *Falls the night* is just as acceptable as *The night falls*. What children appear to do, according to proponents of Universal Grammar, is to set the pro-drop parameter when they are acquiring their native language and then other characteristics which depend on this parameter either 'fall in' or 'fall out', as a consequence.

A second parameter, which we will briefly consider, is the **head (position) parameter**. This has to do with the word-order variation within phrases. Given that, universally, languages have phrases containing a head word and a **complement** (*see* PHRASES), they none the less vary as to whether the head word comes before the complement or after it. In English the head word comes first, as the following phrases illustrate:

(i)   **students** *of physics*   (noun phrase)
(ii) **in** *the kitchen*   (prepositional phrase)
(iii) **go** *with him*   (verb phrase)
(iv) **keen** *on football*   (adjective phrase)

In a language such as Korean, phrases are structured differently. Heads regularly come last. So, in the last example, the Korean equivalent would be *football on keen*. There seem, among the world's languages, to be these two possibilities: a particular language is either a **head-first** language or a **head-last** one.

Evidence such as this suggests that there are universal constraints on parametric variation across languages. In theory there are numerous possibilities for the ordering of heads and complements but in practice this doesn't happen. Chomsky's answer to this is to point to Universal Grammar as imposing genetic constraints on variation. In the case of head parameters, it allows only a binary set of possibilities. This considerably narrows the amount of structured grammatical learning children have to do to acquire their native language. The particular theory that this depends on, known as the **principles-and-parameters theory (PPT)** of language, is the most recent development in Universal Grammar. Given the research evidence that is mounting in its support, it looks set to become the dominant account of what a Universal Grammar might consist of.

Verb.   A term used in the grammatical classification of words to refer to a class of words that typically denote a process or state of being. Conventionally, verbs are often referred to as 'doing' or 'action' words but this only works as a 'rule of thumb', since there are many verbs, e.g. *seem*, *be*, which do not 'act' in any obvious sense. As with other word classes, the criteria used by linguists to distinguish verbs is based on their behavioural characteristics. These principally concern the MORPHOLOGY of verbs – the way in which they can change form to indicate contrasts of TENSE, ASPECT, **person**, and **number** – and their syntactic function. Syntactically verbs **predicate**, or 'make a claim', about someone or something. So in the minimal sentence *The boy laughed*, the verb *laughed* is asserting something about the subject, *boy*.

Verbs are categorised into two main groups: **lexical** and **auxiliary**. Lexical verbs are those which can act as the main verb in a verb PHRASE. They are capable of contrasts of tense, aspect, person, and number. Auxiliary verbs, on the other hand, popularly known as 'helping verbs', are restricted both in form and in distribution. Many of them, such as *can/could* and *shall/should*, have only two forms to indicate present and past. They don't have any 'ing' forms, for instance, such as **canning*, or **shalling*. More restrictive still is their distribution. Because they can never serve as main verbs they must always occur with a lexical verb. Despite these restrictions, however, they are enormously powerful. They are necessary for such operations as asking questions and negation, and for the construction of contrasts of aspect and voice. And, indeed, in verb phrases where they occur, they are also responsible for determining the tense of the phrase.

There are two kinds of auxiliary verb: **primary** auxiliaries and **modal** auxiliaries. The first kind are capable of acting both as auxiliaries and as lexical verbs. *Be*, *have*, and *do* fall into this category. They can occur as main verbs in their own right (*I am a student/I have a bike/I did the washing up*), and as auxiliaries of other verbs. In this latter capacity they are responsible for the generation of both the **progressive** and **perfect** aspect and the **passive** VOICE. The second kind, the modals, as their name suggests, are responsible for the particular MOOD of the verb phrase. They serve to indicate such moods as permission (*can/could*), intention (*will/would*), and compulsion (*must*). Unlike primary auxiliaries they can never occur as main verbs. In recent years the grammar of auxiliaries has attracted a lot of attention particularly by transformational linguists (*see* TRANSFORMATIONAL GRAMMAR), who increasingly see them as part of the **deep structure** of sentences. Interestingly, where they occur in verb phrases they are subject to a fixed order:

Verb phrase order

[MOOD, ASPECT (perfect, progressive), VOICE] + LEXICAL VERB

e.g. *She could*   *have been*   *being*   *beaten*
       (mood)   (aspect)   (voice)   (lexical verb)

Lexical verbs can be divided into **regular** and **irregular**. The irregular variety have forms that English has retained from its Germanic parent. These fossilised forms are embedded in the language, and frequently cause difficulty for learners of English. Fortunately, however, whilst there are thousands of regular verbs, there are less than three hundred irregular ones. The distinction between the two kinds has to do with the formation of the past tense. Regular verbs characteristically form the past tense by adding 'ed', or just 'd' to the stem (*show* → *showed*; *phone* → *phoned*), whereas irregular ones don't. These have an unpredictable past tense. This is because the rules governing their formation are no longer a productive part of the language. So we get forms such as *catch* → *caught*, and *take* → *took*. There are seven main classes of irregular verbs; a useful description of them can be found in Crystal (1988, p. 57). Many irregular verbs have a separate past tense and past participle form (*take* → *took* → *taken*), whereas, in the case of regular verbs, the 'ed' form serves for both. Most grammars, however, still refer to the past participle as the 'en' form in order to distinguish it from the past tense. Using this notation we can say that there are five forms which lexical verbs are capable of:

- The **base** form, listed in the dictionary, which with 'to' makes the 'infinitive': *to wish, to love*

- The **s** form, which occurs in the third-person singular present tense: *I love, you love, he/she/it loves*)

- The **ing** form, or present participle, made by adding **ing** to the base form (often with a change in the spelling): *loving, wishing*

- The **ed** form, or past tense, made by adding **ed** or **d** to the base of regular verbs (sometimes with a change in the spelling), but made in a variety of other ways with irregular verbs: *snowed, broke*

- The **en** form, or past participle, made by adding **en** or **n** to the past TENSE form of some, but not all, irregular verbs (sometimes with a change in the spelling), and in the case of regular verbs by adding **ed** or **d** to the base: *broken, snowed*.

As you can see, this means, in practice, that regular verbs have four forms, whereas irregular ones may be capable of the full five. The most irregular verb in English, however, the verb *to be*, has as many as eight forms. This is surprising since it is also the most commonly used.

Voice. When used as a syntactic term, 'voice' refers to a FEATURE of verb forms that indicates whether the **subject** is the 'doer' or the recipient of the action. There are two forms: **active** and **passive**, as illustrated in the following pair of sentences:

(i)   *The cat chased the mouse*   (**active**)
(ii) *The mouse was chased by the cat*   (**passive**)

In (i) the grammatical subject *the cat* is also the 'doer' (or **agent**) whilst *the mouse* is both the grammatical object and the recipient (or **goal**; *see* FUNCTIONAL GRAMMAR). In (ii), however, they have swapped over their grammatical roles whilst maintaining their functional ones. The cat is still the agent despite being the object and, similarly, the mouse remains the goal despite being the subject. Most **transitive** verbs (*see* TRANSITIVITY) allow this role reversal, although there are some exceptions (e.g. *have*).

The passive differs structurally from the active in requiring a verb phrase composed of a form of the **auxiliary** *be*, followed by the past **participle**. This would be enough to form a complete sentence on its own, i.e. *The mouse was chased*. Indeed, one advantage of the passive is its ability to allow **agent deletion**. A second structural change involves the construction of a 'by' phrase into which the agent, if it is to be expressed, is put. The conversion from one to another entails no change in the logical meaning of the SENTENCE; in the examples above, the chaser and chasee remain the same. However, functional linguists argue that there is a change in **thematic** meaning. This has to do with the information structure of the sentence and, in particular, with concepts of **theme** and **focus**, and **given/new** (*see* FUNCTIONAL GRAMMAR).

Word.   A unit of expression that native speakers intuitively recognise in both spoken and written language. The usual criterion for word recognition is that suggested by the linguist Leonard Bloomfield, who defined a word as 'a minimal free form'. I say 'usual' because there are still difficulties in arriving at a consistent use of the term. First of all, we can distinguish between **phonological** and **orthographic** words (*see* LEXEME). The sound form of a word necessarily differs from that of its written form. Part of the difficulty here is resolved by using the term 'lexeme' to capture the underlying abstract sense of 'word', but as 'word' and 'lexeme' are mutually dependent on each other for their meaning we cannot use one to define the other. We might think that the simplest definition of a word would be semantic, i.e. 'a unit of meaning', but unfortunately this is not adequate. *Kicked the bucket* is arguably a 'unit of meaning' – we can substitute *died* for it very easily – but it is clearly three words.

The most satisfactory criteria for word identification are syntactic. The concept of a word as 'a minimal free form' suggests two important things about words. First, their ability to stand on their own as isolates. This is reflected in the space that surrounds a word in its orthographical form. And secondly, their internal integrity, or cohesion, as units. If we move a word around in a sentence, whether spoken or written, we have to move the whole word or none of it – we cannot move part of a word. And neither can a word be interrupted. Although we might segment a word such as *hospitalised* into *hospital–ise–d*, these segments can only occur in a certain order and we are not free to insert anything between.

This still leaves some problems, however. What do we do about **fused** words like *can't*, *isn't*, or *dunno*, where two or more words are run together? And what about small words such as *a* or *the* that are usually found tied to nouns and don't occur as isolates in the same way as words with more definite lexical content? All of this suggests that there is a certain indeterminacy about the definition of a word. This is in the nature of things and the most sensible solution is to regard Bloomfield's criteria as sufficient for identifying prototypical words (*see* PROTOTYPE THEORY).

Word classes. Most grammars conventionally assign words to certain groupings, or word classes. Older grammars traditionally referred to them as 'parts of speech'. They include NOUNS, VERBS, ADJECTIVES, PRONOUNS, CONJUNCTIONS, and so on. Word classes are important in the acquisition of language because they enable us to construct sentences with a maximum of economy. Knowing that only a verb can complete the following sentence,

$$\text{The boy} \left\{ \begin{array}{l} loved \\ \ldots \\ hit \end{array} \right\} \text{the dog}$$

or an adverb the one below,

$$\text{The boy wrote the essay very} \left\{ \begin{array}{l} badly \\ \ldots \\ easily \end{array} \right.$$

means that we don't have to try out every word in our mental LEXICON to see whether it will fit or not.

The criteria by which linguists assign words to particular classes, however, are less certain. Most people if asked to say what a verb or a noun are rely on what is called 'notional' criteria. These are broadly semantic in origin. They include referring to a verb as a 'doing word', i.e. a word that denotes an action of some sort (*go*, *destroy*, *eat*), and a noun as a naming word, i.e. one that denotes an entity or thing (*car*, *cat*, *hill*). Similarly, adjectives are said to denote states or qualities (*ill*, *happy*, *rich*), and adverbs, the manner in which something is done (*badly*, *slowly*, *well*). As a rule of thumb this works reasonably well, but it's not subtle enough to capture the way in which word classification essentially works. Not all verbs are 'doing' words. The verbs 'to be' and 'to have' clearly aren't. And neither are all nouns necessarily 'things'. Nouns such as 'advice', and 'consequence' are difficult to conceive as entities. We're forced to call them 'abstract' nouns, a recognition that in some way they are not typical. Indeed, notional criteria only work for prototypical class members (*see* PROTOTYPE THEORY), but there are many others for which such criteria are not adequate. The word 'assassination', for example, seems like a verb since it describes a process or action, but it is in fact a noun.

The only secure way to assign words into word classes is on the basis of how they behave in the language. If a word behaves in a way characteristic of a noun, or a verb, then it's safe to call it one. This, of course, means recognising that words can belong to more than one class. It also means recognising that words may be *more* or *less* noun-like or verb-like in behaviour. Word classes are similar to family groupings in that some members are more recognisably part of their class than others. Basic to word behaviour are two sets of criteria, namely, morphological (*see* MORPHOLOGY), and syntactic. Morphological criteria are concerned with the structure of words. Important here are such processes as **inflection**. Most verbs will inflect to show tense (*show* + *ed*), most nouns to indicate plurality (*bat* + *s*), and many adjectives to show the **comparative** and **superlative** (*fat* > *fatter* > *fattest*). But not all. One of the difficulties of relying on morphology alone is that there is no one criterion which all words in a particular class will obey. As a consequence, linguists also use syntactic criteria, in particular the DISTRIBUTION of a word in an individual string. Whereabouts a word can occur in a PHRASE or SENTENCE is an important indication of its class. Using distribution as a criterion we can construct substitution tables such as Table 5.

Using the behaviour of individual words as an indication of word class means that our approach is descriptive rather than prescriptive. And we shall also find that, because of the variable character of words, each class will contain several sub-classes. So there are sub-classes of nouns, verbs, and so on. And because the different classes have features in common it is possible to cross-classify them into larger groups. Linguists differentiate between **lexical** and **grammatical** classes. The former

Table 5

Determiner	Noun	Verb	Determiner	Noun
the	man	chased	the	girl
a	girl	fought	a	cat
+	+	+	+	
this	cat	frightened	this	man
my	bird	hit	my	cat

contain words that have a meaning outside the context in which they are used, and include nouns, lexical verbs, adjectives, and adverbs, whilst the latter consist of words that are only meaningful as part of the syntactic frame (e.g. PREPOSITIONS, conjunctions, pronouns, and auxiliary verbs). Lexical classes are sometimes also referred to as **open** in that they can readily be added to, and grammatical classes as **closed** because they cannot. New nouns and verbs are being formed all the time, but one rarely finds a new preposition or pronoun. As a consequence, lexical classes are usually regarded as **major**, and grammatical as **minor**, classes.

X-bar (X̄) theory.   A system of grammatical analysis that attempts to refine traditional accounts of PHRASE structure. According to the theory, X is a category variable that can stand in for the conventional categories of NOUN, VERB, ADJECTIVE, ADVERB, and PREPOSITION, in standard phrase-structure rules. X-bar theory is a dynamic system and its scope has been considerably extended in recent years. I shall begin by giving an account of its early development before describing later refinements.

The starting point for X-bar theory is the recognition that there are intermediate stages in the formation of phrases that existing rules do not capture. For example, if we take the string *the clever student*, there is no problem in saying what *student* is – it is clearly a noun – nor in saying that the whole thing is a noun phrase. But what of the sequence *clever student*? It seems to be intermediate between the two categories, smaller than a phrase, but larger than a word. Linguists resolve this difficulty by referring to it as a **noun bar**. We could show this new bit of structure as in Figure 20. What this tells us is that the complete phrase consists of a DETERMINER (*the*), plus a noun bar (*clever student*), which in turn consists of an adjective (*clever*) plus a noun, *student*. Nor is this the end of the story, for if we extend the phrase to *the tall clever*

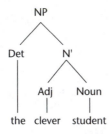

Figure 20   Tree diagram showing a noun bar

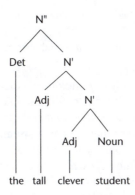

Figure 21   Tree diagram of a pre-modified noun double bar

student, we have yet another intermediate sequence, i.e. *tall clever student*. To cope with this we put another noun bar in the ladder. This time, to show that NP is the final rung, we call it N" (noun double bar), as in Figure 21.

This account is fair enough as far as it goes but noun phrases can also be post-, as well as pre-, modified. In the case of our sample phrase we could extend it with a **complement**, in the form of a prepositional phrase, namely, *the tall clever student **of physics***. In this case we have to recognise a prior stage of formation before the pre-modification, namely, *student of physics*. Absorbing this new bit of structure into our diagram, we can show it as in Figure 22.

Complements exist in a closer relationship to the head than do modifiers. *Tall* and *clever* do not just modify *student* but the sequence *student*

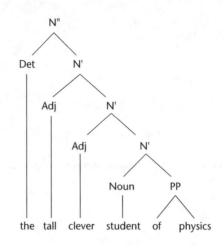

Figure 22   Tree diagram of a pre- and post-modified noun double bar

of physics. Using the family terminology of constituent analysis, complements are **sisters** of the head, whereas modifiers are sisters of the noun bar. In this way we can tie in functional relations to formal ones. At the top of the tree, the determiner acts as a **specifier** expanding the noun bar into a noun double bar, or noun phrase. Interestingly, all phrases, not just noun ones, can be shown to have the same structure. They are all capable of intermediate phrasal categories, or bars, which can be described in a fashion similar to nouns. In the case of verbs, for example, there is an obligatory head – a lexical verb – with various units dependent on it. Specifiers are the **perfect** (*have*) and **progressive** (*be*) auxiliaries (*see* ASPECT) – *has been singing*. Modifiers include 'manner adverbials' (*has been singing **badly***) and prepositional phrases (*has been singing **out of tune***). Complements are those elements that **subcategorise** the verb (i.e. the things which it is obliged to occur with). They may include 'nothing at all', in the case of **intransitive** verbs (*disappeared: see* TRANSITIVITY); noun phrases – *kicked **the ball***; prepositional phrases – *rely **on John***; and SENTENCES – *ask **whether this makes sense***.

Using X as a category variable for the various class labels, it is possible to represent phrase structure as in Figure 23. Summarising the rules for X-bar structure we can say:

1.   The head of a phrase is X, where X stands for noun, verb, adverb, adjective, or preposition.
2.   Complements expand X into X-bar.

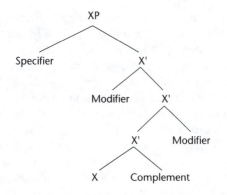

Figure 23   Tree diagram of X-bar structure

3.   Modifiers expand X-bar into X-bar (X-bar can reiterate as often as one wants, thus the diagram shows two such nodes).
4.   Specifiers expand X-bar into X-double bar, or XP.

It should be clear by now that X-bar syntax allows for considerable economy in the description of phrase-structure rules. Instead of having to construct separate **rewrite rules** for each of the categories, they can all be collapsed into one, using X as a category variable. As a consequence, the power and elegance of X-bar theory have made it a principal component of most contemporary syntactic models.

But, like most innovative analytic procedures, it is constantly increasing in subtlety. The account I have given so far is called the primitive X-bar model. Since its adoption by modern generative syntactitions, however, it has undergone a number of refinements. We shall briefly consider these. One limitation of the primitive X-bar model is that although it allows us to describe phrases in a common way, we are still stuck with the conventional rewrite rule for sentences, i.e.

S → NP + VP

(A sentence consists of a noun phrase plus a verb phrase)

On the face of it X-bar syntax doesn't help us with this. Employing the category variable X as in

S → XP + XP

makes the rule too powerful because it does not specify a value for X.

Such a rule would allow sentences to be formed from any type of phrase combination. It's here that X-bar theory makes a startling leap by suggesting that sentences could be considered as just another kind of phrase. On the face of it this is quite a strange idea, and one that cuts completely across traditional categories. In traditional grammar, sentences have the structure of a CLAUSE, not a phrase. The difference is quite significant because, whereas phrases are the result of the projection of a head word (a noun, for example, projects itself by adding on pre- and post-modifiers), a clause is the result of a predication relation between two phrases, i.e. a verb phrase is predicated of a noun phrase (S → NP + VP). But possibly, if we look deeper into the structure of a sentence, we might see that it too is generated from the projection of a head constituent.

The question is 'What constituent could that be?' As we have seen, the main lexical categories (nouns, verbs, adjectives, adverbs, and prepositions) already have their own phrasal projections. Once again, X-bar theory makes an innovative move – this time by arguing that lexical categories are not the only ones that can form phrases: functional categories can as well. In recent X-bar theory, auxiliary verbs, conjunctions, and determiners – classes which provide the framework of a sentence, and with little overt semantic content – are much more important than traditional grammars have suggested. Far from being just the grammatical hinges linking items together, they become the power-house driving the whole engine. In the case of auxiliary verbs, this is something that perhaps should not come as a surprise, given what we know of their importance in framing questions and negations. The auxiliary verb, where it is present, always carries the responsibility for indicating tense and number agreement, as, for example, in the following sentence:

John does like football

Here *does* is in the third-person singular present tense, agreeing with *John*. Were there no auxiliary verb, the task of number agreement and tense would pass to the main verb, i.e

*John like**s** football*

Tense and number agreement are the principal inflections needed for sentence construction. A complete sentence needs an appropriately tensed verb agreeing with its subject. We're not always aware of this because English has a very impoverished inflectional system. But here again X-bar theory makes use of an important concept in modern theoretical approaches to syntax, namely that properties of inflection can be present in a sentence without being visible. So, when we say that English has an impoverished inflectional system, what we really mean is that its system of **marking** inflections is impoverished. This insight has the capacity to revolutionise our understanding of what a sentence is. But the question now arises, 'If inflectional information is invisibly present in sentences, where is it located?' Initially, a number of linguists focused attention on auxiliary verbs, and posited the existence of an auxiliary phrase, or AUXP. This means detaching the auxiliary from the verb phrase, something which would seem to make sense. In the sentence *Jane can't buy books but John can* the process of ELLIPSIS serves satisfactorily to detach *can* from its understood verbal complement 'buy books'. At the same time, however, not all sentences have auxiliary verbs. We could posit the existence of an invisible auxiliary, but this would make things very difficult since auxiliaries do carry some semantic meaning in addition to inflectional information. Including them, even invisibly, would have consequences for the meaning of a sentence. A more radical solution, adopted by current X-bar theory, is to create an **inflectional phrase**. The head of this phrase is a category called **I**. This forms an I bar by merging with a verb phrase, and then is raised to full IP (or I'') by merging with subject elements acting as specifiers. Where there is an auxiliary in the sentence I will be located there. Where it isn't present it will be invisibly located in front of the verb phrase. Illustrations of both possibilities are given in Figures 24 and 25.

The significance of this new level of syntactic description is that it allows us to incorporate sentences within regular X-bar processes. A

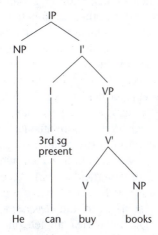

Figure 24   Tree diagram of an inflectional phrase with auxiliary present

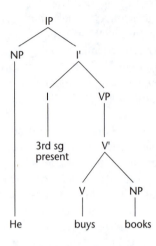

Figure 25   Tree diagram of an inflectional phrase without an auxiliary

sentence is now an inflectional phrase, or IP. Within this phrase the verb phrase acts as the complement of the head I, so producing an I-bar. The specifier for this I-bar is the subject of the sentence: *he* in Figures 24 and 25. We can now replace the traditional formula for a sentence (S → NP + VP) with a new one

IP → NP + I'
I' → I + VP

There are two further refinements to X-bar theory that should be mentioned. They concern the other two functional categories mentioned above: determiners and conjunctions. Let us look first at determiners. Most traditional syntactic analysis treats these as part of the noun phrase. So in the case of our phrase *the clever student* the sequence *clever student* is seen as a N' raised to a full NP by *the* acting as a specifier. Modern X-bar approaches, however, have given much greater significance to determiners, just as they have to auxiliary verbs. In a sense they perform a related function; auxiliary verbs, or more correctly I, serve to locate the verb phrase in time; similarly, determiners locate nouns and their accompaniments in space, whether actual or textual (*this* = near me, *the* = this particular one). Accordingly, many linguists now argue that a phrase such as *the clever student* is really a determiner phrase (DP) with *the* as its head and *clever student* as its noun phrase complement. This would mean the complete phrase having the structure shown in Figure 26.

Such a diagram may at first seem disconcerting, and it has to be said

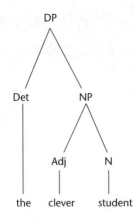

Figure 26   Tree diagram of a determiner phrase

that there isn't complete agreement among linguists about the structure
of such phrases. But it looks as though what X-bar theory is highlighting
is that there may be two kinds of phrases in sentences: the lexical kind
with nouns, verbs, adjectives, and prepositions as their heads (which
provide the inner semantic core), and the functional, or grammatical
kind, with categories such as inflection and determiners as their head
(which provide the superstructure). Into this second kind we can also put
conjunctions or, to use a more recent term, **complementisers**. These
occur all the time in **complex** sentences as, for example, in *Whether/if*
I go or not is up to me. As with auxiliary verbs, contemporary X-bar
approaches see complementisers as adding a new level of structure to
the sentence – in this case, a complementiser phrase with the complementiser *whether* or *if* as its head and the remainder of the sentence, or
IP, as it complement.

  X-bar theory is a complex and sophisticated area of syntax. Its method
of analysis is not always easy to grasp, particularly to students unaware
of the process by which it has developed. But it repays close study, for it
offers arguably the most radical approach to syntax in recent years, and
looks set, in one or other of its incarnations, to become the standard
model of analysis (*see* MINIMALISM).

5 Semantics and Pragmatics

INTRODUCTION

Semantics and pragmatics are the study of meaning communicated through language. Linguists who work in these branches of linguistics are interested in the ways in which words acquire meaning, and the processes by which native users of a language are able to give stable interpretations to word strings. Problems of meaning are arguably among the most significant that ADDRESSERS and addressees experience in communicating with each other. This is principally because of two things: first, the range of possible meanings of which many words are capable; and second, the considerable contextual features that influence how strings are interpreted. We are all aware, in everyday communication, just how much factors such as INTONATION, word stress, and situational context can affect the interpretation of utterances.

One of the initial problems that besets students of semantics and pragmatics is the relative scarcity of useful terminology compared with other LEVELS, such as phonology and syntax. The word 'mean' itself is notoriously imprecise and subject to a variety of different uses in naturally occurring English. We can say:

(i)   *He didn't mean to hurt you*
(ii)   *Her life lost all meaning*
(iii) *The red flag means it's dangerous to swim*

and in each case a different sense is conveyed. In (i) *mean* has the sense of 'intend', in (ii) of 'value', and in (iii) of 'is a signal that'. Using such a slippery term as part of a linguistic vocabulary is, not surprisingly, fraught with difficulties.

Not only that, but there is clearly more to meaning than knowledge about language and language usage. In order to understand (iii), for instance, we have to know something about SIGNS and the way they work. In other words, that objects can represent things, and even concepts, such as danger. The study of signs is termed **semiotics** and some linguists see linguistic meaning as simply a subset of this more general human capacity of making one thing stand for another: letters stand for sounds, words stand for concepts, and so on. But in addition to a general sign-making ability, however, we also need a good deal of encyclopaedic knowledge, that is, knowledge about the world, in order to interpret strings. If we came across the following sentence, for instance,

The telephone dial was made of marzipan

we should know we were in some imaginary world precisely because in the real world telephones are not made of this. Such knowledge cannot really be said to be linguistic in origin. Looking up the word 'telephone' in a dictionary wouldn't tell us anything about what the object was made of. It's something we have acquired as part of our general knowledge.

One of the general points, therefore, that emerges from the work of many linguists is that language underspecifies meaning. According to Nelson Francis, 'Words do not have meanings; people have meanings for words' (1967, p. 119). This seems a radical statement, but in a way it helps to explain the common feeling that words aren't always fully adequate to express what we mean. If this is the case, then one of the first tasks facing students of semantics and pragmatics is to delimit the area of enquiry. What kind of meaning can we usefully describe as 'linguistic' as opposed to that which is of a more general cognitive variety? This is not an easy question to answer, and the many books written on these levels are an indication of the difficulties involved.

A very simple approach to linguistic meaning, and one that is probably unconsciously held by many people, is to suppose that all we need to interpret linguistic expressions is to know the definitions of the meanings of words. We could then assume that when a speaker combines words together in phrases and sentences, the appropriate definitions are also combined and will enable us to arrive at the overall meaning of the utterance. There are several problems with this **definitions theory** of linguistic meaning. One we have encountered already, which is that we need a certain amount of encyclopaedic knowledge as well as linguistic knowledge for interpretation. But a second problem has to do with the sheer **circularity** of definitions. Any definition of a word is itself expressed in words that are dependent on other words for their definitions, and so on, *ad infinitum*. The question is, as Saeed (2003, p. 6) says, 'can we ever step outside language in order to describe it, or are we forever involved in circular definitions?'

A third difficulty with this theory, however, is that it takes no account of the significance of situational context in the determination of meaning. If someone were to say *Well played* to a batsman completing an innings, the meaning would be very different if he was out for nought as opposed to scoring a century. Similarly, *Are you watching this?* said to a friend watching television could be a request to switch to another channel, to turn the set off entirely, or indeed to go to bed. The words themselves are simply not sufficient on their own to determine meaning. We need access to a variety of **extra-linguistic** information about the participants, and the precise nature of the context of an utterance, in order to arrive at a correct interpretation. And indeed, in some instances, it is the body language, the gestures, and facial expressions, i.e. the **para-linguistic features**, which provide the clue to what is meant.

Because of the sheer indeterminacy of utterances and the dependence of linguistic meaning on other types of meaning, linguists characteristically differentiate between two broad but complementary approaches to this area. The first is concerned with **sentence meaning** and is the pursuit of **semantics**, whilst the second is concerned with **utterance meaning** and is the pursuit of **pragmatics**. The difference between them is aptly illustrated by Leech (1983), using two further usages of the word 'mean'. He points out that if we do not understand what someone has said to us, we characteristically say either

*What does **it** mean?*

or

*What do **you** mean?*

In the first instance our request is for information that is independent of both speakers, whereas in the second it is for information directly dependent on the speaker's intention. These are potentially two very different types of meaning.

To understand this, it is important to grasp the relationship between sentences and utterances. Utterances are the most concrete level of language: they are created by producing in spoken, or written, form, a string of words. Sentences, on the other hand, are abstract grammatical elements underlying utterances. If you imagine, for example, two people saying the sentence *Washington is the capital of America*, what we would have would be two utterances but only one sentence. And if more people were to say it there would be, correspondingly, so many more utterances. Similarly in written form, though here the differences would be registered by punctuation and typography. This being the case, we could say that part of the meaning of this string relates to its sentence value (particular words in a certain order) and part to its utterance value (intonation pattern, participants, situational context, and so forth). In practice, it is not always easy to disentangle these two levels of meaning, and there is an on-going debate between semanticists and pragmatists, just as there is between phoneticians and phonologists, as to where to draw the line of separation. None the less it is a useful distinction to work with and one that is still productive in linguistic criticism.

Semantics, then, is concerned with meaning as a product of the linguistic system and, as such, is part of our grammatical COMPETENCE. It focuses on **decontextualised** meaning, as opposed to pragmatics, which focuses on **contextualised** meaning. If this is not sufficiently clear, consider an example used in Geoffrey Finch, *How to Study Linguistics* (1997): the declaration *I love you*. We can give this a certain meaning based simply on what we know of the grammar of the language. We know that *I* specifies the speaker, and *you* the person being addressed, and that *love* is a VERB indicating a range of feeling that is stronger than *like*, but weaker than *adore*. But for a full, context-rich interpretation, we should have to consider who is talking to whom, and the situation in which the utterance takes place. These will all affect *how* the sentence is uttered and understood.

Semantics

Semantic investigation of language operates at two grammatical ranks: word rank and sentence rank. At word rank semanticists explore the relationships that words have with each other within the language as a whole. This constitutes their SENSE, that is, the meaning which a word has by virtue of its place in the linguistic system. There are a number of items in the glossary that deal with aspects of 'sense', such as SYNONYMY, ANTONYMY, POLYSEMY, HOMONYMY, and HYPONYMY. A key idea here, taken from the linguist SAUSSARE, is that words are signs. Their relationship to the world, or their REFERENCE, is symbolic, so that rather than being labels for things they are labels for concepts. The consequence of this is that any individual word, or sign, derives its meaning not from the world, but from its existence within a network, or SEMANTIC FIELD, of related signs.

A development from the study of 'sense' has been the interest within semantics of COMPONENTIAL THEORY. Componential analysts are concerned with breaking down, or 'decomposing', the meaning, or sense, of a word into its atomic components. A word like *man*, for instance, is said to consist of the components, + **Human** + **Adult** + **Male** and *woman* of + **Human** + **Adult** – **Male**. Using these, and other 'atomic' components, semanticists construct grids that relate words in their respective fields in terms of the presence or absence of a particular component. Componential analysis is a staple element of many semantic approaches, but it has been subject to much criticism. To begin with, it clearly works better for some items than for others. Grammatical words, for example, such as *and*, *to*, *for*, do not lend themselves to such analysis. But, more importantly, components such as **Human**, **Adult**, and **Male** could themselves be broken down into smaller components, and so on endlessly, to the point at which it becomes increasingly difficult to distinguish them in any meaningful way. As a consequence, some linguists see componential analysis more as a useful way of looking at the **taxonomic** systems (the ways in which terms are classified) that operate in the language rather than a theory of what meaning is.

At the sentence level semanticists are largely concerned with the truth value of linguistic expressions. In other words with how we establish the real-world correspondence, or otherwise, of statements, questions, and commands, and their internal consistency as linguistic expressions. Semanticists frequently distinguish between **analytic** and **synthetic** truth. A synthetically true statement is true because it is an accurate representation of reality. So, for example, *cats bark* is synthetically false because it does not accord with the facts. An analytically true statement, on the other hand, is true because it follows from the meaning relations within the sentence, regardless of what the situation in the world might be. So the statement *cats are dogs* is false because the sense of *cats* excludes that of *dogs*.

From a semantic point of view both kinds of truth are important in the judgements that we make about the truth or otherwise of linguistic expressions. And at some point they clearly connect with each other since an exhaustive account of the sense of *cat* would eventually include the information 'does not bark'. It is on the basis of both types of knowledge that we are able to construct meaningful sentences of English. At the rank of sentence there is a consensus that, as a very minimum, a semantic theory should reflect an English speaker's knowledge, as in the following examples:

1. That *a* and *b* below are **synonymous**
    (*a*) My sister is a spinster
    (*b*) My sister has never married

2. That *a* below **entails** *b*
    (*a*) The firing squad executed the soldier
    (*b*) The soldier is dead

3. That *a* below **contradicts** *b*
    (*a*) I have lived in Manchester
    (*b*) I have never been to Manchester

4. That *a* below **presupposes** *b*
    (*a*) The Prime Minister visited Northern Ireland
    (*b*) There is a Prime Minister

5. That *a* and *b* are **tautologies**
    (*a*) East is East
    (*b*) When you're dead you're dead

In order to represent the truth value of these and similar sentences linguists draw on the tools of **logic**. Logic is concerned with the rules that govern valid argument and INFERENCE. To some extent these underlie our use of language because they are part of the way in which we make sense of the world and communicate our understanding of it to others. Logical semantics, sometimes called TRUTH CONDITIONAL SEMANTICS, draws largely on propositional logic. Propositions are more abstract than sentences. If we return to our sample sentence *Washington is the capital of America*, we can see that it is possible to produce several different sentences and yet preserve the underlying proposition: *The capital of America is Washington, It is Washington which is the capital of America, The teacher said that Washington is the capital of America*. It is arguable, then, that there is a deep propositional core to language capable of being analysed in formal terms. Semanticists in this tradition use the symbols of formal logic to analyse sentences, reducing them to an abstract representation that will capture their underlying truth value. They are principally interested in the **logical connectives** of English, that is, with words such as *not, and, if, then, or, so*. These are the logical hinges of the language that link propositions together. This is a subtle and complex area that has links with the philosophy of language and requires some training in formal logic to penetrate successfully.

Logical semanticists are often thought of as **correspondence theorists** because they are principally interested in the way in which language corresponds to a correct description of the world as it is. It is on the basis of such correspondences that judgements about truth are made. Some semanticists, however, are sceptical of what is termed the

correspondence theory of truth. They argue that the structure of reality, as reflected in language, is a product of the human mind. This means that we have no access to a reality that is independent of human categorisation. In other words, language doesn't so much *correspond* to reality, as help to *create* it. This fundamentally different approach, sometimes termed **cognitive semantics**, sees language as part of our general cognitive ability, rather than as a set of separate, specialised competences. Semanticists in this school of thought pay special attention to METAPHOR. Cognitive linguists point out that traditional semantic approaches have tended to regard figurative uses of language as anomalous, in other words, as special cases, existing on the fringes of normal linguistic description. Many agree with the proposal by George Lakoff and Mark Johnson (1980) [see also Lakoff (1987), and Mark Johnson (1987)], that metaphor is an essential element in our categorisation of the world and our thinking processes. The consequence of this approach has been the breaking down of barriers between linguistics and other disciplines. Scholars working in literary criticism, rhetoric, ethics, and media, have drawn upon the insights of cognitive linguists in describing the mental structures that constitute our competence in these areas.

Pragmatics

Pragmatics is a relatively newer area of linguistics than semantics. As such, it suffers in particular from the lack of any coherent level of theory. It consists largely of a cluster of approaches that cohere around the preoccupation with the contextual constraints on meaning. In its origins it owes much to the perceived shortcomings of formal logic in coping with natural language. I pointed out earlier that logical semantics makes much of the importance of logical connectives in language use. But pragmatists argue that these often work in ways that formal logic is not entirely sufficient to cope with. For example, the negator 'not' works in logic so that statements such as *John is happy* and *John is not happy* are mutually exclusive. However, in natural language denying that John is happy doesn't necessarily mean he is *unhappy*. We recognise possible states that exist between the two. It is because of this that we can create ambiguous formulations such as *John is not unhappy*. Similarly, in formal logic the quantifier *some* does not exclude the possibility of *all*, so that *Some students passed the exam* does not conflict with *All students passed the exam*. However, if you asked a friend how many people passed the exam and the answer came back *some*, you would naturally conclude that not everyone passed. Examples like these encouraged the idea that language had its own natural logic, in addition to the formal kind proposed by semanticists. Natural logic allows for certain things to be implied beyond those which are obviously stated. These are termed IMPLICATURES.

The study of implicatures is fairly well developed and forms the cornerstone of most pragmatic approaches. The linguist principally associated with implicatures is the philosopher H. P. Grice. He argued that in order for communication to take place in natural language, speakers enter into an unspoken agreement over ways of interpreting what is said. This agreement takes on board the rules by which implicatures work and constitutes a form of cooperation – the COOPERATIVE PRINCIPAL. This principle, with its associated maxims of **quantity**, **quality**, **relation**, and **manner**, has been enormously influential in pragmatic studies. It is not without its critics and it has been subject to a number of revisions, but it remains a key idea in contemporary linguistics.

Equally important in the development of pragmatics has been the rise of SPEECH ACT THEORY, developed by the philosophers J. L. Austin, and J. R. Searle. Speech act theory examines the functional dimension of language. Traditionally, people tend to distinguish between 'doing' and 'saying', that is, between taking action over something and simply talking about it. But in many ways this is a false dichotomy. Looked at from another angle it is possible to see all utterances as kinds of action. They are linguistic events, or acts, in time, calculated to achieve a particular result or effect. The kinds of acts that utterances can achieve will vary from very direct ones, such as those which bind two people together in marriage, or name a ship, to those that give advice or request information. Most slippery of all are indirect speech acts. These are acts that are performed under cover of another act, for example, issuing a command by using a question, *Can you come here please?* In these cases we rely on para-linguistic features such as intonation and stress pattern, as well as extra-linguistic information from the context, to supply a full interpretation. The methodology of speech acts, the various kinds that are performed, and the procedures we adopt in processing them have been fully described in the literature, and although applying them to conversational situations is not always easy, they provide a useful and productive framework for linguistic analysis.

Pragmatics, as I have said, is a very diverse area of linguistic study, but one thing that all approaches have in common is a concern with communicative, rather than simply grammatical, COMPETENCE. Pragmatists focus on what is not *explicitly* stated and on how we interpret utterances in situational contexts. They are concerned not so much with the sense of what is said as with its FORCE, that is, with what is communicated by the manner and style of an utterance. It is, perhaps, not surprising that an adequate explanatory framework does not as yet exist because it is this interface between language and the endlessly diverse world of human meaning that remains the most challenging. And whilst there are on-going debates within linguistics as to the relative merits of semantic and pragmatic approaches, arguably the most fruitful approach for us is to view them as complementary, rather than competing, forms of linguistic analysis.

GLOSSARY

Amelioration. A semantic process whereby a word loses an unfavourable SENSE – for example, *boy*, which originally meant 'male servant' and now simply means 'male child'. The opposing process is PEJORATION. Amelioration is usually studied in HISTORICAL LINGUISTICS.

Antonymy. A SENSE RELATION that exists between words which are opposite in meaning, or SENSE. Antonymy can take a number of forms. **Gradable antonyms** are terms in which the degree of opposition is said to be 'gradable': for example, *wide* and *narrow*, *old* and *young*, *tall* and *short*. In each of these pairs the opposition is not absolute. There are degrees of width, age, and height, so that to say a road is not narrow doesn't mean it's wide, and vice versa. Also, our definition of wide, old, and tall will vary according to the **referent**. A tall man is shorter than a tall building, for instance. Gradable antonyms normally have one item that can be more widely used, or in linguistic terms is un-MARKED. I can say someone is 3 months 'old' or 60 years 'old' without meaning that they are old, but I can really only refer to them as 'young' if they are indeed young, or considered to be so. In this case 'young' is more marked than 'old'.

Complementary antonyms are different from gradable in that the opposition between the terms is absolute. *Alive* and *dead*, *married* and *single*, have an either/or relationship. To say someone is not alive means they are dead, and vice versa – unlike gradable antonyms there are no degrees in between. Having said that, however, it's quite common to find colloquial instances of grading, for example, *He's very much alive*. **Relational antonyms** are also different from gradable ones in that they are not susceptible to degrees of opposition. However, unlike complementary antonyms, they are not 'either/or' in character; we could say, for example, that *husband* is the opposite of *wife*, but not to be a wife doesn't mean you are a husband. Similar pairs are *above* and *below*, and *lend* and *borrow*. Relational antonyms exhibit reversability. This is a logical relationship that allows us to say that if I am your husband then you are my wife, or if you are above me then I am below you, and so on.

Associative meaning.   The meaning that becomes attached to a word because of its use but which is not part of its core SENSE. The principal types of associative meaning are **connotation**, **collocation**, **stylistic meaning**, and **reflected meaning**. Connotation has to do with the communicative value of a word: with meanings that are socially acquired. As such, connotative meanings are less stable than those which represent a word's conceptual sense. The term *man*, for example, has a conceptual sense that is unlikely to change over time and which is composed of the features 'adult', 'male', and 'human'. But if someone were to refer to an acquaintance as *a real man*, we would know that the term carried more meaning than just its core sense. The something extra is its connotative meaning. Just what exactly is connoted is debatable and dependent on a number of cultural variables, but in many respects connotation offers us a greater insight into social attitudes than does conceptual meaning. Words are not simply bearers of neutral cognitive content, as we can see when they are used to discuss sensitive areas of our social and cultural life. The problem of 'race', for instance, is rendered more difficult because words such as *white*, *black*, and *coloured* are connotationally weighted. At the same time, however, connotation provides a rich resource for people who exploit the imaginative possi-bilities of language, whether poets or those writing advertising copy. In spoken language the presence of connotation is often signalled by INTO-NATION. A particular tone of voice, or pattern of stress, can serve to indi-cate a whole penumbra of possible extra meanings.

Collocation refers to the tendency for certain words to occur together. The term itself comes from the verb *collocate*, meaning 'to go together'. A word like *clear*, for example, can be found with a number of nouns, *clear sky*, *clear conscience*, *clear idea*, *clear road*. In each case the term *clear* has a slightly different meaning because of the word it is qualify-ing. In some instances the difference can be quite marked: *strong* has a completely different meaning in *strong tea* than it does in *strong language*, where it is usually a euphemism for 'swearing'. Collocative differences sometimes separate words that are otherwise synonymous: *quiver* and *tremble* are synonyms, but we *tremble* with fear and *quiver* with excitement; similarly humans can *wander* and *stroll* but cows can only *wander*; and *profound* and *deep* can both occur with *sympathy* but only *deep* with *hole*. The distribution of a word within a language is referred to as its **collocational range**. The principle is best expressed by the linguist Brian Firth, 'We know a word by the company it keeps.'

Stylistic meaning is linked to the concept of REGISTER. Words have varying degrees of formality and status within the language. If you take words that cohere around any topic or SEMANTIC FIELD represented in the language you will find a number of terms that differ in associative meaning simply because some are newer or more 'posh' than others. The following words have much the same conceptual sense but differ in association because they belong to separate styles of English:

domicile	(official/technical)
residence	(formal)
abode	(archaic/poetic)
home	(general)
digs	(colloquial)
gaff	(slang)

Reflected meaning is a consequence of the POLYSEMIC nature of many words, that is, their capacity to bear more than one SENSE. Because of this, we sometimes find that when we use a word with a particular sense, one or more of its other senses is reflected in it. An example of this is the term *nuclear* as in the phrase *nuclear family*, in which the term *nuclear* is referring to the 'core' family unit of parents and children, but it's difficult to keep the other sense of *nuclear*, to do with the discovery of atomic energy (as in the *nuclear age*), completely at bay. Reflected meaning bedevils words to do with sexuality. Terms such as *gay*, *intercourse*, *queen*, *fairy*, are often very difficult to use precisely because of this. Reflected meaning allows speakers to indulge in innuendo, ambiguity, and the generation of puns, all of which exploit a potential doubleness of meaning in language by allowing one sense to rub off on another. As such, they are a great resource in the creation of wit and humour.

Cognitive semantics. A term used to describe the semantic approach of linguists who see no separation between linguistic knowledge and general thinking, or cognition. Cognitive linguists tend to adopt a functional view of language, as opposed to the more formal accounts favoured by Chomsky and similar generative linguists. They argue that no adequate account of grammatical rules is possible without considering the meaning of elements. As such, the difference between language and other mental processes is viewed as one of degree rather than kind.

Cognitive linguists are concerned to relate language to basic conceptual structures that they see as part of our experiential world. These structures, or domains, reflect the mental categories that we have formed as part of the inevitable process of being alive. Special attention is given here to METAPHOR. According to George Lakoff and Mark

Johnson, 'our ordinary conceptual system, in terms of which we both think and act, is fundamentally metaphorical in nature' (1980, p. 1). Cognitive linguists view this conceptual system as deriving largely from bodily experience and perception. It is from these that we extrapolate **image schemas**, primitive conceptual structures through which we organise and imaginatively construct the world.

A good example of an image schema is the **containment** schema described by Mark Johnson (1987). This derives from our experience of the human body as a container, that is, the sense we have of inhabiting our own body. This links with other experiences of containment – being in rooms, buildings, and beds, and putting things in bottles or jars – to establish a schema, or framework, that extends over other areas of experience. So, for example, the visual field is often conceived of as a container, *He's coming into view now*, *The car's out of sight*; as are states, *She's in love*, *He's in a temper*. Other schema examples are **path** schemas, which derive from our experience of moving around the world, and **force** schemas, which reflect the sense we have of interacting with animate and inanimate entities. On the basis of the former we conceptualise our lives as journeys and talk of *rushing* to do something and not getting *sidetracked*, whilst the latter give rise to expressions such as being *held up* or feeling *bogged down*.

Cognitive linguists use image schemas to explain a range of semantic phenomena that other approaches are not able fully to penetrate. The meanings of PREPOSITIONS such as *in* and *over*, for example, are notoriously variable in everyday use. In the following instances from Lakoff and Brugman (1988), *over* has several distinct meanings:

(i)   *The plane is flying over the hill*

(ii)   *Sam walked over the hill*

(iii)   *Sam lives over the hill*

(iv)   *The painting is over the mantel*

(v)   *The board is over the hole*

Without going into too much detail here it is possible to see that *over* has a number of related senses, the principal of which are **above-across**, as in the first three; **above**, as in (iv); and **covering**, as in (v). The **above-across** SENSE is viewed by Lakoff and Brugman as the prototypical (*see* PROTOTYPE THEORY) one that they relate to the path schema. This schema allows us to focus on the end point of the journey – its 'across-ness' – if we wish, as in (iii), or to indicate degrees of 'aboveness', as in the difference between (i) and (ii). Similar points are made about the other main senses of the preposition by seeing them as related aspects of the path schema. The 'covering' sense in (v), for example, has a path element latent within it as we can see in the extension *She spread the cloth over the table*. Similar analyses of other prepositional relations are characteristic of the way cognitive linguists are concerned to provide a semantically functional description of linguistic behaviour.

Componential theory (*see also* the Introduction to this chapter). The view that all lexical items can be analysed using a finite set of components (semantic features). Componential analysis developed from a technique devised by American anthropologists in the 1950s for analysing the kinship relations of Native Americans. Basic to the approach is the assumption that individual items can be decomposed into what are termed semantic 'primes', or 'primitives'. It is on the basis of these that we organise our experiential world. One of the commonest examples used by linguists is the set of features that are said to compose the terms *woman*, *bachelor*, *spinster*, and *wife*:

woman	[+ female]	[+ adult]	[+ human]	
bachelor	[+ male]	[+ adult]	[+ human]	[+ unmarried]
spinster	[+ female]	[+ adult]	[+ human]	[+ unmarried]
wife	[+ female]	[+ adult]	[+ human]	[+ married]

Isolating the features of these terms allows us to describe more precisely the conceptual SENSE of words, that is, the stable, or core, meaning that is basic to their individual identity. As a consequence, it enables us to define SENSE RELATIONS more closely. In the case of HYPONYMY (inclusion), for example, we can see that *spinster* is a hyponym of *woman* because its feature specification contains all the features of *woman*. This can be expressed in the following way:

A lexical item P can be defined as a hyponym of Q if all the features of Q are contained in the feature specification of P.

INCOMPATIBILITY can also be dealt with in a similar fashion. The terms *spinster*, *bachelor*, and *wife* are all incompatible and if we look at their feature specification it is possible to see why. In each case they differ from each other in terms of one or more features, despite sharing others, or in formal terms:

Lexical items are incompatible if they share a set of features but differ from each other by one or more contrasting features.

So *spinster* is incompatible with *bachelor* because of gender, and with *wife* because of marital status. It's important to realise, however, that componential analysis doesn't aim to capture the entire meaning of a word. It's only concerned with conceptual, not ASSOCIATIVE MEANING. So the fact that *spinster* has a more negative social meaning than *bachelor*, for example, is irrelevant here.

Despite this, semantic primes are not sufficient on their own to distinguish lexical items. There are, for example, several senses to *bachelor*, not all of which share the exact FEATURES above. In addition to the meaning 'unmarried male', *bachelor* can also mean 'a young knight serving under the standard of another', 'one who has the first or lowest academic degree', and 'a young fur seal without a mate in the breeding season'. To cope with this the linguists Katz and Fodor (1963) make a distinction between **semantic markers** and **distinguishers**. Semantic markers are meant to reflect 'systematic' relations between an item and the rest of the vocabulary. Distinguishers, on the other hand, reflect what is 'idiosyncratic' about an item. In the case of *bachelor*, for instance, we could separate out the feature basis of the different senses by listing the markers for each sense followed by the particular distinguisher (as all the senses share 'adult' we can omit this feature here):

bachelor (N)
i.   (human) (male) [one who has never been married]
ii. (human) (male) [young knight serving under the standard of another knight]
iii. (human) [one who has the first or lowest academic degree]
iv. (animal) (male) [young fur seal without a mate in the breeding season]
(semantic markers are enclosed in parentheses and distinguishers in square brackets)

We could also set this out in a TREE DIAGRAM, as in Figure 27.

Identifying the semantic features of NOUNS is easier than for VERBS, where there is no actual entity for the process of decomposition to focus on. Most analysis of verbs proceeds by separating them into different semantic classes based on the constructions they will allow and then isolating the features that are said to define them. So, for example, Levin (1993) isolates the following elements of meaning which material, or action, verbs can be said to contain:

(change) (motion) (contact) (cause)

If we take the verbs *cut, break, touch,* and *hit*, it is possible to put them

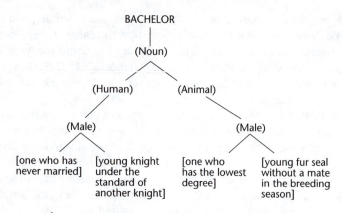

Figure 27 Semantic feature structure of 'bachelor'

into various sets in respect of which components they possess. Levin analyses them in the following way:

cut	(cause) (change) (contact) (motion)
break	(cause) (change)
touch	(contact)
hit	(contact) (motion)

We can test for the existence of these components by using sample sentences and seeing whether verbs with particular features will fit. In the case of *touch*, *cut*, and *hit*, all of which possess the feature 'contact', we can say *John touched/cut/hit James*. In addition, *cut* and *hit* are also verbs of motion and allow *John cut/hit at James* (but not **touched at*). And finally, *cut* can also be used in constructions that cause a change of state, as in *This bread cuts easily* (but not **touches/hits easily*). In this respect it is similar to *break*. Levin summarises this by saying:

> *Touch* is a pure verb of contact, *hit* is a verb of contact by motion, *cut* is a verb of causing a change of state by moving something into contact with the entity that changes state, and *break* is a pure verb of change of state.
>
> (1993, pp. 9–10)

Using this classification other verbs can be similarly assigned:

(i)   *touch* verbs: *pat, stroke, tickle*
(ii) *hit* verbs: *bash, kick, tap*
(iii) *cut* verbs: *hack, saw, scratch*
(iv) *break* verbs: *crack, rip, shatter*

The underlying concern of componential analysis is to arrive at a universal inventory of semantic features that are structurally present in all language. Arguably the most consistent proponent of this has been Ray Jackendoff who, in a series of works, has developed a decompositional theory of meaning that he calls **conceptual semantics**. Jackendoff identifies a number of structural categories, including: **Event**, **State**, **Thing** (or **Object**), **Path**, **Place**, and **Property**. Loosely speaking, 'event' and 'state' tend to be categories present in verbs; 'thing/object', in nouns; 'path' and 'place', in prepositional (PREPOSITION) and ADVERBIAL constructions; and 'property', in ADJECTIVES. These categories can all be sub-categorised by reference to specific semantic components. The event category, for instance, can be broken down to include those features of cause, motion, change, and contact that we have already identified. Similarly, 'thing' can be sub-categorised in terms of the features [± bounded]. This will distinguish between **count nouns** such as *table* and *chair* and **mass nouns** like *music* and *water*. Nouns that are bounded are basically conceived of as units. If we dismantle a chair we can't call the individual pieces a *chair*. Mass nouns, however, are thought of as substances. If we only hear a few bars of a sonata we have still heard *music*. This is reflected in the grammar so that mass nouns, for example, cannot go into the plural, e.g. **musics* (but see p. 104), whereas count nouns can, e.g. *chairs*.

Conceptual semantics is a complex and sophisticated attempt to identify universal semantic categories and map them onto syntactic operations and structures. But in so far as it relies on componential analysis it has inevitably had its critics. A principal difficulty with componential analysis is in the identification of the semantic primes, or markers. Pinning down the sense of words is not easy, even for common items. Also, distinguishing between features that are markers and those that are distinguishers is not unproblematic. How can we be sure that we have enough features, or that they are necessarily the right ones? Consider, for example, the semantic components of *chair* that Katz (1972, p. 40) gives as:

> *chair* (object), (physical), (non-living), (artefact), (furniture), (portable), (something with legs), (something with a back), (something with a seat), (seat for one)

Clearly, some of these features are open to question. Do chairs have to be portable? Is it essential they have legs, or seat only one? Does this analysis cover all chairs or only prototypical ones (*see* PROTOTYPE THEORY)? Once we begin decomposing, it becomes increasingly difficult to be sure about what counts as a prerequisite feature. And at a more practical level, critics of componential analysis have questioned its usefulness in advancing our understanding of language. It can sometimes seem as though all decomposition does is to exchange a simple term for a lot of other terms that can only be understood themselves by reference to other words. Breaking *man* down into (human) (adult) (male) doesn't help us very much if the understanding of 'human', for instance, relies in part on 'man'. The suspicion begins to grow that the process is inevitably circular and that we are simply translating words into their equivalents: something any dictionary does. None the less, despite these reservations about componential analysis as a theory of meaning, many linguists use its vocabulary and methodology as a way of examining the linguistic organisation of words into groups such as SEMANTIC FIELDS and sets.

Cooperative principle.   A term derived from the philosopher H. P. Grice and important in the study of conversational structure. Grice's principle assumes that people cooperate in the process of communication in order to reduce misunderstanding. The principle itself states, 'Make your contribution such as is required, at the stage at which it occurs, by the accepted purpose or direction of the talk exchange in which you are engaged' (cited in Malmkjaer, 1995, p. 355).

In order to comply with this principle speakers need to follow a number of subprinciples, called by Grice **maxims**. These fall into four categories, of quantity, relation, manner, and quality:

1. **Maxims of Quantity**
   (a) Make your contribution as informative as is required for the current purposes of the exchange.
   (b) Do not make your contribution more informative than is required.

2. **Maxim of Relation**
   Be relevant.

3. **Maxims of Manner**
   Super maxim: be perspicuous. More specifically:
   (a) Avoid obscurity.
   (b) Avoid ambiguity.
   (c) Be brief (avoid unnecessary prolixity).
   (d) Be orderly.

4. **Maxims of Quality**
   Super maxim: try to make your contribution one that is true. More specifically:

(a) Do not say what you believe to be false.

(b) Do not say that for which you lack evidence.

At first sight one limitation of these maxims appears to be their assumption that communication is simply a process of exchanging information. Grice is naturally aware that there are many other reasons for engaging in conversation, and that other maxims may influence speakers and listeners, but his assumption is that they are additional to what he regards as core requirements. They represent a kind of baseline for talking. Unless there is evidence to the contrary, we assume, as listeners, that speakers will tell the truth, estimate what we need to know and package the material accordingly, keep to the topic, and give some thought to us being able to understand them. The maxims, then, are best regarded not as rules but as implicit principles on which successful communication is built. As such, they can be departed from in two main ways. Speakers can choose either to **flout** or to **violate** them. Floutings are different from violations. Violating a maxim involves some element of communication failure: providing too little, or too much, detail, being irrelevant, or too vague. Floutings, however, are *apparent* rather than *real* violations. They enable us to comply with the maxims indirectly rather than directly. So, for example, sarcasm, calling out *nice one* about something you hate, can be viewed as a form of flouting since it only appears to violate the maxim of quality. And many, apparently irrelevant, replies are often indirectly relevant. Indeed, such is our natural tendency to cooperate that we will go a long way before assuming that something said to us is nonsensical. Novelists flout the maxim of manner when they disrupt the story by using flashbacks or digressions, but we trust, as readers, that the narrative will eventually come together. If it doesn't, we would conclude that the maxim had been violated.

Floutings, in other words, allow for a certain measure of creativity in communication. Participants are aware of an underlying tension between the simple maxim and its flouted form and it is this that gives rise in many instances to indirect SPEECH ACTS. The maxims are also the source of what Grice calls conversational IMPLICATURES. These are implied meanings that exist in addition to what is explicitly stated. So that, for example, if I ask you who has eaten my chocolates and you reply *John was in your room this morning*, I am entitled to assume, by the maxim of relevance, the implicature 'John ate your chocolates'.

The cooperative principle has been refined in two main ways. First, by the addition of the **politeness principle**. This was suggested by Leech (1983) as a way of explaining why people feel the need to be indirect in conveying what they mean. The politeness principle enjoins people to be tactful and polite unless there is a specific reason not to be. It has two formulations, one negative: 'Minimize (other things being equal) the expression of impolite beliefs', and the other positive: 'Maximize (other things being equal) the expression of polite beliefs' (Leech, p. 83). One of the things it does is to account for so-called 'white lies'. These ostensibly break the maxim of quality but are felt by most people to be different from other lies in that they are intended to be cooperative rather than to mislead. Leech shows that where there is a clash such as this the politeness principle will normally take precedence. The second refinement is more radical in nature. Some linguists follow the lead of Sperber and Wilson (1986) in arguing that all the maxims of the cooperative principle can be incorporated within the injunction to be relevant, since not telling the truth, being insufficiently informative, and presenting information in a haphazard way, are neglecting the demands of relevance. **Relevance theory**, as it is sometimes called, has developed over the last twenty years and has acquired a sophisticated theoretical base. Relevance theorists are interested in the way we process information and operate within models of reality, which allow us to assess the relevance or otherwise of utterances. There is still continuing debate, however, as to whether relevance theory sufficiently accounts for all the factors involved in the cooperative principle.

Entailment.   A logical relationship between two sentences such that the truth of the second sentence necessarily follows from the truth of the first. So, for example, sentence (1a), below, entails sentence (1b):

(1a)   *John killed Bob*
(1b)   *Bob died*

The entailment here is a consequence of the semantic relationship between *kill* and *die*. We know that there are various ways to die and that being killed is one of them. In other words, an important part of the sense of *killed* is contained within *die*. This kind of entailment, in which the sense of one lexical item is included within another, is based on a hierarchical relationship between items, known as HYPONYMY. Another example of such an entailment is the following pair:

(2a)   *I bought a cat*
(2b)   *I bought an animal*

In this case sentence (2a) entails sentence (2b) since a cat is a kind of animal. Another way of putting this is to describe (2b) as the **entailment** of (2a). Notice, however, that the relationship is not reversible. Saying that I have bought an animal does not entail that I have bought a cat. It could be a dog, or a parrot, or any other animal. Similarly, to state that Bob died does not entail that John killed him.

One of the principal difficulties that students regularly have is distinguishing entailment from PRESUPPOSITION. This is another logical relationship involving statements that are dependent on one another. The big difference is in the nature of that dependence. In the sentences above, negating (a) means that (b) can be either true or false. In other words, the entailment fails. So, for example, saying that I didn't buy a cat leaves completely open the question of whether or not I bought an animal. This would not be so if the relationship were one of PRESUPPOSITION. In the sentences below, (3a) presupposes (that is, assumes) the truth of (3b):

(3a) *The King of England left for Peru yesterday*
(3b) *There is a King of England*

but even if we negate (a) the presupposition holds:

(4a) *The King of England did not leave for Peru yesterday*
(4b) *There is a King of England*

The importance of entailment to linguists is that it enables them to analyse what are called the **truth relations** of sentences. These are independent of their empirical, or actual, truth. This means that (1b) and (2b) are automatically entailed respectively by (1a) and (2a). On the basis of these, semanticists interested in the logical dimension of the language can construct **truth tables**. Table 6 shows the truth relations that exist between (1a) and (1b), and between (2a) and (2b). The symbols p and q represent the first and second sentences in each sequence and the

Table 6   Truth table for entailment

p		q
T	→	T
F	→	T or F
F	←	F
T or F	←	T

T = TRUE; F = FALSE

arrows → and ← show the direction of a relation 'when . . . then'. So the first line reads 'when p is true, q is true', and the last line reads 'when q is true, p can be either true or false'.

The entailments we have looked at so far are lexical in origin, that is they derive from the lexical relationship between individual words. But entailment can also be syntactic in origin. Active and passive versions (*see* VOICE) of the same sentence will entail one another, so for example (5a) and (5b) below entail each other:

(5a)   *John killed Bob*
(5b)   *Bob was killed by John*

These sentences have the same set of entailments. That is, they **mutually entail** each other. Or, to put it another way, they **paraphrase** each other.

Extension.   A semantic process whereby a word expands in meaning. There are two main ways in which this can occur. First, by **generalisation**. This occurs when a word with a restricted SENSE takes on a wider, or more general one. The word *virtue*, for example, originally denoted a male quality only, but now, of course, can apply equally to both sexes. More frequently, words that originally had a strongly emotive sense acquire a looser and much weaker one. This has happened to words such as *sensational*, *monstrous*, *ghastly*, *abominable*, *phenomenal*, and *horrid*. This is sometimes referred to as **weakening.**

Second by **transference**. This occurs when a word is transferred from one SEMANTIC FIELD to another. For example, railway terms, such as *track*, *train*, *switch*, and *rails*, all belong originally to other fields: a *track* is a path, a *train* is a procession, a *switch* is a twig or small branch, whilst a *rail* is a piece of wood. It is characteristic of language development that when we want a new term for something, we first of all try and adapt an existing one before inventing a new one. One particular form of transference that is especially productive is **metaphorical transference**. Many words acquire figurative meanings in addition to their more 'literal' ones. A good example is parts of the body, *eye, hand, foot*, which have all been extended in this way: *eye of the needle, hand of the clock, foot of the bed*, and so on. Metaphorical transference is a key process in the development of POLYSEMY.

Force.   The contextual meaning of a linguistic item, frequently signalled by INTONATION. Force is an aspect of utterance-meaning rather than sentence-meaning (see p. 138). If, for example, someone says *I like* *your hat*, we need to know more than the SENSE and REFERENCE value of the words in order to interpret them correctly. We have to be alert to the possibility of irony in the speaker's tone, particularly if there is anything odd about the hat, in which case the speaker might actually be implying the reverse of *like*. Indeed, ironical statements characteristically oppose force and sense, as in *nice one* said sarcastically.

The analysis of force is more the concern of pragmatics rather than semantics (see p. 142). At issue here is not so much linguistic, as **extra-linguistic**, meaning. In other words, those elements of meaning that are not explicit in the language itself and for which reference to a dictionary would only be of limited help. As we have already said, intonation plays an essential part here, but so does stress. You have only to think of the ways in which the stress pattern of any simple sentence could be varied to see the differing interpretations possible from an actual utterance. The sense of *I'm not going out tonight* is clear enough, but its force will depend on where we place the **nuclear** stress. The other main way in which force is communicated is by thematic arrangement. We tend to make the most important parts of our utterances more prominent by thematising them, that is, by positioning them at the beginning. Newspapers frequently do this to draw attention to the most dramatic bits of the news, but creative writers also do it. Rearranging *The rain came down* to *Down came the rain* doesn't alter the sense of the line but it does alter its force because now the emphasis is on the physical descent of the rain rather than its simple existence.

Homonymy.   A relation that exists between words that have the same form but unrelated SENSES. Homonyms may have the same phonological or graphical form, or both. Examples of the former are *sight/site* and *rite/right*. These are **homophones**. Examples of the latter are *lead* (of a dog), and *lead* (on the roof). These are **homographs**. And some homonyms are homophonic and homographic: *mail* (armour) and *mail* (post), *cleave* (unite) and *cleave* (part). The difficulty for linguists is to distinguish between POLYSEMY and homonymy. At the theoretical level the distinction is clear enough in that homonyms are separate lexical items. The relationship between them is purely accidental. It is similar to discovering that one has a lookalike somewhere to whom one is totally unrelated. In the case of polysemy, however, we are dealing with a single lexical item that has acquired more than one sense. In practice, however, the distinction is often difficult to make. The most straightforward solution is to take word origin, or etymology, as the principal criterion. But that would lead us to decisions that are counter-intuitive. *Pupil* (eye) and *pupil* (student) have a common origin and are therefore, by an etymological criterion, polysemic. But the senses are so unrelated that most people would intuitively classify them as separate lexical items, that is, as homonyms. A similar problem exists with *sole* (fish) and *sole* (shoe). Arguably a more useful approach is to look for a common core of meaning existing between the senses, and to set the matter of etymology aside.

Hyponymy. A hierarchical SENSE RELATION that exists between two terms in which the SENSE of one is included in the other. Terms such as *daisy*, *daffodil*, and *rose* all contain the meaning of *flower*. That is to say, they are all **hyponyms** of *flower*. The more general term is called the **superordinate** or **hypernym**. Much of our vocabulary is linked by such systems of inclusion: *red* is a hyponym of *colour*, *flute* of *musical instrument*, and *hammer* of *tool*. Sometimes a word may be superordinate to itself in another sense. This is the case with *animal*, as shown in Figure 28. The first occurrence, opposed to *vegetable*, is the sense contained in the phrase 'the animal kingdom'. The second occurrence is synonymous with *mammal*, and the third with *beast*. Hyponymy is a vertical relationship that is fundamental to the way in which we classify things. Most dictionaries rely on it for the provision of definitions ('a chair is a type of furniture', 'a flute is a type of musical instrument', and so on). The set of terms that are hyponyms of the same superordinate term are **co-hyponyms** (for example, *red*, *black*, and *yellow*, in the colour system). Another way of describing the relationship is to say that the individual colours are **sisters** of the parent term **colour**. As such, they exhibit INCOMPATIBILITY. That is, something cannot be all red and all green, a flute cannot be a violin, or an apple a peach.

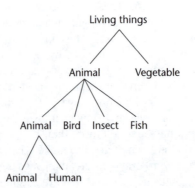

Figure 28 Diagram of the hyponymic sense relations of 'animal'

Implicature. A term derived from the work of the philosopher H. P. Grice and now frequently used as part of the study of conversational structure. Implicatures result from the process of implication that speakers and listeners rely on in the production and interpretation of utterances. All communication uses implied knowledge or PRESUPPOSITIONS, on the basis of which we draw certain conclusions. The term in general use for this implied knowledge is 'implication'. Grice's term 'implicature' is an attempt to give a more formal linguistic status to it. All sorts of things can have implications: actions, events, and so on, but only linguistic events carry implicatures.

Grice distinguishes between two kinds of implicature: **conventional implicature** and **non-conventional implicature**. The first sort is a consequence of the natural, rather than formal, logic that utterances characteristically employ. The introduction to this chapter refers to the example of natural logic in the utterance *Some students passed the exam*, which, although it doesn't formally conflict with the statement *All students passed the exam*, would normally be taken as implying 'some students didn't pass the exam'. In Gricean terms this is a conventional implicature precisely because it is one that we all automatically make irrespective of the context. Non-conventional implicatures, by contrast, depend for their interpretation on a wide range of contextual information, including information about the participants, and their relationship with each other. Take a simple statement such as *I like you*. The implicatures we are likely to derive from this will depend on what we know of the speaker and the circumstances in which it is being said.

There is, however, a sub-class of non-conventional implicature that has aspects of conventionality in it, and it is this class that has been most influential in pragmatic theory. Grice refers to it as **conversational implicature**. Conversational implicature arises from the necessity we are under in communicating to make our utterances coherent, clear, and orderly. What guarantees these features is the COOPERATIVE PRINCIPLE. This, with its associated maxims, enables us to make INFERENCES over and above what is explicitly stated. So, for example, if you are asked if you have any pets and you reply that you have two cats, the listener is entitled to conclude that that is the limit of your pets, even though you haven't exactly said so. Conversational implicature is important in the study of DISCOURSE analysis, although debate still continues about the precise status of the cooperative maxims.

Incompatibility. A SENSE RELATION that exists between words in a SEMANTIC FIELD where the choice of one excludes the other. So, for example, it is a contradiction to say *This instrument is a piano and a* *violin*, since the SENSE of *piano* excludes that of *violin*. Similarly, in the field of fruit we cannot say *This fruit is an apple and a banana*, or, in colour, *This colour is red and black*. Because these words are mutually exclusive members of the same field we say they exhibit incompatibility. At the same time, however, the exclusion is not a form of ANTONYMY. *Apple* is not the opposite of *banana*, nor *red* of *black*. But there are occasions when the distinction between antonymy and incompatibility is a fine one. The terms *woman* and *man*, for example, are commonly thought to be opposites, but not being a woman doesn't necessarily mean you are a man. It is more correct to label *woman* as incompatible with *man*. What we are saying, then, is that antonymy will inevitably involve incompatibility, but not the reverse. Senses can be incompatible without necessarily being antonymous.

Inference.   The process of deduction that listeners characteristically employ in interpreting utterances. Inference is crucial to interpretation because a good deal of meaning is implied rather than being explicitly stated. The amount of inferring that speakers expect listeners to undertake depends on the degree of shared knowledge between them. In the following examples the speaker relies on the listener to flesh out the utterances with the appropriate inferences:

  (i) *I cleaned the house today. My mother-in-law is coming.*
       Inference: the speaker cleaned the house **because** his/her mother-in-law was coming.

  (ii) A: *Where are my socks?*
        B: *Have you looked in the drawer?*
            Inference: the socks are in the drawer.

Most inferences are derived automatically from utterances and are part of the way in which consecutive sentences are assumed to be coherent. In the examples below, the words in bold are inferred by the listener to refer back to an antecedent NOUNPHRASE:

  (i) *I dropped the vase.* **It** *broke.*
  (ii) *I saw the boss yesterday.* **The old fool** *still doesn't know who I am.*

Another instance of automatic, or routine, inference is what linguists call **bridging inferences**. These occur in sentences where speakers rely on general or background knowledge to fill in the gaps, as in:

(i)   *I entered the room.* **The ceiling** *was beautiful.*

(ii)   *I walked on the beach.* **The tide** *was out.*

In these cases, because it is a matter of general knowledge that rooms have ceilings and that tides occur on beaches, the listener is able to draw the appropriate inference linking the two sentences.

Limitation.   A semantic process whereby a word contracts in meaning (for example, *meat*, which originally meant 'food' and now simply means 'the flesh of animals'). An echo of the older, more extensive meaning can be heard in the proverb *One man's meat is another man's poison*. The opposing process is EXTENSION. Limitation is usually studied in HISTORICAL LINGUISTICS.

Meronymy.   A SENSE RELATION that describes a part–whole relationship between the SENSES of words. *Cover* and *page*, for example, are meronyms of *book*. Meronymy is similar to HYPONYMY in reflecting a hierarchical relationship between words. A typical system might be as shown in Figure 29.

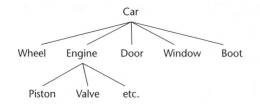

Figure 29   Diagram of the meronymic sense relations of 'car'

Metaphor.   Characteristically, a process in which one SEMANTIC FIELD of reference is carried over, or transferred, to another. So, for example, in the sentence *The ship ploughed the water*, the language of farming is transferred to the activity of sailing. In traditional literary criticism the semantic field being described, in this case 'sailing', is referred to as the **target**, and the semantic field being used for the comparison, 'farming', is referred to as the **source**. Other, more traditional terms are **tenor** and **vehicle.**

There are two main positions on the role of metaphor in language. The first, often called the **classical** view, can be traced back to Aristotle. Basically, this sees metaphor as a kind of decorative addition to ordinary language. Metaphor is regarded as something outside normal language, requiring special forms of interpretation. A version of this is often adopted in the **literal language theory**. According to this, metaphor is a form of anomaly, or deviation, which a hearer recognises as such before employing strategies to construct the figurative or non-literal meaning. These usually involve lifting the SELECTION RESTRICTIONS on words. For example, we register the sentence *All our yesterdays have lighted fools the way to dusty death*, as anomalous, or deviant, because the verb *light* doesn't allow us to select *yesterday* as an appropriate subject. Only things with the semantic feature + concrete can be lit, and references to time don't have this. As a consequence, we interpret the sentence by suppressing this feature, and any others that block interpretation, and highlighting those that are in common. In this particular instance, one FEATURE that a day and a candle could be said to share is transience, in that neither lasts very long.

The difficulty for linguists following this approach, however, is to describe the set of rules that governs when and how selection restrictions may be lifted. One of the most influential attempts is that provided by S. Levin (1977). Levin bases his account of metaphor on the work carried out by Katz and Fodor into semantic primes. Taking as his example *The stone died*, he argues that the anomaly of this sentence lies in the incompatibility of the features for *stone* and *die*. In the case of *stone* these are:

physical object
natural
non-living
mineral
concreted

and for *die*:

process with result, namely, that some **living** entity *x* ceases to be living:
(adapted from Levin, 1977)

The semantic features that are incompatible here are 'non-living' and 'living'. What happens in the case of metaphor, Levin argues, is that one feature transfers across and neutralises the other, so allowing us to provide an acceptable interpretation. If 'non-living' transfers to *die* it produces the interpretation 'The stone ceased to be', whereas if 'living' transfers to *stone*, it produces the interpretation 'The natural physical object died'. Levin develops a number of what he calls 'construal' rules, which he argues govern when and how such feature transfers can occur. These typically employ processes of **disjunction**, **conjunction**, or **displacement**. Levin's approach has its attractions but it has not been without criticism. In the first place, because of the concern to find a non-metaphorical, literal equivalent, it reduces interpretation to the level of translation. And secondly, the status and existence of the so-called semantic primes are not beyond question (*see* COMPONENTIAL THEORY).

The second approach, often called **romantic**, views metaphor not as an anomaly requiring special methods of interpretation, but as an integral part of language and thought. From this standpoint there is no real distinction between figurative and non-figurative language since all language is essentially metaphorical. An extension of this view can be found in the work of cognitive semanticists, though they usually adopt a weaker version of the romantic position in which some distinction is made between literal and figurative language. Of principal importance here is the work of George Lakoff and Mark Johnson (1980), who see metaphor as a naturally occurring feature of language, and a consequence of the way in which we reason and think about the world.

Lakoff and Johnson distinguish three basic kinds of metaphors. The first consists of **structural** metaphors of the sort 'X is Y', where one thing is experienced and understood 'in terms of another' (1980, p. 5). This is what most people conventionally understand as metaphor. Lakoff and Johnson illustrate this with various metaphors surrounding the concept of argument, e.g. *An argument is war*, *An argument is a building*, *An argument is a container*, and so on. These metaphorical concepts, as they call them, develop through the mapping of one kind of experience onto another. They underlie such expressions as *He defended his argument*, *His argument is founded on ...*, and *His argument includes the idea that ....* The second kind of metaphor they call **orientational**. These are concerned with the way in which we spatialise experience. They arise from our awareness of our own bodies and the way they function in a predominantly physical environment. So, for example, the fact that *up* is connected with things that are pleasant and good (*His spirits rose*, *I'm in peak condition*, *Things are looking up*), and *down* with the reverse (*He's feeling down*, *Sales are down*, *That was a low thing to do*), reflects our sense of the importance we attach as physical beings to standing up as opposed to lying down: the former being associated with activity and alertness, and the latter with sleep and death. Similar metaphorical correspondences are constructed on the basis of our physical awareness of *in/out*, *front/back*, *on/off*, and *near/far*. These correspondences allow us to project our orientation onto situations and things around us. We experience ourselves as having an inside and an outside, a front and a back, and correspondingly we talk of being on the *inside* of a decision, or of some activity as *a front* for something else.

The third kind of metaphor is **ontological**. These arise from our experience of objects as 'discrete entities or substances' (1980, p. 5.). Lakoff and Johnson argue that in order to conceive of things in the first place we need to be able to identify, categorise, and group them. In other words, we confer entity status on them. This is largely done by reference to prototypical (*see* PROTOTYPE THEORY) members of the class of things in question rather than any set of defining features. Ontological metaphors are typically used to 'comprehend events, actions, activities and states' (p. 30). They give as an example a race, viewed as a discrete entity – *Are you going to the race?* – in which an event in time is conceptualised as an object. Metaphorical correspondences allow us to extend entity status to a wide range of experiences based on processes such as 'referring', 'quantifying', and 'identifying'.

Cognitive semanticists argue that because of their presence in speakers' minds, metaphors exert influence over a wide range of linguistic behaviour. The tendency in English, for example, of using the physical domain as a way of conceptualising the mental, is important in the development of POLYSEMY. The verb *see* has two meanings: one physical, meaning 'to perceive with the eyes', and the other mental, meaning 'to understand'. The linguist Sweetser (1990) points out that in Indo-European languages generally there is a tendency for verbs of sense perception to shift in this way. We can see it again in the way the word *taste* has developed the meaning of choice or preference.

Pejoration.   A semantic process, sometimes referred to as **deterioration**, in which a word takes on a negative evaluation, for example *gossip*, which originally meant 'god-relative' and now means 'idle talk'. Similarly *officious*, which once had the meaning 'kindly', now means 'interfering'. The opposing process is AMELIORATION. Pejoration is usually studied in HISTORICAL LINGUISTICS.

Polysemy.   A SENSE RELATION in which a word, or LEXEME, has acquired more than one meaning (as distinct from HOMONYMY, in which two lexemes happen to have the same sound, or written form). The term *flight*, for example, can mean all of the following: (i) the power of flying; (ii) an air journey; (iii) a series of steps; (iv) a digression; (v) a unit of the air force. These senses are clearly related and it is possible to see how they might derive from the same word. Many NOUNS acquire new meanings by having a literal and a metaphoric meaning, for example, parts of the body, *eye*, *leg*, *hand*, and *foot*, applied to *needle*, *chair*, *clock*, and *bed*.

And some nouns acquire a concrete and an abstract SENSE. So *text*, *book*, and *thesis*, can be used to refer to a specific item, as in *I've had my thesis bound*, or to a more general one, as in *I agree with your thesis*. Words that are capable of more than one meaning are **polysemic**, as opposed to those that can only bear one meaning, termed **monosemic.**

Presupposition. A term used in both semantics and pragmatics to refer to assumptions implicitly made by speakers and listeners that are necessary for the correct interpretation of utterances. The statement *I'm sorry it's raining*, for example, presupposes that it is raining. The presupposition also holds if the statement is negated: *I'm not sorry it's raining*, also presupposes *it's raining*. This is an important difference between presupposition and ENTAILMENT, a logical relationship with which presupposition is sometimes confused. Presupposition deals with the necessary preconditions for statements to be true. So the sentence *My cat was run over yesterday* assumes as a necessity the truth of *I had a cat*.

Presupposition allows us the freedom not to make everything absolutely explicit in our communications. If we had to spell out all the details every time we spoke, then communicating would be an extremely lengthy and tedious business. Being able to assume a certain amount of knowledge on the part of listeners makes it possible to take shortcuts. The degree of shortcutting, however, depends on the context in which communication takes place. A certain amount of presupposition is implicit in the linguistic system and can be studied just like entailment, in terms of its **truth conditions**. This is the concern of semanticists for whom presupposition is a matter of formal logical relationships. The examples already given illustrate this strict view. We could call this **sentence presupposition**. Many sentence presuppositions are produced by the presence of certain words. Linguists term these **lexical triggers**. For example, there is a class of verbs, such as *regret* and *realise*, that are called **factive** verbs because they presuppose the truth of their complement clauses. Compare sentences (1a) and (1b) below. Only the sentence with the factive verb *realise* presupposes (1c). The non-factive verb *think* has no such presupposition.

(1a)   *John realised that it was raining*
(1b)   *John thought it was raining*
(1c)   *It was raining*

Similarly, compare (2a)–(2c):

(2a)   *Sarah regretted going out*

(2b)   *Sarah considered going out*

(2c)   *Sarah went out*

The problem with an account of presupposition that is limited to a truth-based semantic approach, however, is that it doesn't take full account of all the presuppositions that speakers and listeners make in interpreting communications. To begin with, some presuppositions clearly depend upon our knowledge of the world. Compare the following sentences:

(3a)   *She tripped before getting in the car*

(3b)   *She died before getting in the car*

(3c)   *She got in the car*

(3c) is presupposed by (3a) but not by (3b). The reason for this is simply that we know that someone who has died cannot get into a car. The issue here is pragmatic rather than strictly semantic. The matter is made more complex when we consider that many presuppositions are the result not of sentence form but of intonation. In the following cases, for example, the sentences are exactly the same but uttered with a different stress pattern. The consequence is the production of different presuppositions:

(4a)   *Jenny admired **JOHN***

(4b)   ***JENNY** admired John*

In (4a) the presupposition is *Jenny admired someone*, whereas in (4b) it is *someone admired John*.

This second kind of presupposition, which depends on **extra-linguistic** and/or **paralinguistic** (*see* NON-VERBAL COMMUNICATION) information, we can term **pragmatic** or **utterance presupposition**. In any communication there is a certain amount of presumed knowledge independent of purely semantic knowledge. The degree and kind of assumed knowledge depends on a wide range of factors that linguists broadly refer to as **context**. If you ask someone whether they want a cup of coffee and receive the reply *It will keep me awake*, your respondent is assuming you know whether or not they wish to stay awake. This background presupposition cannot be recovered from the form of the answer itself, but must necessarily be there for it to count as an appropriate reply. What is at issue here is the degree of shared knowledge that both parties have. This form of presupposition is vaguer and less codifiable than its stricter semantic counterpart. Most pragmatists who study it approach it in terms of communicative strategies such as the COOPERATIVE PRINCIPLE, which involve interpretative principles based on INFERENCE and IMPLICA-TURE. Stylistically, presupposition is exploited in a range of discourse types, including advertisements, newspapers, and fiction. The injunction *Don't put up with back pain*, for example, carries the implicit presupposition *You have back pain*.

Reference.   The relationship between words and the things, activities, properties, relationships, etc. in the outside world, to which they refer. Words differ in the degree of reference they allow. So, for example, proper NOUNS, or names, are highly referential. We know that nouns such as *London* or *Gloria* refer to a particular place or person. On the other hand, words like *as*, *to*, *for* and, *and*, so-called 'function words', appear to have no reference at all: it's impossible to indicate anything in the outside world to which they correspond. A more difficult case are abstract nouns. When we talk about *honesty*, *beauty*, or *virtue*, we are not directly referring to anything in the outside world, although we may well have an event, activity, or person in mind. The degree of possible reference here would seem to be very weak, and hence the term *abstract* noun. Some reference is also more general and less specific than other kinds. The statement *I like that tree*, for example, is using *tree* to refer to a specific object, whereas *I like trees* is using *trees* to refer to the species. This is a form of 'generic' reference. Even names can be used in this way, as in *Gloria is a nice name*, where *Gloria* is not referring to any particular person but to the name itself. Being able to tell whether a word is being used with generic or specific reference is sometimes important in determining the meaning of an utterance. Just think of the misunderstandings that might arise from the utterance *I'm looking for a woman*.

Some linguists limit the term 'reference' to specific reference, that is, the activity of picking out precise things, or **referents**, in the world. Generic reference they see as the process of **denotation**. According to this account, words denote by indicating activities, events, or things, but not necessarily in a specific manner. Reference is thus a particular form of denotation. Linguists also differentiate between 'constant' and 'variable' reference. Expressions such as *the Tower of London* and *the Vatican* have **constant reference**, while expressions such as *I*, *you*, and *she*, have variable reference. To know who is being referred to by these pronouns we need to know a lot about the context in which they were uttered.

Reference is clearly an important dimension of meaning and indeed some early semantic accounts give it a high priority. The ancient notion that words are really names for things, or **nomenclaturism**, is effectively a reference view of language. But modern semantics adopts a more complex perspective in which reference is only one dimension of word meaning. Equally important is SENSE. If we return again to the statement *I like that tree* we could say that the only reason we can use the word *tree* to refer at all is because we have the concept of 'treeness' in our minds. In other words, we have to have some SENSE of what the word means before we can apply it. This division suggests that SENSE is primary in that it allows reference to take place. Words are thus labels for concepts rather than things.

Selection restrictions.   Semantic restrictions on the co-occurence of linguistic items. VERBS, for example, are commonly said to select their **subjects** and **objects**. The verb *eat*, for instance, will select for its subject a NOUN PHRASE with an animate reference. This will allow us to say *He/the cat/the man is eating a banana*, but not *The stone/the peanut is eating a banana*. Similarly, the object of *eat* has to be edible, so that we can't eat a brick or a house. Nouns will also normally select dependent constituents with which they are compatible. This is especially the case with adjective combinations; so we find *tall trees* and *tall people*, but not **tall cushions* or **tall ants*.

The concept of selection restrictions arose largely as a consequence of the work of generative grammarians such as CHOMSKY. He realised early on that whilst the rules of syntax might operate autonomously in producing WELL-FORMED strings, the question of whether such strings were ACCEPTABLE or not was largely a semantic issue. As a consequence, some linguists (e.g. Katz and Fodor) have turned more particularly to considering the relations between syntax and semantics. Items in the LEXICON are decomposed into their semantic FEATURES, on the basis of which particular verbs or nouns are said to select items with which they can co-occur. So, for example, in the case of *eat*, the verb is marked with the feature + animate, which means that it can only combine with a subject similarly marked. This restriction will be indicated in the lexicon: i.e. [+ [+Animate]].

Problems arise with the strict application of selection rules in that many expressions, notably figurative ones, frequently violate them. We might complain about an onerous job *eating our time*, or read a children's story about ants that distinguishes between *tall* and *short* ants, without feeling that any of these usages were unacceptable. One way of coping with this is to see figurative language as a special case in which the normal selection restrictions are allowed to be lifted. The issue then for linguists is to describe the set of rules that captures such exceptions (see METAPHOR for further discussion).

Selection restrictions can most usefully be studied in the context of COMPONENTIAL THEORY since the semantic features which influence co-occurrence are seen as deriving from the semantic primes, or components, of lexical items.

Semantic field.   An area of meaning containing words with related SENSES. Semantic field theory derives very largely from the work of German and Swiss scholars in the 1920s and 1930s. According to this theory, meanings of words cluster together to form fields of meaning, which in turn cluster into even larger fields until the entire language is encompassed. So, for example, we can identify a semantic field of madness containing words like *insane*, *demented*, *batty*, *schizophrenic*, *paranoid*, some of which are synonyms of *mad*, and others which are types of madness. This field belongs in turn within a larger one of mental states, which includes a wider selection of words. Or again, we can identify a field of running including words such as *sprinting*, *running*, and *jogging*, which itself clusters into the field of human motion.

Basic to field theory is the view that words occupy a certain amount of semantic space within the language, which is distributed among the specific lexical items available. So, for example, the field of residences is divided up into *castle*, *maisonette*, *house*, *bungalow*, and *flat*, to name just a few. These terms constitute the lexical set, or lexical field, which realise the semantic field. The meaning of any one of them is affected by the other terms to which it is related. As a consequence, fields are constantly expanding and contracting. If the term *maisonette* were removed from the set, then one of the others, possibly *house* or *flat*, would expand to occupy the space. Not surprisingly, field theory is very useful in the contrastive analysis of different languages. Languages differ quite widely even in apparently basic lexical divisions, and fields such as temperature, kinship, colour, parts of the body, and animal and vegetable worlds, divide the semantic space differently with respect to them.

A natural consequence of field theory is the idea that words, or more particularly the senses of words, define themselves against each other. So, for example, in the field of medical personnel, part of our understanding of *doctor* is 'not *nurse/surgeon/matron* or *orderly*'. Also fundamental to field theory is the assumption that words can belong to more than one field. In addition to meaning 'insane', for example, *mad* can also mean 'angry', and as such, belongs within the field of anger. SENSE RELATIONS utilise fields to establish relationships based on SYNONYMY, ANTONYMY, HYPONYMY, MERONYMY, POLYSEMY, and INCOMPATIBILITY. These serve to illustrate the philosopher Ludwig Wittgenstein's oft-quoted view that 'the meaning of a word is its use in the language'.

Sense. The meaning a word has within a language – limited by some linguists to a word's conceptual or propositional meaning. Sense is usually discussed in relation to REFERENCE, which is the other principal 'meaning' relation words have. The study of sense owes much to the concept of words as SIGNS. According to this view words are symbolic entities deriving their meaning from the place they occupy in the linguistic system. If, for example, you were asked what the meaning of the word 'red' was, one way of answering would be to point to all the red things around. But all that this would tell you was what 'red' referred to (in other words, its reference). A more linguistic way would be to place 'red' within a SEMANTIC FIELD of meaning, in this case colour, and then proceed to relate it to other colours in the field: similar to orange, different from black, inclusive of burgundy, scarlet, and crimson, and so on. The meaning that derived from the totality of these relationships, or SENSE RELATIONS, would be what linguists call 'sense'. Sense is the semantic meaning which *red* has in any context. A good analogy here is with money, another symbolic system. To establish the value of 20 pence you could either point to all the things it was possible to buy with it – in linguistic terms, its reference – or indicate its place in the monetary scale: twice ten pence, a fifth of a pound – linguistically, its 'sense'. The term 'value' is relevant to both money and language here. Following SAUSSURE, linguists use it to refer to the combination of both reference and sense in a word's meaning. So we could say that the **value** of 'red' comprises all the things in the world to which it refers together with its place in the linguistic system.

Some linguistic approaches, principally COMPONENTIAL ANALYSIS, use sense quite extensively in an attempt to build a semantic model of the language. But it's important to bear in mind that a word's conceptual sense doesn't exhaust its meaning within the linguistic system. Words also have ASSOCIATIVE MEANINGS derived from **connotation**, **collocation**, **stylistic variation**, and **reflection**. The problem is what significance to give associative meaning in relation to the account we have so far given of sense. We could see it simply as an extra layer of meaning, and in some respects this is true, but this approach has the disadvantage of making associative meaning peripheral. Another solution is to see sense as a composite of conceptual and associative meaning. This involves expanding our understanding of sense and it has the advantage of enabling us to talk of both conceptual and associative sense, giving equal weight to both. And finally, bear in mind that sense is only concerned with a word's meaning within the linguistic system. Its contextual meaning, or FORCE, may be quite different. This is more properly studied within pragmatics.

Sense relations.   The semantic relationships that words contract with each other within the linguistic system on the basis of their SENSE. The principal relationships are SYNONYMY, ANTONYMY, POLYSEMY, HYPONYMY, MERONYMY, and INCOMPATIBILITY.

Speech act theory.   A theory originally developed by the Oxford philosopher J. L. Austin in the 1930s and expounded in a series of lectures that he gave at Harvard in 1955. These were subsequently developed in 1962 as *How to Do Things with Words*. The approach has been greatly developed since by the philosopher J. R. Searle.

Speech act theory argues that when we use language we are performing certain acts. Traditionally philosophers have distinguished between actions and speaking on the basis that speaking about something is quite different from doing it. As a consequence, all we can do of utterances is ask whether they are a correct representation of reality, not whether they work or not. Austin substantially challenged this by demonstrating that utterances can be regarded as events in a similar way to other actions. There are three types of acts that utterances can be said to perform: a **locutionary act**, an **illocutionary act**, and a **perlocutionary act**. A locutionary act, or locution, refers simply to the act of saying something that makes sense in the language (in other words, that follows the grammatical rules of language). An illocutionary act is one that is performed through the medium of language: stating, warning, wishing, promising, and so on. And finally, a perlocutionary act is the effect the illocutionary act has on the listener: such as persuading, convincing, deterring, misleading, surprising, and so forth. Let's take, as an example, requesting a favour. The locution would consist of the words being uttered in a grammatical sequence; the illocution, the act of requesting; and the perlocution, the persuasion of the ADDRESSEE, provided, of course, that the request was successful.

Speech act theory tends to concentrate largely on illocutions. Locutions and perlocutions, coming before and after the illocutionary act, although important, are of less central interest. When Austin first began his study of speech acts he attempted first of all to distinguish between a class of utterances that he called **performatives** and those that he termed **constatives**. Performatives are a special group of utterances the saying of which actually performs the action named by the verb. For example:

act of marriage   *I pronounce you man and wife*
act of naming a ship   *I name this ship the 'Saucy Sue'*

act of closing a meeting	*I declare this meeting closed*
act of a **wager**	*I bet you a fiver*
act of apology	*I apologise*

In order for these utterances to count as performatives various conditions have to be met. Only certain people can pronounce you man and wife, for example, whilst if you apologise and clearly don't mean it you have not really apologised. The right context has to be matched with the right form of words. Austin termed these conditions **felicity conditions.**

Constatives consist of all those other utterances, such as statements and questions, where actions are being described or asked about rather than explicitly performed, as in *I cooked the cake* and *Can you cook the cake?* The test of whether an utterance can be classed as a performative or not is whether the word *hereby* can be inserted before the verb. In this respect *I hereby declare this meeting closed* is unproblematic, whereas *I hereby cooked the cake*, or *Can you hereby cook the cake?* are not. But Austin quickly realised that the distinction between performatives and constatives was artificial since even constatives are performing some kind of act although of a more purely linguistic kind than performatives. *I cooked the cake* is performing the act of stating. We have only to recast it as *I hereby state that I cooked the cake* to see this. And similarly, *Can you cook the cake?* is performing the act of enquiring. We can recast this as *I hereby enquire whether you can cook the cake*. As a consequence Austin abandoned the distinction between performatives and constatives and distinguished instead between **explicit** and **implicit** performatives. Explicit performatives are those which have a performative VERB, that is, a verb that names the action being performed (for example, *affirm, allege, assert, forecast, predict, announce, insist, order, state*). These are sometimes referred to as **speech act verbs** since they are all verbs of 'saying'. Implicit performatives lack a saying verb, but none the less assume the presence of one. So, for example, *Beware of the bull* can be expanded to *I warn you to beware of the bull*, and *Come and see me sometime* is expandable to *I invite you to come and see me sometime*.

We thus arrive at the view that all utterances constitute speech acts of one kind or another. In some cases the type of act is explicitly marked by a speech act verb, whereas in others it is more implicitly signalled. Since the early work on speech acts much effort has been directed towards categorising the types of acts possible in language. Some are so fundamental that they are grammaticalised into distinct sentence types. **Declarative** SENTENCES are used for the act of stating, **interrogative** sentences for asking questions, and **imperative** sentences for giving orders and making requests (*see* MOOD). But these are just a few of the many that are available to speakers. Taxonomies of speech act types provided by theorists vary in detail but one of the most widely used is that proposed by Searle (1976, pp. 10–16). He divides all acts into five main types, as below:

1. **Representatives**, which commit the speaker to the truth of the expressed proposition (paradigm cases: asserting, concluding)

2. **Directives**, which are attempts by the speaker to get the addressee to do something (paradigm cases: requesting, questioning)

3. **Commissives**, which commit the speaker to some future course of action (paradigm cases: promising, threatening, offering)

4. **Expressives**, which express a psychological state (paradigm cases: thanking, apologising, welcoming, congratulating)

5. **Declarations**, which effect immediate changes in the institutional state of affairs and which tend to rely on elaborate extra-linguistic institutions (paradigm cases: excommunicating, declaring war, christening, marrying, firing from employment)

Speech acts of the kind we have been looking at so far can all be described as **direct speech acts** in that there is a match between **sentence meaning** and **speaker meaning** (i.e. the form of the utterance coincides with what the speaker is intending to convey). However, much of what we say is not so direct. We often use statements, for example, to make requests, and even orders. The statement *It's cold in here*, for instance, could be classed, under Searle's classification, as a representative, since it's manifestly asserting something. But a listener might also detect an extra or indirect meaning, 'Can you close the window?' In this case we could say that the utterance is performing an **indirect speech act**: the speaker means what the sentence means, but something else as well. One of the principal reasons for the employment of indirectness in utterances is that speakers and listeners perceive it to be more polite. This is particularly so in the area of requests and orders. If we want the marmalade passed down the table we are unlikely to issue a simple instruction *Pass the marmalade*, but often couch our request in the form of a question: *Can you pass the marmalade please?* In this case the direct act is a question about the hearer's ability to pass the marmalade. It could conceivably be answered by him/her saying *yes* and doing nothing. Both participants are aware, however, that action is expected. What indirectness appears to do is allow the listener some freedom to comply and, in doing so, concede him/her a degree of power.

If it's the case that the meaning of utterances is in large part indirect, then this raises the problem of how listeners arrive at a secure interpretation of them. How are we to know if *I'll see you tonight* is a promise, a threat, or simply an announcement? This is a greyer area of speech act theory since we are encountering here a fundamental problem of language, namely, the extent to which it underspecifies meaning. The only approach we can take here is pragmatic. Searle suggests that in understanding indirect speech acts we combine our knowledge of three elements. These elements are: the felicity conditions of direct speech acts, the context of the utterance, and the principles of conversational cooperation, such as those provided by the COOPERATIVE PRINCIPLE. The felicity conditions, as we have seen, have to do with the speaker being in an appropriate situation to make the utterance. I cannot promise you my gold watch, for example, if I don't possess one. The context of the utterance is the situation in which it is made. This usually gives the clue as to how it should be interpreted. And the conversational principles are the baseline assumptions which speakers and hearers conventionally hold about relevance, orderliness, and truthfulness. The process of combining these elements draws heavily on INFERENCE because much of what is meant is not explicitly stated. It is here that the work of speech act theorists links up with the more general approach of H. P. Grice and his interest in **conversational** IMPLICATURES.

Synonymy.   A SENSE RELATION that exists between words which have a similar meaning or SENSE (for example, *drunk/intoxicated*, *mad/insane*). English is particularly rich in synonyms because of the influx into it of words from a variety of languages. *Royal*, *regal*, and *kingly*, for example, are synonymous terms that have derived from French, Latin, and Anglo-Saxon respectively. Although, theoretically, it is possible for two words to be completely synonymous, that is to say, identical, it is very rare for this to happen. Total synonymy would mean that words were interchangeable in all linguistic environments. Such is the nature of language, however, that there is invariably some difference. Synonyms frequently differ **stylistically**. *Steed* and *nag* have the same conceptual sense but belong to different styles of English: the first is poetic and rather archaic, the second slang. **Connotational** differences are also fairly common. *Hide* and *conceal*, *obstinate* and *stubborn*, *tight* and *stingy*, are all synonyms but most users would feel that one term in each pair had a slightly stronger meaning than the other. And many synonyms also differ in their **collocational range**, that is, the words with which they can co-occur. *Powerful*, *mighty*, and *strong* look interchangeable but they won't all occur with *tea*, *ocean* and *language*, and where they do occur the meaning is likely to be different in each case: *powerful language*, for instance, has a different meaning from *strong language*.

Truth conditional semantics. The study of the propositional meaning of utterances and the logical conditions for establishing their truth or otherwise. Unlike the approach of many other linguists, who are concerned with exploring and mapping the conceptual structure that underlies language (*see* COMPONENTIAL THEORY *and* COGNITIVE SEMANTICS), truth conditional semantics, or **formal semantics**, is preoccupied with how language relates to reality. You might think that all semantics must have this as its aim, and in one sense this is true. But whereas other theoretical approaches see human beings as using language to represent, or even construct, reality, truth conditional semantics focuses exclusively on the referential properties of language. Language is seen as corresponding to the world in an almost literal sense. So, for example, knowing what a SENTENCE like *The sun is shining today* means, involves knowing what situation in the world this would correspond to, or fit. On the basis of such knowledge we could judge the statement to be either true or false. In other words, what is at issue here is the logical basis of utterances. Truth conditional semantics assumes that we are all, as users of the language, concerned with the conditions that allow us to determine the objective truth, or otherwise, of utterances.

Examining the logical foundation of language means employing the **metalanguage** of formal, or propositional, logic in the description of sentences. Not surprisingly, this is a highly complex and difficult area of semantics, and really requires some formal training in the use of logical symbols. Sentences are translated into mathematical-type formulae and then subjected to rigorous truth tests. So, for example, there is a set of symbols for the logical connectives of English: *not, and, or, if ... then*. Using these symbols it is possible to represent some of the standard logical operations of English as in Table 7. These formulae will capture the logical relations of the sentences below:

1. *John is not coming*
2. *John arrived late and missed the train*
3. *Either John will go to the meeting or I shall*
4. *Either John will go to the meeting or he won't*
5. *If John passes his driving test I'll eat my hat*
6. *John will go to the meeting if he is able to*

One of the advantages of logical formulae is that they capture differences between apparently similar usages. The *either/or* connectives in 3, for example, are logically different from 4 because they allow for the possibility of both propositions being true, that is, 'John will go to the meeting **and** I shall go to the meeting'. Similarly, *if* has a different meaning in 5 as opposed to 6. In 5 it is logically possible for me to eat my hat even if John fails his driving test, whereas in 6 it is a necessary condition of John going to the meeting that he is able to.

Table 7

	Connective	Syntax	English
1	¬	$\neg\,p$	it is not the case that **p**
2	∨	$p \vee q$	**p** and **q**
3	∧	$p \wedge q$	**p** and/or **q**
4	$\vee_e$	$p \vee_e q$	**p** or **q** but not both
5	→	$p \rightarrow q$	if **p**, then **q**
6	≡	$p \equiv q$	**p** if and only if **q**

NB: **p** and **q** stand for sentence constants, or propositions

It is important to recognise here that logical connectives are interpreted differently in formal semantics from the way they are in ordinary discourse. In normal conversation, for example, 5 would be taken to imply that I would only eat my hat if John passed his test. And similarly, the propositions in 3 would usually be taken by most people to be mutually exclusive. There is a distinction, in other words, between natural logic and formal logic. In terms of natural logic, for example, we should assume in 2 that John's being late caused him to miss the train but in fact the truth value of the propositions doesn't depend on that. There is nothing in the sentence which necessitates that logical link other than the mere fact of lineal order. Formal logic doesn't aim to capture all the meaning of utterances. It is simply concerned with their abstract, propositional core. As a consequence, no distinction is made between the following sentences, all of which use the conjunction connective, as in 2:

7. *She was poor and she was honest*
8. *She was poor but she was honest*
9. *Although she was poor she was honest*

Again, the truth value of these propositions is independent of the particular conjunction being used despite the fact that the sentences do not mean the same.

For some linguists, particularly those more interested in pragmatics, the failure to take account of natural logic is a limitation of truth conditional semantics. But for others it is a necessary simplification in the process of laying bare the logical skeleton of language. The fact that we rarely encounter it simply in skeleton form doesn't matter. Most of the operations that we perform in language, from the employment of tense and modality to the use of terms such as *all*, *every*, and *some*, have as their basis a formal logical structure. The attempt to capture this, albeit in the abstract language of symbolic logic, is proving to be one of the most exciting developments of contemporary semantics.

6 Linguistics: the Main Branches

INTRODUCTION

The last three chapters have dealt with the core areas of linguistics. Between them, phonetics/phonology, syntax, and semantics/pragmatics constitute the principal LEVELS of linguistics. Whatever branch of the subject we look at we shall inevitably find ourselves talking about them. We use the metaphor of a tree here because this seems the best way to capture the relationship between these core areas, collectively the 'trunk', and the individual disciplines, or 'branches', which sprout from them. Changing the metaphor, we could think of the core as the hub of a wheel with the various branches as the individual spokes radiating out. The diagram in Figure 30 shows the main ones, followed by a brief definition of each:

sociolinguistics – the study of language and society.
stylistics – the study of language and literature.
psycholinguistics – the study of language and mind.
computational linguistics – the simulation of language by the use of computers.
comparative linguistics – the study of different languages and their respective linguistic systems.
historical linguistics – the study of language change over time.
applied linguistics – the study of language teaching. (You will sometimes find that stylistics and comparative linguistics are treated as sub-branches of applied linguistics.)

The branches have become more numerous over the years as the subject has grown but, arguably, the principal developments in linguistics in recent years have been in stylistics, sociolinguistics, and psycholinguistics. As a consequence, a majority of the terms discussed in this chapter are from these branches. The chapter begins, however, with a short introduction to each of the major branches identified above, followed by detailed entries, alphabetically arranged, as usual, on key items.

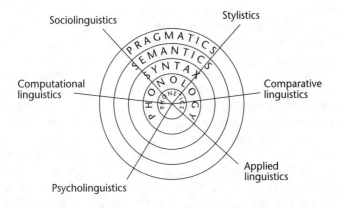

Figure 30   The major branches of linguistics

Source: Adapted from Jean Aitchison, *Teach Yourself Linguistics* (1999). Reproduced by permission of Hodder & Stoughton Ltd.

Applied Linguistics

Applied linguistics is the most practical of all the linguistic branches. Its concern is with the application of linguistic theories and procedures to the issues of everyday life. With such a loose definition it is easy to see why the territory covered by this branch is so indeterminate. One could argue, for instance, that sociolinguistics and psycholinguistics, are more properly part of applied linguistics, since, to some extent, they are both concerned with using the insights of linguistics in a practical way. Sociolinguistics is used by demographers, for example, in studying population changes and, as such, feeds into the development of social and regional policy-making, whilst psycholinguistics can be useful in the planning of a national language policy. But in practice, both these disciplines have developed their own theoretical foundations that enable them to be considered as branches in their own right. One way of distinguishing the areas that overlap with applied linguistics is to talk, as some do, of applied psycholinguistics and applied sociolinguistics, as opposed to their more 'pure' parents. All we are really acknowledging here is the general point, that most branches of linguistics will, necessarily, have a practical application somewhere. Remembering the tree metaphor we are using, it is in the nature of branches to be interconnected.

Some of the most frequently encountered fields of application that have emerged in recent years are **clinical linguistics**, the analysis of language disorders (e.g. speech defects such as stuttering); **neurolinguistics**, the study of brain activity in relation to core linguistic activities such as, speaking, listening, writing, reading, and signing; and **forensic**

linguistics, the use of linguistic techniques in connection with the law, more particularly, to investigate crime. The latter has recently come to prominence because of a number of high profile court cases in which, by using grammatical and lexical criteria, it has been possible to demonstrate that witness statements were tampered with. Within this field linguists also sometimes distinguish a separate domain of **forensic phonetics**, concerned with such issues as speaker identification, speaker profiling, and tape authentication. But by far the most developed field of applied linguistics, and the one most usually associated with the term, is the teaching and learning of foreign languages. In the case of English, applied linguistics refers to teaching the English language to non-native speakers. The courses in which this teaching takes place are variously called TEFL (Teaching English as a Foreign Language), TESL (Teaching English as a Second Language), ELT (English Language Teaching), and ESOL (English for Speakers of Other Languages). The terminology differs between English and America usage.

The question of how best to teach English to non-native speakers has spawned a variety of different methodologies and approaches over the years, but it is true to say that modern approaches have been deeply influenced by contemporary developments in linguistics. Older approaches tended to take their cue from written forms of the language with idealised sentences and pronunciation forms. Today, however, most textbooks adopt a communicative approach. Their aim is for the speaker to acquire **communicative competence** in the language, that is, the ability to apply the rules of grammar appropriately in the correct situation. So, for example, native speakers know when to abbreviate utterances. The answer to the question 'Where are you going tonight' is likely to be 'To the pictures', rather than 'I am going to the pictures'. And they know when to use idiomatic as opposed to more formal English, or when it is admissable to miss out syllables or reduce vowel sounds in running speech. The concept of register is an important one to acquire in order to become a fluent user of the language. All of this is predicated, firstly, on the primacy of speech (i.e. that English language learning is first and foremost about learning to talk in English) and, secondly, that learning a language is an intuitive process. Whilst learning English may involve some hard work learning vocabulary and grammar, we are, nonetheless, programmed linguistically to acquire language, and those methods work best which work with the learner's innate capacities.

English for Specific Purposes (**ESP**) is a localised area within English language teaching which has grown significantly in recent years. In ESP, the nature of the course is determined by the particular needs of the learners. So, for example, would-be business men might need some instruction in business English. Similarly, there are books and courses in the use of scientific English, English in technology, marketing English, and so on. In general, it has become common to distinguish two main branches of ESP: **English for Academic Purposes** (EAP) and **English for Occupational Purposes** (EOP), or **English for Vocational Purposes** (EVP) in America. This distinction is a way of recognising the broad split between so-called 'academic English', the variety used by the educational establishment in writing essays, reports, and papers, and those varieties favoured by various business corporations, such as the law, commerce, and politics, in which many of us lead our working lives.

Computational Linguistics

Computational linguistics is concerned with the use of computers in the study of language. Broadly speaking, this occurs in two ways. Firstly, computers can be used as a means of exploring how we generate and intepret language. You may well have noticed that much of the current literature about linguistics employs the metaphor of computing. The brain is frequently visualised as a processor, scanning material in order to generate an output, or decode an input. This is not an accident, and is, in itself, a product of computer technology and its accompanying mind-set. If linguistic operations can be translated into mechanical processes, then the possibility of developing computer programmes that can simulate the linguistic activity of the brain comes a step nearer. We have only to think of the complexity of these operations to realise what a considerable task this is. The brain is able, from a finite set of rules, to generate an infinite number of well-formed word strings. Successfully producing a computer which could do that would, in effect, mean creating a machine which could think for itself, a prospect envisaged in the character of Hal, the computer in *2001: A Space Odyssey*. Such a prospect may still be science fiction, but in the meantime computers are telling us a lot about how the brain works as it scans, selects, and sorts the oral/aural information that carry the linguistic code.

One of the principal offshoots of this interest in brain simulation lies in the field of **speech processing**. Speech processing takes two forms: first, the development of systems capable of converting written text into spoken output (**speech synthesis**) and, second, the conversion of speech input into written form (**speech recognition**). Most people will have come across commercially produced speech synthesizers at some point (for example, they are used by telephone services such as directory enquiries to give us a particular number we are after). In terms of replicating human speech they are good enough to provide us with the information we require, but no one would be fooled into thinking this was natural speech. The problem in replicating speech is in capturing not only the phonetic structure of the language, but also the features associated with connected speech, such as stress, intonation, and vowel reduction. It is similarly the case with speech recognition. Because naturally occurring speech is so messy, any computer program capable of turning speech into written form must be able to predict what the most likely sequences in the language are in a similar manner to the way we do. There has been significant progress in speech processing in recent years, but, not surprisingly, research is still a fair way off from the ultimate goal of producing a system capable of performing mechanically what we do naturally.

The second way in which linguists use computers is as a tool for analysing texts, oral as well as written. It is here that computational linguistics overlaps with another branch of the discipline, **corpus linguistics**. In linguistic terms a 'corpus' (plural: corpora) is a collection of linguistic material that can be used for scholarly analysis. The original usefulness of such corpora lay in the analsyis of **dead languages** (languages no longer used as a medium of communication), where the only surviving material lay in written texts. Since then all kinds of corpora have been collected of both spoken and written language. The ability to store such material on computers vastly increases its usefulness. Computer programs can be developed that enable linguists to search collections for particular word formations, or syntactic patterns. One of the first such collections was the 'Brown University Corpus of American English', dating from 1961, which consisted of 500 written text samples of about 2000 words each, drawn from a range of American publications. A corresponding corpus of British English, known as the 'Lancaster–Oslo/Bergen corpus', was compiled in 1982. Others include the 'Oxford Text Archive', which contains texts of various languages and historical periods. Clearly, such corpora are of invaluable assistance to lexicographers. If the lexicographer is searching for every common occurrence of a word such as 'hefty', then the corpus can be scanned using a **concordance program**, to show the distribution of the item, and, as a consequence, its use in the language.

Modern corpora include spoken as well as written language, but in order for this to happen the oral text has to be transcribed into written notation, and, ideally, in a form that also indicates prosodic features. Not surprisingly, the electronic availability of written material far exceeds that of oral. The use of corpora by scholars is increasing rapidly. If you are studying children's language, for example, it is extremely useful to have at your fingertips a ready-made resource that can be searched, sorted, and analysed by a custom-made computer package. The use of corpora to determine issues of **acceptability** and **well-formedness**, however, has not been without its critics, principally because it seems to fly in the face of Chomsky's stress on the importance of the intuition of native speakers. In other words, if you want to know whether a particular usage is well-formed or not, the conventional generative approach is to ask a native speaker of the language rather than interrogate material collected from miscellaneous sources. But, as most linguists acknowledge, the competence of native speakers varies considerably. Moreover, because corpus studies include different varieties and registers of a language, they can illuminate usage in ways not discoverable from intuition alone.

Using computers to analyse text has considerable advantages. Because of the speed and accuracy with which they work, computers can carry out tasks that would take a researcher a lifetime if done manually. Computers have been used by literary critics to determine the authenticity or authorship of certain historical texts. Usually this is done by computing the frequency with which particular stylistic features occur. On a larger scale, computers can be used as discourse processors to analyse syntactic constructions and semantic patterns within naturally occurring speech. But there are certain difficulties here. Analysing text as discourse means more than simply investigating isolated sentences. It involves understanding the way sentences relate to each other, what some linguists refer to as the **textuality** of the text. All discourse has a functional structure to it by which we introduce topics, elaborate on them, provide examples, and give summaries. Not only that, but SPEECH ACT THEORY has made us aware that we use language to achieve certain goals: that saying is a form of doing. Developing a computer program that can process utterances in the way our brains do is a tall order, not least because interpretation has an element of indeterminacy about it. How is it possible, for example, to build into a computer the sort of background knowledge about the world that human beings draw on when they are listening to or reading a text? These are some of the problems that computational linguists have to grapple with. We are back again to the conundrum of developing a computer capable of performing like a human being.

Historical Linguistics
All languages change over time and, consequently, all languages have histories. Reconstruction of a language's past is the concern of historical linguistics. It involves studying what Ferdinand de Saussure, the

great Swiss linguist, termed the DIACHRONIC axis of language. A majority of linguists are concerned with a language's SYNCHRONIC state, or its present-day form. But some are interested in how languages have developed over time in order to arrive at their current form. Tracing a language back over time is no simple task. In the case of recent history we can call on the help of written records, of course. These will tell us about changes in grammar and meaning. And they can also tell us something about changes in pronunciation too. Knowing that the word *thrust* was frequently spelt *frust* in Elizabethan English is a good indication of how the word used to be pronounced (and still is, of course, in modern day London English). Rhymes that work in medieval poetry but don't now are also a useful way of reconstructing older forms of the language. But what about further back, before written records began? Language existed in spoken form several millennia before the invention of writing. How is it possible to track backwards into unrecorded history?

Up until the nineteenth century knowledge about the historical roots of language was largely confined to knowledge about the history of Latin. Scholars had been aware for some centuries of the close links between the so-called Romance languages, Spanish, French, Italian, and Portuguese. All of these languages are 'daughters' of Latin, a consequence of the Roman colonisation of Europe. Roman soldiers intermingled with the native peoples of the continent, producing various pidgins based on Latin. Once these became the dominant form of communication they developed into full-blown languages. The person usually credited with extending our knowledge of the history of language beyond the boundaries of Europe was a British judge, Sir William Jones, who had a passion for languages (see p. 3). A noted Orientalist, who spent the later years of his short life in Calcutta, Jones noticed resemblances between Latin and Greek, and the ancient Indian language Sanskrit. To be strictly correct, he was not the first to observe these resemblances. But as the most prominent Oriental scholar of his day, he was the first to go public, and announce to the scholarly world, as he did in 1786, that 'all three languages must have sprung from some common source, which perhaps no longer exists'. During the next century, scholars throughout Europe began comparing languages spoken in Germany, Eastern Europe, and India, with the Romance languages descended from Latin (Spanish, French, Italian, and Portuguese). In each case it appeared there were systematic correspondences in sounds and vocabulary items which suggested that, not only was Jones's hypothesis correct, but that the net of languages that comprised this family was very large indeed. They were helped in this direction by the publication in the nineteenth century of texts and glossaries of older European languages such as Gothic and Old Norse, which were no longer spoken. From all of these sources it was possible to trace back a series of changes occurring over several millenia to a common parent. This parent was called by linguists 'Proto Indo-European' ('Indo-European', indicating the geographical boundary of its descendants, and 'proto' because it's a reconstructed, i.e 'hypothetical' language). The precise manner in which this was done came to be known as 'the comparative method'. It's a process of internally reconstructing speech sounds using words from different languages that are cognate, i.e. words which have a common ancestor. Cognate situations occur where two languages, A and B, with no borrowing relationship, share similar vocabulary items. In such cases linguists posit the existence of a third language, C, from which A and B have independently borrowed. Where C no longer exists it has to be reconstructed, and in order to do that we need to know something about how words change their linguistic form over time. This was largely the achievement of one man, Jacob Grimm a nineteenth-century German linguist, better known perhaps for his collection of fairy tales, who formulated a series of rules, known as 'Grimm's Law', designed to capture the systematic changes that occur within speech sounds.

One of the correspondences that Grimm noted between languages in the Indo-European family was that words that begin with 'p' in the Romance languages, characteristically start with 'f' or 'v' in German and English. So the English word *father* is *vater* in German, *padre* in Italian, *pere* in French, and *pai* in Portuguese. This is a systematic, rather than an occasional, difference. In these, and other cases, the argument for a common parent is strong. But which form is likely to be the oldest? To answer this we need to notice that 'p' and 'f/v' belong to different consonant classifications: 'p' is a **voiceless plosive** (plosives are sounds that involve complete interruption of the air-flow – see also VOICE) whereas 'f' and 'v' are **fricative** sounds (i.e. produced with friction). Now, what Jacob Grimm pointed out was that voiceless plosives change into fricatives far more often than the other way round. So, on the basis of phonetic probability it is far more likely that 'p' represents the older pronunciation. Equally important is the fact that once a sound change occurs it affects most of the items in a language's vocabulary.

Working backwards in this way it was possible for linguists to suggest that the original word for 'father' in proto Indo-European was probably pronounced something like */pəter/ (*indicates a conjectural form). Grimm also established several other sound changes of a similar sort. In the intervening years, since the work of Grimm, studies by other scholars have increased our understanding of what proto-Indo-European was probably like. The vocabulary, with lots of words for animals and farming (e.g. *lamb, grain, millstone, honey, axe*) and a strong emphasis on kinship terms, suggests a fairly settled agricultural community. The speakers of this language probably inhabited the steppes of southern Russia as much as 5,000–10,000 years ago. By about the third millennium the language had split into various dialects which were carried by migrating tribes into Europe and Asia. It is these dialects, developing over time, from which all the languages of the Indo-European family, including Latin, Greek, Sanskrit, Celtic, Persian, and Germanic, have descended (see Figure 1, p. 4)

Beyond 10,000 years, however, comparative methods can't help us very much. If we ask the question 'what was the parent of Indo-European?' we enter territory that is highly speculative and hypothetical. In the 1960s a couple of Russian scholars did formulate the hypothesis of a father language of Indo-European, which they called 'Nostratic' ('our language'). This great ancestor was supposed to have been the parent of several other language families, including Afro-Asiatic, Dravidian, and Altaic, families from the Caucasus and north-east Asia. And since then, others have proposed the existence of an even wider grouping called 'Super Nostratic', which included language families from Africa (Nilo-Saharan) and from America (Eskimo-Aleut). A lineage of some sort must exist, given that language had a single origin, but reconstructing it with any degree of certainty is largely guesswork.

In recent years a more productive method of reaching back into the pre-history of languages has been developed. Instead of relying on evidence of cognateness and working backwards to a parent, a method which must logically become increasingly speculative as the evidence becomes thinner, this new approach looks at the likely geographical spread of languages, and maps this against the presence or absence of certain features. 'Population typology', as it is called, is the brain-child of Johanna Nicholls of the University of California. She has observed a number of language features that increase remarkably the further east one travels. Some languages, for example, distinguish between the use of 'we' to include only those present at the time of talking, and the use of 'we' to mean people not present. Tok Pisin, spoken in New Guinea is one such language. The distinction between inclusive and exclusive use of 'we' is a feature present in very few European languages (as few as one in ten have it). But the further east one travels, the more frequent it becomes. An estimated 56% of south-east Asian languages have it, and 89% of Australian languages. A similar finding has emerged from Nicholls's study of a range of other features. Languages in the eastern part of the hemisphere are more likely to distinguish grammatically between possessions that can be separated from us (such as 'my books') and those that can't (such as 'my finger'), and they are also more likely to indicate noun plurality (more than one thing) by inflecting the verb rather than the noun.

The low rate of occurrence in the west of the features that Johanna Nicholls has observed would seem to indicate they are not recent in origin. We can surmise this because, for most of recorded history, the dominant linguistic influences world-wide have been western in origin. The movement west of peoples in search of new homelands, new wealth, and new territories, was a linguistic as well as a material expansion. Given this scenario, the most likely explanation for the concentration of these features in the east is that they represent older linguistic forms which have withstood the pressure of linguistic imperialism from the west. In pre-history it seems that language expanded out of Africa into Asia, Australia, and Europe. The spread was from east to west rather than the other way round. The subsequent rise of the west may have reversed that trend, but the work of Johanna Nicholls would suggest that if we want to investigate what languages were like when the various families were beginning to form we should look to the east, to the peoples and languages of the Pacific and the New World areas.

Stylistics

Stylistics is concerned with using the methodology of linguistics to study the concept of 'style' in language. Every time we use language we necessarily adopt a style of some sort: we make a selection from a range of syntactic and lexical possibilities according to the purpose of the communication. The study of style has traditionally been the preserve of literary criticism, but since the rise of linguistics there has been a more systematic attempt to provide a 'linguistic' foundation for literary effects, as well as a concern to broaden the scope of enquiry to include non-literary texts: recipes, car manuals, sermons, and so forth.

In many respects stylistics is a twentieth-century development from the classical study of **rhetoric**. Interest really began with the publication in 1909 of a work on French stylistics by the linguist Bally, a pupil of Ferdinand de SAUSSURE. Other European linguists were gradually attracted to the subject, and in the ensuing decades its influence spread. It wasn't until the 1960s, however, that it penetrated American and British universities, largely as a consequence of developments in descriptive linguistics, and the perceived shortcomings of traditional literary criticism.

There are various sub-branches of stylistics, reflecting the diversity of approaches that exist within the field itself. **General stylistics** is used as a cover term to refer to the analyses of non-literary varieties of language. The main focus of such studies is with establishing principles that can account for the choices made by individuals and social groups in their use of language. The way a text communicates has to do with a host of variables, such as the CONTEXT (the background situation), the TENOR (the relationship between the participants), the FIELD OF DISCOURSE (the topic), the MODE of discourse (spoken or written), and the CHANNEL (telephone, letter, face to face). If we take any of these they divide into yet more variables; context, for instance, can mean social, cultural, or linguistic. The problem for linguists is to establish a principled framework that can cope with the almost infinite acts of communication which occur between individuals or groups. One of the most influential models has been that of Roman Jakobson, the Swedish linguist, presented at a conference at Indiana University in 1958. Despite the brevity of Jakobson's paper, most discussions of the factors affecting style have taken his model, which seeks to match six general functions of language to their corresponding situational partners, as a starting point (see Table 8). The idea underlying this model is that all language is oriented in some way towards one or more features of the communicative situation. Language which is oriented towards the situational context, for example, is likely to be referential in nature (a discussion of the weather will contain lots of references to the elements), whilst language directed at the ADDRESSEE is likely to be conative, i.e. persuasive, interrogative, or directive. The other functions can be paired as below:

Phatic language (greetings, leave-takings, and so on) – oriented towards the contact or channel of communication.
Emotive language (the expression of feelings and attitudes) – oriented towards the ADDRESSER.
Metalingual language (language about language, e.g. requests for clarification, *I don't understand/can't read that*) – oriented towards the code.
Poetic language (verbal play, e.g. figurative devices, humour, and so on) – oriented towards the message.

Jakobson's model is sufficiently abstract to cope with most stylistic varieties and can be useful as a starting point for classifying different language types. Once we move beyond genre description, however, it has proved more difficult to link precise grammatical devices or structures with individual functions, partly because, in practice, most varieties fulfil more than one function. But it is also due in part to the fact

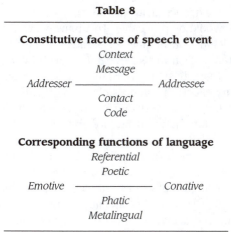

Table 8

Constitutive factors of speech event

Context

Message

Addresser ——————— Addressee

Contact

Code

Corresponding functions of language

Referential

Poetic

Emotive ——————— Conative

Phatic

Metalingual

that we lack an agreed methodology for analysing texts. Of those in current use, however, probably the most widely employed is that based on the linguist Michael Halliday's functional/systemic model of the language (*see* FUNCTIONAL/SYSTEMATIC GRAMMAR). Halliday places great emphasis on the semantic and grammatical relationships that CLAUSES establish between the **participants**, the verbal **processes**, and the **circumstances** represented in the grammatical form of utterances. Different types of verbs allow different relationships and in so doing encode a view of the world. In this way a clause can be said to be a representation of the world. At another level, clauses also act as messages in the way information is prioritised by positioning within the clause. These kinds of **thematic relations** reflect the value participants place on particular items. At a third level, clauses operate as exchanges between participants, and have an interpersonal function. Important here is the concept of MOOD and the particular SPEECH ACT which is being performed, whether that of stating, directing, or something more complex.

Hallidayan grammar provides a useful framework for examining the DISCOURSE level of texts, whether spoken or written, because it seeks to link structure to semantic or pragmatic effects. As a descriptive method this is fine. Difficulties arise, however, when we try to move beyond description to evaluation. This is a particular issue in **literary stylistics**, where the focus is on trying to give an objectively based account of literary merit, or worth. In the early days of stylistics it was sometimes suggested that linguistics would end the kind of impressionism that was thought to beset traditional literary criticism, by grounding judgements on hard linguistic evidence. Thus, it was argued, the literary worth of a particular work would be proveable. This naïve view is no longer held, having fallen victim to a number of assaults, none more devastating than that of Stanley Fish in '*Is there a Text in this Class?*' (1980). Fish makes the point that whilst one may link particular grammatical devices to certain literary effects, it's impossible to say that they cause them to happen. To begin with, it's very difficult to say what a 'literary' effect is because the boundary between literary and non-literary texts is itself problematic.

The influence of **reader-response theory**, with which much contemporary stylistics has joined forces, has been to suggest that judgements about literariness and literary worth are communally arrived at through agreed ways of reading and interpreting texts. In other words, that it is readers who decide what is literary or not. As a consequence, most stylistic analyses today acknowledge the importance of intuition and interpretation in the appreciation of texts and aim to provide descriptive linguistic support for judgements, rather than replacing them with some hypothetical 'objective' criterion. In this respect, one of the most significant concepts that linguistics have contributed to literary criticism is **foregrounding**. This notion derives from the work of the Russian Formalists, notably Victor Shklovsky (1917), according to whom the main purpose of art was to make people see the world in a new way, through **defamiliarisation**, or 'making strange'. This was achieved by highlighting, or making prominent, particular textual features, thus foregrounding them. Inevitably, this entailed breaking the norms of the standard language, with the result that one characteristic of literariness, it was argued, was a degree of linguistic deviance.

Other sub-branches of stylistics include **critical linguistics**, **affective stylistics**, and **stylostatistics** (or **stylometry**). Critical linguistics is concerned with the way in which a writer's use of certain stylistic features encodes what are considered to be the hidden power relations in texts. It came into prominence after some initial work by linguists at the University of East Anglia, Norwich, published in *Language and Control* (Fowler et al., 1979). Critical linguistics, and its offshoot **critical discourse analysis,** make use of a wide variety of insights drawn from sociology, politics, and media studies, as well as mainstream linguistics, to analyse the relationships that exist between powerful elites and their various clients, customers, or subjects. A key term for workers in this field is **ideology**, thought of here in a neutral way, as the pattern of ideas or underlying assumptions by which people live their lives. Of the other two sub-branches, **affective stylistics** is associated with critics such as Fish (above) who are concerned with the mental operations involved in the process of reading, and **stylostatistics** with the use of computers to quantify stylistic patterns adopted by authors. One of its principal uses is in the determination of authorship in cases where this is contested or uncertain (*see also* COMPUTATIONAL LIGUISTICS).

Sociolinguistics

Sociolinguistics, or the study of language in relation to society, is a relative newcomer to the linguistic fold. It wasn't until the early 1960s, largely as a result of William Labov's work in America, and Peter Trudgill's in Britain, that it developed into a recognised branch of linguistics. Before then there had been a long tradition of studying DIALECTS, usually in remote rural areas, as part of language surveys, but with an agenda largely dictated by concerns to record and preserve historical features of the language. This kind of **dialectology** was inherently conservative and was part of larger, comparative language studies pursued under the discipline of **philology**. Labov was one of the first linguists to turn his attention away from rural, to urban, subjects, in an attempt to analyse the contemporary features of American speech.

Sociolinguistics is in many ways a blend of sociology and linguistics. It is sometimes referred to as the 'sociology of language', although that label suggests a greater concern with sociological rather than linguistic explanations, whereas sociolinguists are principally concerned with language, or, to be more precise, with what Dell Hymes crucially calls 'socially constituted' language (Coupland and Jaworski, 1997, p. 14): with the way language is constructed by, and in turn helps to construct, society. Its popularity has grown very much as a reaction to the more 'armchair' methods of generative (*see* GENERATIVE GRAMMAR) linguists of the Chomskyan school (*see* CHOMSKY). Generative linguists examine 'idealised' samples of speech in which utterances are complete, in a standard form of the language, and free from PERFORMANCE errors. Sociolinguists, on the other hand, are more interested in 'real' speech, within and among communities. Their overriding concern is with the way in which language varies according to the social context in which it is used and the social group to which it belongs: Labov terms this 'secular linguistics'. The social variables that influence speech include personal factors such as age and education, as well as more general ones like nationality, race, and gender. All of these have a bearing on language use.

The standard way in which sociolinguists investigate such use is by random sampling of the population. In classic cases, like those undertaken in New York by Labov, or in Norwich by Trudgill, a number of **linguistic variables** are selected, such as 'r' (variably pronounced according to where it occurs in a word) or 'ng' (variably pronounced /n/ or /ŋ/). Sections of the population, known as **informants**, are then tested to see the frequency with which they produce particular variants. The results are then set against social indices which group informants into classes, based on factors such as education, money, occupation, and so forth. On the basis of such data it is possible to chart the spread of innovations in ACCENT and dialect regionally. One complicating factor, however, is that people do not consistently produce a particular accent or dialect feature. They vary their speech according to the formality or informality of the occasion. So tests have to take into account stylistic factors as well as social ones. Interestingly, the findings that have emerged from such studies show that some variables are more subject to stylistic variation than others. What appears to happen is that people monitor their production of a variable they are particularly conscious of, whilst those they are less conscious of, they ignore. The first kind of variable is termed a **marker** and the second an **indicator**. Most innovations start as indicators, with certain social groups unconsciously producing them; a good example is 'h' dropping. If successful, they become adopted more widely by other groups, for whom they become markers. At a final stage a feature may become so distinctive of a certain section of the public that it becomes a **stereotype**. Such changes are examples of **change from below**, that is, from below conscious awareness. Once a feature has emerged into consciousness, however, and particularly if it becomes a stereotype, there may be attempts to check its progress by reintroducing some supposedly 'correct', and therefore more prestigious, form. This has happened in the case of 'r' dropping in parts of America, and 'h' dropping in New Zealand and Australia, where vigorous attempts have been made to reintroduce these vulnerable sounds in the environments in which they are most likely to disappear. Both of these cases are examples of **change from above**, rather than below.

A major object of Labovian-type sociolinguistics is to understand how and why languages change. At its core is a very precise, empirical methodology, and its procedures are based on established ways of working in the social sciences. Since these classic studies, however, changes in methods of enquiry have altered the way in which sociolinguists gather their material. In particular, procedures using **participant observation**, in which observers immerse themselves in communities, rather than relying on random sampling for the collection of data, have yielded more refined accounts of linguistic behaviour. The work of James and Leslie Milroy (1987) on working-class speech in Belfast, for example, has demonstrated the importance of **social networks** in mediating speech habits. Networks operate their own group dynamics and influence speech in a subtler way than the simple class categories, used by more conventional methods of sociological enquiry, would suggest.

Although the 'hard edge' of sociolinguistics is concerned with accent and dialect, there is much else in the subject besides. Since the growth of so-called 'political correctness' the relationships between language on the one hand, and gender, race, and ideology, on the other, have been extensively explored, and we have, as a result, learnt much about the way in which language not only mirrors social reality but, more controversially, constructs it. The degree to which it does this is still debated, and to a certain extent depends on insights from social anthropology and philosophy, but it gives to sociolinguistics a distinctive modernity and relevance.

At its outer edges sociolinguistics merges into the related area of stylistics and, in particular, DISCOURSE ANALYSIS. Two sub-branches, **ethnomethodology** and the ETHNOGRAPHY OF COMMUNICATION, are concerned with style in its contextual and communicative dimension. The first is devoted to analysing conversation and the rules, or principles, that govern turn-taking. Knowing when to speak and what counts as a reply, as opposed to an interruption, are important socialising factors in language use. The second is concerned, on a much broader scale, with the effect of social and cultural variables on what is loosely termed 'linguistic behaviour'. Knowing whether to call someone 'Mr Jones', 'Jimmy', or 'Jones', for example, depends on a number of factors to do with the situational context, the nature of our relationship, and the cultural assumptions within which we are speaking. 'Terms of address', as they are known, are a complex area of study, not least because customs differ between countries and nationalities.

Psycholinguistics

Psycholinguistics is the study of the mental processes underlying the planning, production, perception, and comprehension of speech. A principal aim of modern linguistics, since the Chomskyan revolution (*see* CHOMSKY), has been to arrive at an understanding of the way in which our minds work, and in this respect it could be argued that psycholinguistics, with its unique blend of psychology and linguistics, is the most significant of all the linguistic branches. Not surprisingly, because it covers a very large territory, the boundaries of psycholinguistics are rather fluid. One important sub-branch is concerned with psychological constraints on the use of language (e.g. how memory limitations affect speech production and comprehension), yet another with the investigation of speech disorders (**clinical linguistics**, **aphasiology**). All of these areas have been enriched in recent years by technical information about language and the brain (**neurolinguistics**).

Probably the best developed branch of the subject, however, is the study of language acquisition in children, the most important outcome of which has been the establishment of **stages of acquisition** (*see* CHILD LANGUAGE). Recent studies of language acquisition all suggest that children are tuned into language from a very early age. If, as some linguists argue, we imagine the brain as having a language processor, consisting of various modules (*see* MODULARITY) for processing and producing speech, then learning a language is rather like the tuning-in process that a television set must go through before it can successfully decode electrical impulses into light and sound patterns. And once the switches are thrown in the direction of a particular language, it seems that our language programming is virtually set. If we attempt to learn a second language later in life we can rarely achieve the mastery we have attained in our native tongue. At the same time, acquiring a language is more than a mechanical process of tuning in. Television sets have to decode signals but they don't have to 'interpret' them. Interpreting language entails more than decoding it for the simple reason that language underspecifies meaning. When a child says *Mummy shoe*, the listening adult has first of all to extend this into a complete utterance, *Mummy put my shoe on*, and then to decide on the SPEECH ACT that is being performed – is it an announcement, question, request, command, etc. Language has a social and human dimension that interacts with the programming device to produce the full range of language forms. Typically, children will both OVER- and UNDER-EXTEND words and constructions in the effort to match their own private world to that around them. Studying language acquisition, therefore, can never be simply a matter of mapping which constructions emerge at particular ages. Just as important is the issue of what language is used for, and how it relates to the child's emerging sense of self.

One of the hotly debated issues in current psycholinguistic studies, not unrelated to this discussion, is the extent to which language activity can be seen as the responsibility of discrete language modules in the brain, or as the output of general cognitive abilities used in thinking and conceptualising about anything. Some psycholinguists argue that syntactic processing, the way in which we produce and recognise WELL-FORMED strings, is carried out separately from other processes performed by the brain, whilst others argue for a more wholistic view of linguistic and other competences. Much of the debate has centred on evidence from the study of language disorders and of language impairment resulting from strokes or mental illness. This has shown that some language abilities can exist separately from others. Schizophrenic patients, for example, can often produce strings that are syntactically well-formed but which make little or no sense. More radically, however, it has emerged from the study of deaf and dumb patients that the general cognitive abilities involved in mathematical and logical reasoning are unimpaired by the lack of significant linguistic functions. Nevertheless, it is still a large step from evidence of this kind to the conclusion that language is a wholly discrete cognitive ability processed in a series of autonomous stages by autonomous components. The distinctive way in which language is interwoven with other human activities would suggest otherwise.

The problem would, perhaps, be easier to resolve if agreement existed on which areas of the brain are specifically responsible for language. However, the location is agreed on only in outline and the details remain very controversial. In the majority of human beings language is located in the left half of the brain. Within this, the production of speech is controlled mainly by forward portions of the brain, in an area tradition-ally know as **Broca's area**, after the nineteenth-century French neurol-ogist Paul Broca, who in 1861 wrote a paper in which he claimed that a patient with damage to the frontal area was only able to produce the word *tan*, though he was well able to comprehend speech. Speech comprehension, as such, is located towards the back of the brain's left side in an area called **Wernicke's area**, after another nineteenth-century neurologist, this time German, who in 1874 published a paper demonstrating the importance of the rear of the brain for understanding language. Since then, however, experiments have shown that there is considerable variation within humans and that damage to these areas does not always result in the impairment predicted. Nowadays, there is more emphasis on the links between different areas of the brain, and the way in which information is carried via neurotransmitters, than on iden-tifying precise locations for language activity.

What is at issue here is the relation between **brain** and **mind**. In popular thought these terms are often used interchangeably, but it's important not to confuse them. The brain is the physical organ in the skull that controls bodily behaviour and thought, and, like any other organ, its operations can be observed. The mind, on the other hand, comprises the mental and emotional capabilities that make us human. In contrast with the brain, it's not a physical organ and not open to direct observation. Clearly our minds are dependent on our brains, but no one has yet managed to correlate their workings in any precise way. In an earlier age theologians were exercised with trying to find the exact loca-tion of the soul in the body. Attempting to determine the boundaries of the mind is proving no lesser task.

Psycholinguistics, however, is only indirectly concerned with the brain; its principal target is the human mind. As such it has gained considerably from the discipline of psychology. Indeed, it is sometimes referred to as 'the psychology of language', although strictly speaking this is more the domain of psychology than of linguistics. None the less, our understanding of the way in which language is both produced and comprehended has been greatly enriched by reference to psychologically-based models. Making an utterance involves selecting the appropriate information one wishes to share (for whatever purpose), arranging it in such a way that its topic and focus are clear and will attract the attention of our addressee, and performing it successfully. There are various kinds of mental knowledge required here, including the conceptualisation of the message, its formulation in terms of a linguistic structure, and its phonological processing. At each stage it is possible for mistakes to occur, resulting in speech errors (*see* ASSEMBLAGE ERROR). These are immensely valuable to linguists because they allow them to make inferences about the precise strategies used in speech production. Comprehending utterances is equally complex. Most psycholinguists distinguish two types of process: **perceptual processes**, which register written or spoken language; and **comprehension processes**, which interpret language. In practice these processes operate together. Lexical, syntactic, and semantic knowledge all interact with perceptual input, so that we normally begin to recognise and interpret a word before we have heard it completely. The strategies we use to coordinate this disparate information have been the subject of considerable debate, which in turn has generated various explanatory models and theories (*see* DERIVATIONAL COMPLEXITY THEORY *and* GARDENPATH SENTENCES). At the same time, however, it's important to bear in mind that language comprehension is not solely the preserve of autonomous linguistic processes. We also rely on non-linguistic cues from texts, and a knowledge of characters, entities, and events not explicitly mentioned, for a full interpretation. If an action takes place in a restaurant, for example, the listener can infer the presence of a kitchen, even though it may not be explicitly mentioned. This side of psycholinguistics connects with discourse analysis and is concerned with how we make sense of texts. Evidence suggests that we do so by constructing **mental models** or **schemas** based on our knowledge both of the world around us and of its representation in language. On the basis of such knowledge we have access to a range of **scripts** or **scenarios**, which characteristically structure our expectations, and which are constantly being adjusted as we read or listen. It is these that enable us to build on, and make sense of, propositions and ideas with which we are presented through the medium of language.

GLOSSARY

Accent

(1) The set of pronunciation FEATURES that identify where a person is from, regionally or socially. It's important not to confuse accent with DIALECT, which refers to varieties differentiated by grammar and vocabulary. By contrast, accent is concerned solely with auditory effects. Most accents are regional or national (so there are West Country, Manchester, Scottish, American, and Australian accents). However, some are **social accents** and relate to the cultural and educational background of the speaker: in Britain, the best example of such an accent is **received pronunciation** (RP), the regionally neutral accent associated with public schools, the BBC, and the Civil Service. People who use RP often think of themselves as having 'no accent'. As a consequence, accents are popularly conceived of as deviations from the norm, and a social stigma often attaches itself to those, usually urban ones, which are considered least elegant. But, in linguistic terms, all accents are equal and, despite its non-regionality, RP is as much an accent as Cockney. RP is distinctive, however, in being paired exclusively with standard English dialect. This is not the case with other accents. A Cockney accent, for example, can be used with either Cockney or standard English dialect.

Despite its image as the 'King's, or 'Queen's English, it is clear that RP is as much subject to change as any other accent. Linguists generally distinguish three main types of RP: **conservative RP**, spoken by older RP users, including the Queen herself, typified by tense VOWELS (see Chapter 3) and a clipped manner; **advanced RP**, spoken by younger members of the Royal Family, with more drawling vowels; and **general** or **mainstream RP**, spoken by newscasters, journalists, and professional people generally. Noticeably, this latter variety seems to be acquiring some of the features of Cockney and it is not uncommon to hear the occasional **glottal stop** (see p. 46) in words like *quite* and *alright*, spoken by otherwise mainstream speakers. Nowadays the speech of both conservative and advanced RP speakers is likely to seem 'affected', and it may well be that RP itself is losing some of the image it has acquired as an icon of 'correct' pronunciation.

(2) The emphasis that makes a word or syllable stand out in a stream of speech. This prominence may be the result of loudness and intensity (**stress**), pitch change (INTONATION), length, or a combination of such factors. English is sometimes referred to as a **stress-timed** language, which means that there is a tendency for accents to fall at fairly regular intervals in speech. It is this which accounts for the particular rhythm of

English. In the following utterance, for example, an UNMARKED pronunciation pattern would alternate accented with unaccented syllables:

IF i've TOLD you ONCE i've TOLD you TWICE

There's nothing to stop us, of course, accenting any of the syllables, but in so doing we would be registering a particular meaning. The usual practice of speakers is to accent the **lexical** items and leave **function** words unaccented. In this respect you might notice that the unaccented items in the example above are all function words (PRONOUNS, and auxiliary VERBS). The study of this aspect of linguistics is termed **prosody.**

In literary stylistics prosody takes on a special meaning, particularly in the study of poetry, where analysts are concerned with **metrics**, or **metre**. Even with these more formalised patterns of accentuation, however, it is still the case that the rhythms of English verse are predominantly founded on those of natural speech, and much of the subtlety of poetic writing comes from the interplay between metre and speech rhythm.

Accommodation. A sociolinguistic theory associated with the linguist Howard Giles, which tries to explain why people modify their style of speaking in order to make it more, or less, like that of their ADDRESSEE(S). According to the theory, part of the way in which we cooperate, and show our friendliness to others, is by altering our manner of speech so as to converge with theirs, much as two people may adopt a reciprocal posture. Thus, a characteristically RP speaker may become less so in the company of someone with a regional accent, and vice versa, of course. Alternatively, should we wish to emphasise the difference between us and our addressee, we could achieve this by ensuring that our style of speaking diverged from theirs.

Addresser/addressee. The two principal participants in any linguistic act of communication. The addresser is the author, and the addressee is the intended recipient, of the message. The paradigm situation envisaged here is a basic one involving a speaker and a listener, or a writer and a reader. However, complex acts of communication may involve various intermediaries. In the case of an advertisement, for example, it is not always clear who the author is. It could be the advertising company or the organisation on whose behalf it is working. Some linguists cope with this ambiguity by employing the concept of a corporate addresser, but this isn't an entirely happy solution and still leaves the issue of authorship vague. A somewhat sharper distinction exists

between addresser and **sender**. In the paradigm situation these participants are one and the same, but in other circumstances they may not be.
An official letter may be sent by special courier, for example. Similarly,
at the other end of the spectrum, the concept of addressee requires
sharpening in order to distinguish the various possible recipients of a
message. A letter may be read by someone other than the person it's
intended for, and so might many advertisements. In such cases it's
helpful to distinguish between the **receiver** and the addressee.

The situation becomes even more complex if we try and fit literary
communication into this framework. Novels can have a number of
different addressers and addressees. The novelist is the main addresser,
but s/he has more than one incarnation. There is the actual author – the
person who has written the book – and an implied author, or fictional
presence, within the text. The two are not necessarily the same, as
readers often discover when they compare the biography of an author
with what can be learnt about him/her from the novel. The implied
author is often identified in literary criticism as the 'narrator', although
in first-person novels the situation may be even more complex. Critics
differ here as to whether they choose to distinguish between these two
authors as **primary** and **secondary** addressers, or to call the implied
author the addresser and the actual author, the sender. And just as there
are different authors there are different readers, notably the reader
intended by the author (the implied reader), and the person who actually
reads the book (the actual reader). Again, it is helpful here to distinguish
between the addressee and the receiver.

Anaphora/anaphoric reference.   The term 'anaphora' comes from a
Greek word meaning 'carrying back'. It is used in stylistics to describe
the cohesive ties that link SENTENCES to those which precede them.
Anaphoric reference, in other words, is a form of DISCOURSE connection
that enables the reader to see the sentences s/he is reading as constituting a text. Its counterpart is CATAPHORIC (or 'forward looking') reference.

Anaphoric reference is typically achieved in three ways. Firstly by **co-
reference**, in which pronouns and sometimes determiners refer to
items previously mentioned in the text, as in *Finish your homework. **It**
will save time*, where *it* refers back to *Finish your homework*. Secondly, by
substitution – using *do* and *one* – usually to avoid repetition, as in *I like
his car. It's a new **one***, and *His cat scratches. If it **does**, just tap it on the
nose*. And thirdly, by **ellipsis**, for example: Q. *Where are you going?* A. [*I
am going*] *To the pictures*. Failures of anaphoric reference are frequently
encountered in the speech and writing of young children, who will talk

about *him* or *her* without having indicated who is being referred to. Novelists may also omit anaphoric reference, in this case deliberately, in order to create the illusion of a pre-existing world, as in the opening sentence of John Fowles's novel, *The Collector*: 'When she was home from her boarding-school I used to see her almost every day sometimes, because their house was right opposite the Town Hall Annexe.' See also EXOPHORIC/ENDOPHORIC REFERENCE.

Assemblage error.   A mistake in speaking or writing in which sounds, syllables, or words, are mixed up. The most common assemblage errors are slips of the tongue (or pen): *bake my bike* (take my bike); *par cark* (car park). These sorts of errors are known as **transpositions**, or **metatheses**. The first kind (*bake my bike*) are **anticipations**: the early anticipation of the *b* of *bike* interferes with the initial segment of *take*. The second (*par cark*) are **reversals**, commonly associated with the nineteenth-century clergyman William Spooner, who regularly transposed sounds in this way. Other slips may involve **blends**, in which two words are run together – *grastly* (grizzly + ghastly); or **selection errors**, in which the wrong word is selected – *before the place closes* (before the place opens).

Assemblage errors provide important evidence for the linguist about how language production is planned. For the most part, speakers/writers have the correct items but assembled in the wrong order. This suggests that we do not plan what we are going to say or write word by word, but in larger chunks – PHRASES and CLAUSES – since the items must have been chosen in advance of actual production. The problem, then, is largely a processing one, and the task for the psycholinguist is to investigate what happens in the production programme to cause these errors.

Bioprogram(me) hypothesis.   Hypothesis associated with the linguist Derek Bickerton that argues that humans possess a universal linguistic 'bioprogram' that enables them to develop language. Bickerton developed his hypothesis as a consequence of studying the CREOLE spoken among the children of workers on Hawaiian sugar plantations (1981). Bickerton was struck by the capacity of these children to generate for themselves a complete language when their parents could only speak a variety of PIDGIN. They were able to do so, he suggested, because they were biologically programmed to. Bickerton also argued that his hypothesis explained the linguistic similarity of Creoles around the world. They were similar because the biological program was innate, and universal. The excitement generated by the hypothesis has been due largely to the fact that Bickerton appeared to have found first-hand evidence of the existence of UNIVERSAL GRAMMAR.

Since then, Bickerton has gone on to look at how the bioprogram might have evolved in humans (1990, 1995). Crucial to the evolution of language is the development of **grammar**. Bickerton argues that early man, *Homo erectus*, who lived around 1.5 million years ago, possessed a very rudimentary linguistic capability, which he refers to as **proto-language**. In a sense this is language without a proper system – such as word order or **inflections** – for showing grammatical relationships. The evolution of a capacity for grammar within the human brain was what enabled *Homo sapiens*, who emerged around 300,000 years ago, to develop language proper. In other words, *Homo sapiens* was in a similar situation to the children of the Hawaiian plantation workers in having to develop a language relying only on his/her own innate capacities.

Caregiver language.　A polite term for what is colloquially called 'motherese' or 'baby-talk'. This is the language spoken to children by those who look after them. Many people when speaking to very young children adopt marked INTONATION patterns, speaking slowly, at a higher pitch than normal, and often employing made-up words, such as *moo cow*, *baa lamb*, and *bow wow*. The effect of such language on children is probably limited to reinforcement of articulatory processes. There's little evidence that children actually acquire any grammatical or lexical knowledge from such interactions. At a later stage, adults may help by providing children with **expansions** of their utterances. So, for example, if a child says *Shoes dirty*, a parent may expand this into a complete sentence by replying *Yes, your shoes are dirty*. It used to be thought that expansions were a principal agent of children's development in providing a model for children to aim at, but recent research suggests that more productive are **recasts**. These are responses in which the parent repeats what the child says in an alternative form and continues the conversation, for example, *They're not very dirty. Let's clean them, shall we?*

Cataphora/cataphoric reference.　'Cataphora' is from a Greek term meaning 'forward looking' (as opposed to ANAPHORA). It is used in stylistics to describe the cohesive ties between items and those which come after them: typically between a PRONOUN and a following NOUNPHRASE of some kind: ***That's*** *what I like to see,* ***an empty plate***. Because of its anticipatory quality, cataphora can be used to create suspense: *Over in the corner* ***it*** *lay, a small untidy heap. As Michael approached he saw* ***a perfectly formed human shape***. Cataphoric reference is a more stylised device than anaphora and is less frequently encountered in ordinary discourse (*see* EXOPHORIC/ENDOPHORIC REFERENCE).

Channel. The technical means by which a message is transmitted. For some linguists it is synonymous with MEDIUM, and it is acceptable to use it in that way. However, a useful, if fine, distinction can be made between them. Medium, in linguistic terms, is more concerned with the physical form a message takes. If we consider speech to be a primary linguistic medium of communication, for example, then clearly it can be transmitted in a number of ways: by telephone, television, radio, or face to face. Similarly, writing can appear electronically on a computer screen, or on the printed page of a book. All of these technical communication aids are channels.

In stylistics 'channel' is one of a number of variables that affect the style, or REGISTER, we adopt in speaking or writing. Most people, for instance, will speak differently over the phone than face to face. Without the visual clues to tell us how a message is being sent or received, we have to pay more attention to phrasing and INTONATION. It's partly because of this extra demand on speech that the telephone can sometimes seem intimidating. Characteristic of much communication today is the use of **multiple channels**, in which one channel is embedded in another, as in a discussion broadcast over the radio. In this case both the primary channel of face-to-face interaction and the secondary of radio broadcast would subtly affect the medium of speech. You only have to compare a football commentary over the radio with one transmitted via television to become aware of this.

Child language. The language ability of children, which differs from that of adults. It's commonly assumed by people with little linguistic knowledge that children learn language by imitating adults, but no amount of imitation can explain children's ability to produce structures like *Me throwed the ball*, or *No daddy go*, which they cannot have heard. Utterances like these indicate that children are devising rules for themselves rather than simply copying adults. As they get older they modify these rules in the light of fresh information that comes their way. The nature of these rules, and the way in which children formulate them, is still a matter of controversy, but there is a large body of opinion that believes that children are guided by innate linguistic principles (*see* UNIVERSAL GRAMMAR), and that language is **maturationally controlled**, i.e. we are biologically programmed to acquire language (provided the environment is normal). Additional evidence for this comes from the frequently observed fact that children all seem to go through very similar stages in their development. The following programme is a typical one for an English-speaking child:

1–6 weeks   **Vegetative sounds**:   primitive vocal sounds reflecting baby's biological state and connected with eating, passing motions, and so on. Baby is learning to control air flow and produce rhythmic sounds.

6–8 weeks   **Cooing**:   more settled and musical sounds, quieter, low-pitched and usually consisting of a vowel preceded by a back consonant. Strings of cooing noises emerge as baby learns control of its tongue.

3–4 months   **Vocal play**:   sounds more definite and controlled. Baby is experimenting with different sounds.

6–12 months   **Babbling**:   syllabic sequences, at first repetitious, *bababa*, and from about 9 months becoming more varied, with syllables joined together in a kind of proto-speech or **scribble talk**. An important component of such 'talk' is the production of adult-like intonation patterns.

12–15 months   **Single words**:   utterances of just one word, *gone*, *dada*, *teddy*, *shoes*; 60% of words have a naming function, 20% express an action. These are frequently **holophrases**, that is, single words that represent a larger unit: so *shoe*, for example, might mean *I want my shoe*. Typically, children will also simplify pronunciation, replacing fricatives with stops, *tee* instead of *see*, velars with alveolars, *don* instead of *gone*, omitting consonants at the ends of words, *ha* instead of *hat*, dropping unstressed syllables, *nana* for banana, and harmonising vowels and consonants, *wouwou* (window), *gog* (dog). These practices may continue for a considerable while, and in the case of awkward consonant clusters and difficult sounds, even up to school age.

18–24 months   **Two-word stage**:   two words brought together to make primitive SENTENCE structures, *Cat jump* (subject+ verb), *Shut door* (verb + object). Simple negatives emerge, combining *no/not* with another word, *no sit*, *not there*; and also simple questions, using intonation, *Daddy gone?*

2–3 years	**Telegraphic sentences**: sentence patterns filled out with extra CLAUSE elements, *Daddy got car* (SVO), *You go bed now* (SVOA). Inflections appearing, regular past tense and plural. Use of 'wh' words for questions, *Where daddy going?* Use of negatives within constructions, *You no do that, Mummy not got that.*
3–4 years	**Full sentences**: clauses strung together to express more complex thoughts using linking devices, *cos, and, so.* Adult-type negatives occur, linking negatives to auxiliary verbs, *You've not got one, She isn't going,* and also adult-type questions, using subject auxiliary inversion, *Is that a car?*
4–5 years	**Sorting out**: learning of adult forms of irregular inflection patterns for plurals and past tense, and case forms of plurals: *He gave the cheese to the mice,* instead of *He gived the cheese to the mouses.*
5–10 years	**Adult stage**: acquisition of cohesive devices for linking sentences together, complex patterns of subordination, and production of passives.

As this timetable makes clear, the major stages of language learning are achieved by the age of five. Although the child will become more proficient linguistically after this, the basic structure of his/her language system is now in place. What is not shown here, however, is the communicative, or functional aspect of a child's development. We need this to complete the picture because, however we view language acquisition, it can never be simply a mechanical process of biological programming.

The linguist Michael Halliday has done more than anyone else to examine the functional dimension of child language. His work emphasises the link between language and other communicative processes that the child uses to signal his/her needs and demands. A crucial stage in the pre-linguistic stage of development is when the child uses gestures symbolically as a form of 'signing': signalling a request by closing and opening a hand round an object, rather than grabbing it, or pressing a finger on a toy which is being tossed up and down, signalling 'do it again'. When, during their first year, children begin making speech-like sounds they take a step towards using language, instead of actions, as a symbolic system. These systems are individual to the child – they are his/her own language. An example from Halliday's research into his own son Nigel's speech showed that *na* meant 'Give me that', *yi* 'Yes I want that thing there', whilst other syllabic utterances meant 'I'm here', 'Let's look at this', and 'That's funny' (see Halliday, 1985). From his observations Halliday identified seven main functions that this kind of **proto-language** fulfilled:

(i)   **Instrumental**: 'I want'.
(ii)   **Regulatory**: 'Do as I tell you'.
(iii)   **Interactional**: 'Me and you'.
(iv)   **Personal**: 'Here I come'.
(v)   **Heuristic**: 'Tell me why'.
(vi)   **Imaginative**: 'Let's pretend'.
(vii)   **Informative**: 'I've got something to tell you'.

According to Halliday, (v), (vi), and (vii) develop later than the rest and are more specifically linguistic. From his account, one of the principal reasons for children moving beyond this proto-language stage is the relative paucity of meaning which is capable of being conveyed. It's impossible to mean more than one thing at a time, or to refer to things not present, or in the past. To do that one must be able to take the individual elements and recombine them, i.e. one must have a grammar. Proto-language is inevitably a two-tier system in which meaning and sound are directly related, whereas language is a three-tier system. In between the other two lies a middle tier of grammar (see Figure 31). At some stage in his/her development a child leaves the two-tier system and adopts the three-tier one. It is this leap which is unique to humans and that cannot be replicated by animals.

Proto-language: MEANING
↓
SOUND

Language: MEANING
↓
SYSTEM OF WORDS
↓
SOUND

Figure 31   The three-tier system of language

Source: Based upon M. Halliday, *Spoken and Written Language* (Melbourne: Deakin University Press, 1985).

Code.   In its simplest sense a code is a system of rules that allows us to transmit information in symbolic form. By this definition human language is a code. It consists of words that symbolically represent ideas, events, and objects in the world outside, and which, when put together in certain sequences, enable us to communicate. In order to be able to use the code we have to learn a variety of rules, or **subcodes**, governing the phonology, syntax, and semantics of language. Some of these are common to all languages and constitute a **universal code**, and others are specific to individual languages.

A code, then, is basically a SIGN system, and using it to refer to language entails the recognition that words are signs, a view that has become deeply rooted in modern linguistics ever since the work of the Swiss linguist SAUSSURE. A characteristic of sign systems is that messages can be converted from one system (or **primary code**) into another (or **secondary code**). Morse code and semaphore are both, in this respect, secondary, therefore, in being based on language. Linguists sometimes talk about the processes by which we transmit and receive language as **encoding** and **decoding**. This can give the impression that activities such as speaking and listening are largely mechanical. Clearly, understanding what someone is saying to us involves more than simply turning the stream of sound which we are receiving back into words. We have to be able to interpret prosodic features such as stress and INTONA-TION, both of which contribute to meaning. The concept of code copes with this by treating such features as part of the subcode of PHONOLOGY, within which prosody has its own rules for assigning meaning to utter-ances. So, providing we remember to use the terms 'decode' and 'encode' with this more expanded, rather than narrow sense, they will serve well enough.

It is also worth remembering that language is only one sign system among many. The NON-VERBAL behaviour that accompanies speech (commonly called 'body language') is also a form of signalling, employ-ing its own complex system of communicating. Indeed, in a general sense, all aspects of human behaviour function as signs, from the way we dress to the cars we drive. The study of these sign systems, or codes, is the pursuit of **semiotics**. The success of this field of study among modern communications theorists is evident from the way in which most disciplines in the humanities have their respective codes. There are cultural codes, aesthetic codes, theatrical codes, and literary codes. All of them are based on the idea that we make sense of what we see and hear by drawing on an implicit system of signs encoded in a text, a painting, a play, or a even a social event. Because of the extensive way in which it is used, 'code' can sometimes seem a vague and pretentious term, but providing we keep in mind its primary sense it remains very useful.

Code-switching.   The shifting by speakers between one DIALECT, or language, and another. Many native English speakers will switch between speaking regional dialect, or non-standard English, casually among friends, and standard English for professional or business purposes. **Bidialectalism** as it is sometimes called has received the overt support of many linguists as a way to approach the difficulty that schools face in giving appropriate recognition to the local dialect of children whilst at the same time respecting their entitlement to acquire standard English. **Bilingual** speakers, of course, do more than simply switch dialects. People who are fluent in two or more languages may regularly switch from one to the other according to the situation, the person being addressed, or even the topic.

Cohesion/coherence.   Terms frequently encountered in DISCOURSE ANALYSIS that refer specifically to the way in which sentences, whether in spoken or written form, cohere together to form a meaningful text. It is part of the quality of a text that it is not just a series of disconnected sentences but possesses what the linguist Michael Halliday terms **textuality**. Our ability to create and recognise such sequences, according to Halliday, constitutes our **textual competence.**

The terms themselves have a slightly different meaning that is important linguistically because it forms the basis of a useful distinction. Cohesion signifies the **surface** ties which link units together. The key work in identifying these has been undertaken by Halliday and Hasan (1976). They identified a range of ties at various linguistic LEVELS, phonological, syntactical, lexical, and semantic, which serve to hook sentences onto each other. Some of the principal devices here are **lexical**, involving the use of SYNONYMS or HYPONYMS: *He turned to the* **ascent** *of the mountain. The* **climb** *was steep/I bought some* **daffodils**. *They're very practical* **flowers**. Others are more grammatical and involve strategies such as **co-reference**, **substitution**, and **ellipsis** (*see* ANAPHORA).

Cohesiveness used to be considered by language teachers as a basic requirement for texts. But since the work of Halliday and Hasan more emphasis has been placed on coherence as a criterion of textuality. It's possible for a sequence of sentences to be cohesive without being coherent. The following utterance uses the cohesive device of substitution to tie the sentences together but the result is clearly not coherent: *A castle is a piece in chess. There's one at Windsor.* The speech of schizophrenics is characterised by incoherent cohesion. A good example of such speech is that of the character Benjy in William Faulkner's novel *The Sound and the Fury*. A text may in fact be coherent without any cohesive links at all. The following two sentences have nothing to tie them together but are nevertheless logically related in the minds of both speaker and listener: *I must tidy the house. My mother-in-law's coming tomorrow*. This utterance could easily be made cohesive by the insertion of *because* between the sentences but it's clearly not necessary in such a context. We know the two are causally related partly because of the logical sequence of assertion followed by explanation, which is one of the discourse frames we habitually use, and partly because we know in the real world what a visit by a mother-in-law may entail.

These examples would suggest that cohesion doesn't render a text coherent. Rather it seems to signal coherence for purposes of either clarity, emphasis, or elegance. Coherence is concerned with the way in which propositions are linked together in a logical and sequential manner. Our expectation of such linkage is a basic convention of communication and underlies both the COOPERATIVE PRINCIPAL and the production of SPEECH ACTS. As such, coherence depends, crucially, on INFERENCE, that is, our ability to detect and interpret meanings not necessarily present in the text. This is part of our PRAGMATIC knowledge and as a consequence must take into account features such as CONTEXT and audience. Speaking to someone from a different culture, for example, we may need to use fairly explicit cohesive devices in order to signal actively the logical connections we are making, whereas with someone we know very well we can afford to take all kinds of discourse liberties.

Context.   This is a very widely used term in linguistics and, as a consequence, any account of its meaning will involve us in specifying exactly how it is being used. In a general sense it refers to that which comes before or after something. In the case of a SENTENCE, or utterance, it could be the sounds, words, or PHRASES, which surround a particular verbal item. So, for example, in the sentence *Peter went to the pictures. He went alone*, we know who *he* refers to because of the preceding item *Peter*. This kind of context is called **verbal context**, or sometimes simply the **co-text**. Co-text means 'accompanying text', i.e. those sounds, words, phrases and so on, which accompany each other in the particular sentence or utterance. Verbal context is also important in semantics, in determining the actual SENSE with which a word is being used. The word *flight*, for example, has a number of different senses, including 'a series of steps', 'a journey by air', and a 'digression'. But to know which of these is most appropriate in the title *The flight of the* *bumble bee*, we need to take into account the meaning of the item *bumble bee*.

The kind of context we have been talking about so far can, in general terms, be thought of as the **linguistic context**, that is, the context provided by the linguistic system itself. Equally significant, although more difficult to define, is the **situational context** in which utterances take place. If you ask someone whether they want a cup of coffee and the reply is *Coffee keeps me awake*, then, clearly, in order to know whether this means *yes* or *no*, we need to know more than the simple meaning of the words being used. The ability to interpret utterances correctly involves us in processing not just the words, but the situational context in which they are being used. But the problem for linguists is in deciding just how much of a given situation we need to know in order to carry out the task of interpretation. Some of the contextual variables, such as the relationship of the participants (father/daughter, employer/employee), and the particular form of communication being used (telephone, letter), can be dealt with by other DISCOURSE categories such as TENOR and CHANNEL. But there still remains an indeterminate area of situational context, much of which we may take for granted in interpreting an utterance. A seemingly innocent question about coffee will vary in contextual meaning according to whether it is said in a café, on top of a bus, in a time of coffee shortage, or in a culture which regards coffee drinking as decadent. The list of variables is almost infinite.

To cope with the spread of possible contexts many linguists make a broad distinction between **micro-context** and **macro-context**. The micro-context is the immediate one in which an utterance occurs. The principal features it incorporates are **setting** and **occasion**. The first of these indicates the place where a discourse event occurs, and the second, the particular circumstances which occasion it – a row with a neighbour, a proposal of marriage, and so on. The macro-context, as its name implies, includes the more 'remote' environments in which communication occurs. Any communicative act assumes a framework, or background, of shared values and beliefs. The factors which are important here are geographical, social, and cultural. The separation of wider and immediate features in this way enables us to describe the impact of context on linguistic meaning more clearly. None the less, it still remains an indeterminate area of stylistic analysis if only because situational context is essentially extra-linguistic in character. As such, it's the point at which language and the world at large interact.

Covert prestige.   A term used in sociolinguistics to describe the way in which non-standard forms belonging to regional DIALECTS are positively valued by speakers. The existence of such prestige helps to explain why there are not more RP and standard English speakers than there are. Some communities clearly value non-standard forms, chiefly as a means of reinforcing group solidarity and local identity, even though this is not always a matter of conscious awareness.

Evidence for covert prestige has usually come from what sociolinguists call 'under-reporting', a classic instance of which is detailed in Peter Trudgill's 'Norfolk study' (Trudgill, 1974). As part of his analysis of Norfolk dialect Trudgill asked informants to take part in a 'self-evaluation test' in which they reported on what they believed themselves to be saying, which he compared with what they actually did say. Using a range of linguistic variables he was able to show that perceptions of speech habits were often at variance with actual usage. In the case of **yod dropping**, for instance (the dropping of /j/ before /u/ in words such as *beauty* and *tune*), as many as 40 per cent of informants claimed to use the non-standard form (*booty*, *toon*) when in fact the tape recording showed them using the standard form. Even allowing for the influence of tape recorders on linguistic behaviour (*see* OBSERVER'S PARADOX) this represents a remarkable disparity. The conclusion which Trudgill drew from this is that 'Speakers . . . report themselves as using the form at which they are aiming and which has favourable connotations for them, rather than the form which they actually use' (1983, p. 91).

Trudgill discovered that covert prestige was more common among male speakers, a finding which correlates with the frequently observed phenomenon that women value standard forms of speech more highly than men: 'A large number of male speakers, it seems, are more concerned with acquiring *covert prestige* than with obtaining social status (as this is more usually defined). For Norwich men (and we can perhaps assume, for men elsewhere) working-class speech is statusful and prestigious' (1983, p. 92).

Creole: *see* PIDGIN.

Deixis/deictic.　From a Greek word meaning 'pointing' or 'showing'. In stylistics 'deixis' refers to those features of language which orientate our utterances in time, space, and speaker's standpoint. So, for example, the TENSE system is deictic because it locates events in the present or the past. Similarly, words such as *here*, *there*, *this*, and *that*, are normally deictic because they locate items in space relative to the person who is speaking: my *here* is your *there*. The first-person pronouns *I* and *we* and the second-person pronoun *you* are also deictic in this respect. This form of deixis is EXOPHORIC in character in that it is situationally, or contextually, bound.

A secondary form of deixis is ENDOPHORIC and serves to locate items textually. In the following example *this* points forward CATAPHORICALLY to the next sentence: *This is important. Don't go out*. Additionally, terms like *this* and *that* can be used to locate things emotionally. Linguists refer to this as **displacement**. In the utterance *Get that animal out of here*, the demonstrative *that* as well as pointing to the particular animal conveys the speaker's dislike. Similarly, *this* frequently occurs in jokes and anecdotes as a means of indicating familiarity: *There was this man* (i.e. a particular man).

Derivational complexity theory. A theory associated with the linguist George Miller and popular for a time in the 1960s, which argued that the relative difficulty which listeners have in comprehending a sentence correlates with the number of transformations it has been subject to (*see* TRANSFORMATIONAL GRAMMAR). So, for example, a **kernel** sentence such as *The boy hit the girl* would be easier to understand than *Was the girl hit by the boy?*, where the original sentence has been subject to two transformations (interrogative + passive). This theory seems initially attractive, and for generative grammarians it appeared to provide additional evidence for the existence of transformational processes. However, tests of speech comprehension indicate that people do not decode sentences by starting from their kernel form and then adding on the transformations. There is, in fact, little correlation between difficulty of comprehension and transformational complexity. Most linguists do not regard transformational grammar as a representation of the knowledge speakers possess about relationships within language but as a set of instructions for processing language. Moreover, such have been the changes to transformational approaches that the model underlying the derivational complexity theory is now out of date.

Dialect. A geographically based language variety with distinct syntactic forms and vocabulary items. It's usually distinguished from ACCENT, which refers solely to features of pronunciation, although on occasions 'dialect' is loosely used to include accent. Many dialects are regional in origin and belong to a particular area. So Cornwall and Northumberland, for example, have distinctive words and grammatical constructions which native speakers of those regions will often use. These rural dialects used to be the pursuit of early sociologists concerned with describing and recording dialects as relics of a more linguistically diverse history. Since then **dialectology** has switched away from traditional dialects to the study of so-called 'modern' or urban dialects. Principally important here has been the American sociolinguist William

Labov, whose early work on the speech of New Yorkers influenced a generation of sociolinguists. The difference between traditional and modern dialects is well illustrated by Peter Trudgill (1990, p. 5) with the following example:

> *Hoo inno comin* (traditional dialect)
> *She ain't comin* (modern non-standard dialect)
> *She isn't coming* (modern standard dialect)

In addition to regional and urban dialects there are also national and international varieties, such as Scottish and American. Some people also use the term to refer to varieties used by social groups, in the sense of **class dialects**, although it is probably better to use the term **sociolect** for these and keep 'dialect' for geographical varieties.

It's important to bear in mind that the term 'dialect' is purely descriptive. There is no implication that one variety is in any sense better than any other. However, people often have their own preferences and will frequently seek to exalt these into judgements about linguistic correctness. The issue of 'correctness' arises particularly in relation to **standard English**, which is popularly regarded as not a dialect, because of its national status and its non-regional character. Historically speaking, however, the basis of what is now standard English was the local dialect of the region bounded by Oxford, Cambridge, and London. Its elevation has been the consequence of a number of social and cultural factors, but these shouldn't hide from us the fact that it is still a variety of the language, albeit a non-regional and socially normative one, and therefore can still be thought of as a dialect.

Standard English is unique among dialects, however, in not being paired with a particular accent. It's possible to speak it with any kind of accent, Geordie, Cockney, Welsh and so on. But the same is not true for other dialects. It's difficult to imagine Cockney dialect, for example, being spoken with anything other than a corresponding Cockney accent. One might perhaps get away with using another urban accent but not with using **received pronunciation** (*see* ACCENT). Standard English's claim to 'standardness', however, rests on two interrelated facts: first, that it is the variety of the language which is taught, and secondly, that it is also the medium of teaching, i.e. other subjects are taught using it. This in turn is only possible because standard English, unlike the other dialects, is a written variety. As such, it is codified in dictionaries and grammars and subject to what linguists call **minimum variation of form** and **maximum variation of function**. This means that syntactic and orthographic variation in standard English is limited (there is usually only one way to spell a word, for example), whilst at the same time it is used in a wide variety of contexts – the law, medicine, the church, politics, and so on. By contrast, regional and urban dialects, commonly referred to as **non-standard English**, are restricted in function and have no fixed orthographic form. This poses a problem, of course, if writers wish to use dialect in novels or poetry, as they sometimes do, to create a sense of authenticity. Usually they resort to **eye-dialect**, which involves spelling words in an unconventional way to indicate the presence of a dialect speaker. However, because the spelling system is only loosely phonetic the result is often merely quaint. If we saw the line *Wot e sez is* we should be inclined to think the speaker a Cockney, but it actually represents the standard pronunciation more accurately than does the conventional orthography.

Because of the social value attached to certain dialects many speakers learn dialect-switching (or CODE-SWITCHING). This usually involves switching from a regional or urban dialect to the standard one and corresponds to degrees of formality. So one might speak local dialect to friends but not when being interviewed for a job. In this sense 'dialect' overlaps with the term REGISTER. The distinction made between these terms by Michael Halliday (1978) is that register varies according to use, and dialect according to user. But in practice dialect often takes on a register function. The adjective derived from 'dialect' is **dialectal**.

One of the fuzzy areas of sociolinguistics is the exact distinction between 'dialect' and 'language'. This might seem obvious at first in that dialects are simply subdivisions of languages, but the issue is not so clear cut. Normally, speakers of different dialects can understand each other whereas those of different languages can't, i.e. dialects are mutually intelligible. This criterion isn't always sufficient, however. Along the Dutch–German border, for instance, the dialects of both languages are so similar that speakers can often understand each other fairly well; much better in fact than speakers from this area of Germany can often understand a Swiss or Austrian speaker of German. Nevertheless, we still class Dutch and German as different languages, not dialects. These kinds of comparisons force us to acknowledge that linguistic criteria alone are not enough to distinguish dialects from languages. Also important are cultural, political, and historical factors, the two most important of which are **autonomy** and **heteronomy**. Languages are autonomous in that they are independent, standardised varieties with a life of their own. This applies to both German and Dutch. Dialects, on the other hand, are heteronomous, or subordinate to another variety. So different dialect users of German will nevertheless look to German as their standard language and will read and write in German. Similarly,

Dutch speakers of whatever dialect will look to Dutch, not German, as the source of authoritative usage.

What this alerts us to is a problem that perennially affects linguistics. That is, the extent to which dividing linguistic and social phenomena into discrete entities has any basis in reality. As Peter Trudgill has pointed out, although it is possible to speak of Norfolk dialect and Suffolk dialect, there is no clear linguistic break between them. Travelling from one region to the other it is clear that many of the linguistic characteristics that make up these dialects change gradually. There's no sudden change at the county boundary. Moreover, it could be argued that there is more than one Norfolk dialect in that differences occur between eastern and southern parts of the county. It would be more accurate to say, in such circumstances, that there is a **dialect continuum**. The reality, then, is more complex than may often at first appear and it is as well to keep this in mind. Terms such as 'dialect' are enormously useful in distinguishing sets of FEATURES which are common to a particular region, but it is rarely the case that any one feature is exclusive to that area. At the level of individual usage all we have are speakers, and they are as varied in their linguistic make-up as in everything else.

Diglossia (diglossic). Some languages have two very different varieties co-occurring through a speech community, each with a different range of social function. If you are in Greece, for example, you might well find native users of the language writing in one form, 'Katharevousa', but speaking another, 'dhimotiki'. Such a situation is 'diglossic'. It's usually the case that one form (sometimes called 'high') is used for the more serious purposes of education, politics, and commerce, and the other (or 'low' variety) for domestic and informal settings. Whilst the 'high' is more prestigious, the 'low' is thoroughly acceptable in the contexts in which it is used. This is an important point and one that enables us to distinguish the situation in England from diglossia. In the first place, English dialectal varieties are regional in character whereas diglossic varieties aren't, and secondly, non-standard forms are clearly stigmatised in a way that prevents them being regarded as acceptable alternatives. Diglossic situations may also be found in Egypt, where both classical Arabic and colloquial Arabic are used, and in Switzerland, where speakers use High German and Swiss German.

Historically, it is likely that the Romance languages (such as French, Spanish, and Italian) arose from diglossic situations in which a high Latin was used for education, religion, and serious purposes, and a Latin vernacular for everyday speech. Such situations exist today in communities in the Pacific and Caribbean where both a standard variety of English and a pidginised (*see* PIDGIN) form exist side by side.

Discourse (analysis). 'Discourse' is one of those elastic terms that one sometimes encounters in linguistics. It's often used quite loosely to mean any sequence of language in written or spoken form larger than a SENTENCE. The distinctive aspect of 'discourse', however, is that it stresses the communicative dynamics of language. In this sense analysing discourse means investigating all those features that are part of the total communicative act: CONTEXT of utterance, TENOR of relationships, MODE of discourse, and so on. All those features which are part of what the Russian critic Mikhail Bakhtin has called the 'concrete living totality' of language. This sense is equivalent to that of the French term **discours**, which includes fiction and poetry as types of literary or narrative discourse. Linguists who use the term in this more comprehensive sense will also use the term **text** more liberally and talk of written as well as spoken texts.

Other linguists, however, restrict the term 'discourse' to spoken language. This is true of early discourse analysts, such as M. Coulthard and J. Sinclair at Birmingham University, who extensively studied teacher/pupil and doctor/patient exchanges. Discourse in this sense is viewed as a series of connected utterances, the equivalent in spoken form to a written text. Nowadays, however, many discourse analysts tend to adopt the more liberal, and continental, definition of discourse, although it is arguably still true that the real advances of discourse analysis, as far as linguistics is concerned, have been in the analysis of spoken language. In this respect it has succeeded in highlighting many elements of speech which conventional grammars often ignore. The importance of INTONATION as an interactional way of signalling meaning and intention, and of **tone units** generally in the organisation and structure of utterances, has been greatly advanced by viewing speech as discourse.

One of the difficulties that discourse analysts have traditionally faced in investigating speech, particularly at the level of conversation, has been its apparently casual and loosely structured quality. By concentrating on more tightly controlled interactions Coulthard and Sinclair managed to limit interference from the more spontaneous features of speech, but in so doing restricted the usefulness of their approach. None the less, the model they employed, with various modifications, has been much copied by later analysts. Its value lies in the way it divides up interactions using a ranking scale which is hierarchical in nature:

TRANSACTION

EXCHANGE

MOVE

ACT

At the top of the scale, 'Transaction' describes the total sequence between the participants. This will normally consist of smaller sequences, or 'exchanges', which are usually topic-based and involve the exchange of information of some kind. A typical exchange involves the basic 'moves' of **initiation**, **response**, and **follow-up**:

(a) *What time is it?* (initiation)

(b) *Seven-thirty* (response)

(c) *Thanks* (follow-up)

Each move here represents a SPEECH ACT – requesting, informing, thanking – and in this way discourse analysis is able to use and extend the work of speech act theorists such as J. R. Searle and J. L. Austin.

As we have noted, however, this model works best for more formal interactions between two participants. Problems arise with spontaneous conversations where several people are contributing in an apparently random manner, such as a chat in a local pub. Deciding where exchanges begin and end, and what moves and acts are being performed, is often difficult, and of limited usefulness anyway. These kinds of complications have led many discourse analysts to concentrate more on how people behave and cooperate in the management of discourse rather than on trying to apply abstract models to raw speech data. Observing conversational behaviour in this way is the concern of a school of discourse analysis called **ethnomethodology**. Ethnomethodologists study the conventions of conversation such as **turn-taking**, i.e. how people know when it's their turn to speak, and the use of **adjacency pairs** – the formulaic pairing of utterances, *greeting–greeting*, *apology–acceptance*, which allows people to negotiate stock situations. They analyse strategies for beginning and ending a conversation, how topics enter and disappear, and the ways in which acts of politeness and face-preservation are performed. On the basis of such analyses ethnomethodologists seek to establish the underlying 'norms' or rules of conversation that speakers and hearers implicitly follow.

With such a large agenda it is not surprising that discourse analysis continues to have a wide appeal. Linguists are not the only people interested in speech behaviour; so are sociologists, anthropologists, and psychologists. Discourse analysts, then, come from a 'broad church' of related disciplines, each with its own particular view of the subject. But if we stick with our linguistic perspective we could say that discourse analysis is centrally occupied with two main linguistic functions: the **interpersonal** and the **textual** – the interpersonal because it is focusing on the way in which we use language as a means of interacting with others, and the textual because it also focuses on our ability to construct COHERENT/COHESIVE 'texts'. This is the case whether such texts are in written or spoken form.

Displacement.   The ability to communicate about matters removed in time and place. This is one of the distinguishing FEATURES between animal and human communication systems. Animals can signal information about the here and now but are generally unable to do so about things which happened yesterday, or in another place. Some creatures, like bees, have a limited capacity for displacement: **bee-dancing** can communicate geographical information about the location of nectar.

Ethnography of communication.   The study of language in relation to the social and cultural variables that influence communication. All societies have their own rules or conventions about how language should be used in social interaction. There are rules about how to address someone – title, first name, or surname – and rules about degrees of politeness and deference. Knowing these conventions is important in interpreting human behaviour and understanding correctly the significance of what is said to us. If we telephoned someone in Japan, for instance, we might be perturbed to be greeted with total silence. But, as Peter Trudgill (1983) points out, many people in Japan expect the caller to speak first. There is, in fact, quite a wide diversity of telephone behaviour around the world. In France it's quite normal for callers to apologise for the intrusion and to identify themselves before asking to speak to someone, whereas American and British callers behave differently. A British caller might simply ask for someone and if they're not there, ring off, only at the last minute possibly giving his/her name. Similarly, there are conventions about the order of talk, and the amount of silence which can be accepted in conversation. Some communities, such as in Britain, usually only allow one person to speak at a time, whereas in the Caribbean, it's not uncommon for several people to speak at once. At the other extreme, some Native American groups tolerate silences between contributions of a considerably greater length than is the norm elsewhere.

Ethnography is a wide and diverse aspect of sociolinguistics. It has been chiefly important in the study of communicative COMPETENCE.

Linguists who study this area take into account all those extra-linguistic variables (e.g. CONTEXT, CODE, TENOR, CONTACT) that influence speech events, and seek to construct principles which govern human interaction.

Exophoric/endophoric reference.   A pair of terms used to describe the principal ways in which texts refer either externally to the world outside (exophoric), or internally to themselves (endophoric). Exophoric reference is contextual, or situational, reference. So, for example, the PRONOUNS *I* and *you* are exophoric in the utterance *I like you*, where they refer outward to participants in the discourse – as opposed to the third-person pronouns *he/him*, *she/her*, which are typically endophoric and require textual antecedents in order to make complete sense. So the utterance *He likes her* requires us to indicate who is being referred to, as in: *John phoned Jane. He likes her.* Exophoric reference is particularly common in spoken interactions where items in the world about us are the topic of conversation. In the following utterance *that* has exophoric reference whilst the third-person pronoun *it* which begins the next sentence is endophoric: *I like that. It will match my hat.* Endophoric reference has two main forms: ANAPHORIC ('looking backwards') and CATAPHORIC ('looking forwards').

Field of discourse.   One of the variables significant in determining the REGISTER we adopt in communicating. It refers, very broadly, to the subject matter, or subject area, which forms the basis of our communication. There are, frequently, a set of terms particular to each field, and which we interpret in relation to the field. The term 'free kick', for example, means something different in the field of sport than it does in general use. Topics such as the weather or the economy all have their own individual LEXICONS. If we hear the phrase *trough of low pressure* we know instantly that we are listening to the weather forecast. Sometimes 'field of discourse' may denote a type of discourse rather than a specific subject. So linguists will talk about the field of journalism or advertising, since both have their own distinctive set of lexical items.

'Fis' phenomenon.   An observed phenomenon of children's speech which indicates their ability to identify words they cannot themselves pronounce clearly. The classic demonstration of this, recorded by the linguists Berko and Brown, concerns identification of the word *fish* in adult speech:

> One of us, for instance, spoke to a child who called his inflated plastic fish a
> *fis*. In imitation of the child's pronunciation, the observer said: 'This is your

fis?' 'No,' said the child, 'my *fis.'* He continued to reject the adult's imitation until he was told, 'That is your fish.' 'Yes,' he said, 'my *fis.'*   (Berko and Brown, 1960, p. 531)

Numerous instances of the 'fis' phenomenon have been observed since the original one. The linguist N. Smith (1973), for example, records that his son could perceive the difference between words such as *mouse* and *mouth* long before he could produce it. All the evidence makes the same point, namely, that children have a more accurate representation of words than they can accurately produce themselves. Caution has to be exercised, however, because the problem is not always one of production: a child can sometimes produce the problem sound in other words. In such cases it may be that the child has not consistently learned which tongue and lip movements are linked to which sounds, with the consequence that production is not secure.

Garden-path sentences.   These are sentences in which listeners are initially led astray because a sentence is capable of more than one meaning. In the following sentence, for example, the word *punch* would normally be interpreted by most listeners as a blow, until they got to the end and realised that it referred to a drink: *John reeled from the effect of Bill's powerful punch despite his high tolerance of alcohol.* Misinterpretations such as these provide linguists with valuable clues about how people process language. Some think that we compute one meaning initially, and only go back and compute another if it becomes implausible or contradictory. This would explain the surprise people get on discovering their original interpretation was wrong. However, research has shown that people take longer to process ambiguous fragments than they do unambiguous ones, which suggests that rather than computing one meaning listeners compute at least two and then immediately pick one on the basis of context. This is not to say that they are actively aware of ambiguity as such; the assumption is still that there is only one meaning, which the context will clarify.

Idiolect.   The speech habits of an individual. Each of us is unique in the way in which we use language. Although our speech may predominantly belong to a particular DIALECT, none the less the selection of features we make within that variety will differ from that of other users of the same dialect. In a sense we all have our own dialect: a product of where we were born, our age, sex, education, race, and nationality. Katie Wales (1989) likens it to a finger-print. When sociolinguists study dialect they are really studying an abstraction made up of the regularly recurring FEATURES of speakers in a particular speech community. Idiolect is a useful term, not only in sociolinguistics, but also in stylistics. Authors can be said to have their own idiolect in the sense that each will have their own set of individual stylistic features. Some writers also habitually construct characters with distinctive language traits. Many of Dickens's comic creations, for example, are characterised in this way.

Isogloss/isograph.   A line drawn on a map to mark the boundary of an area in which a particular linguistic feature is used. A number of isoglosses falling in one place suggests the existence of a DIALECT boundary. There are various types of isoglosses depending on the feature in question: an **isophone** marks the limits of a phonological FEATURE; an **isomorph** marks the limit of a morphological (*see* MORPHOLGY) feature; an **isolex** marks the limit of a lexical item (*see* LEXICON); and an **isomeme** marks the limit of a SEMANTIC feature (e.g. when the same words have different meanings in different areas).

Medium/mode.   These terms are sometimes used interchangeably in **stylistics** (see p. 187), although some linguists do attempt to distinguish them. Medium refers to the physical means by which a message is transmitted. In communication theory this could be almost anything, from the human body to clothing. As far as language is concerned there are two main media: speech (**phonic medium**) and writing (**graphic medium**). Occasionally 'medium' is also used to refer to the CHANNEL of communication, that is, the technical means of transmission. A message in the phonic medium (speech) can be transmitted via several different channels: telephone, television, radio, and so on.

Speech and writing, then, are the distinctively linguistic media. The relationship between them, and the dynamics of addresser/addressee interaction that each involves, have been the subject of much study. At one time it used to be thought that writing was simply speech in another form. We now know that this isn't so. Writing involves a quite different attitude towards language and a different relationship between participants. Because it's a visual medium, rather than an oral one, it alters the way we perceive ourselves as linguistic beings. Cultures that are wholly oral typically have a semi-magical view of language, in which words are part of the objects or people that they name. This is the source of spells and incantations, as well as oaths. The dynamics of orality and literacy are a central feature of communication theory.

At a less theoretical level, however, we have to acknowledge that speech and writing, although separate media, are not entirely discrete forms. A good deal of writing – dramatic dialogue, lectures, and much poetry – is written to be spoken. It is also true that people's speech is frequently influenced by things they have read. Characteristic, then, of advanced literate cultures, is what linguists call **complex media**, in which speech and writing are intertwined. It's here that distinguishing between medium and mode can be useful. Those who make this distinction use the term 'mode' to indicate the particular format or genre which a piece of writing, or speech, adopts. Letters, monologues, reports, poems, and sermons are all constructed according to certain conventions either of speech or of writing, or both. They have a **rhetorical mode**. One of the rhetorical conventions of letters, for example, is the greeting formula 'Dear Sir/Madam' with its various degrees of informality 'Dear Mr Jones/Jim'. When we read these greetings we interpret them conventionally (i.e. according to the rules of the genre).

Mentalese.   The hypothetical 'language of thought' in which ideas are considered to exist prior to their expression in linguistic form. The concept of mentalese is an attempt to answer one of the perennial problems of linguistic enquiry concerning the relationship between thought and language. What kind of thought is possible without language is a question that has received a variety of answers. To George Orwell, in *Nineteen Eighty Four*, the abolition of words such as 'freedom' and 'equality' from the language by Big Brother would mean these ideas were no longer thinkable. As a consequence of the modern belief in the MODULAR structure of language, however, most linguists tend to argue that language is a distinct faculty, quite separate from the general ability to think. Evidence for this comes from research into two groups of people: first, those who have very little or no language, such as deaf and dumb adults, who can none the less understand mathematical processes and logical relations; and secondly, severely mentally subnormal children who can speak fluently, although without making much sense. The psycholinguist Jean Aitchison (1992, p. 61) quotes the example of Marta: *It was no ordinary school, it was just good old no buses*.

If thought can exist independently of language the question arises as to what form it exists in. It's here that the concept of 'mentalese' comes in. To its exponents, mentalese is a logically based programme that uses symbols to represent concepts. 'People do not think in English or Chinese or Apache,' argues Steven Pinker (1994, p. 81); 'they think in a language of thought.' Being linguistically competent means 'knowing how to translate mentalese into strings of words and *vice versa*' (p. 82). The concept of mentalese owes much of its currency to the work of the American psychologist Jerry Fodor, who popularised it in his book *The Language of Thought* (1975).

Modularity (of language).   The property of being composed of separate components, or 'modules'. Many linguists believe that language is a modular system, by which they mean that language is a self-contained system largely independent of other cognitive programmes. The model for this is based very much on computer science. Basic to it is the notion that language systems operate various subroutines that are separately wired in the brain and which interact with each other to produce language. So, for example, the PHONETIC component could be said to operate various modules which deal with different properties of the sound signal. There is a lot of evidence to suggest that these properties are separately processed and only then put together. One part of the processor deals with tonal qualities and helps us to determine whether someone is angry or kindly, another part deals with speech recognition and enables us to recognise who is speaking to us, whilst a third part decodes the message. This model of speech perception is supported by research into the capacities of stroke victims, some of whom can recognise who is speaking without being able to understand what is being said, and vice versa. Similarly with intonation, some victims respond to tone of voice but without having either of the other two abilities.

Non-verbal communication (NVC).   Communication that takes place other than through words. There are two types of NVC that are relevant to linguistics. The first is **vocal** communication, or **paralanguage (paralinguistic)**. This refers to all those non-verbal, but vocal, aspects of language which accompany the words we utter. Important here are **prosodic** FEATURES such as loudness, pitch, and stress, significant in INTONATION, as well as more general features, such as giggles, snorts, grunts, and sighs, which communicate 'attitude'. The second is **non-vocal** communication. This consists of what is more commonly known as body **language**, and includes gestures, facial expressions, posture, and eye movement.

Clearly, paralanguage is of more obvious interest to linguists than non-vocal communication since it involves the human voice. None the less, both forms are important in the process of communication. In the case of the non-vocal variety, it is frequently crucial in providing feedback to the speaker on how his/her message is being received.

Observer's paradox.   Formulated by the sociolinguist William Labov, this states that: 'The aim of linguistic research in the community must be to find out how people talk when they are not being systematically observed; yet we can only obtain this data by systematic observation' (cited by Freeborn, 1986, p. 146). Most people will tend to alter their speech if they know they are being observed, thus rendering any systematic analysis of their actual linguistic usage extremely difficult. The obvious solution would be not to tell informants, but linguists being, or wishing to be considered, decent people, regard such a course of action as unethical.

The observer's paradox poses more of a problem for linguists using the classic Labovian method, whereby informants are randomly sampled. Those using a participant observation approach which involves becoming part of a group and carrying out observations over a substantial period of time are less likely to encounter it. Labov himself developed a number of strategies for coping with the problem. These included taking advantage of natural breaks, such as interruptions, or a break for tea, and leaving the tape recorder running, or asking people to talk about some event in their lives which might engender strong feelings and enable them to forget about being recorded. Even so, a researcher might have to wait a long time before the particular DIALECTAL features being observed appeared sufficiently frequently to be analysed. S/he might also have to wait a considerable time to observe STYLE SHIFTING, the capacity of speakers to adjust their style of speech to the situation. This is why some researchers ask informants to read a word list or a passage – tasks that are normally performed with a more self-conscious delivery, and that enable comparison with more casual speech. In his early research into the use of 'non-prevocalic r' – the sounding of 'r' when it doesn't occur before a vowel (as in *fourth* and *floor*) – in New York speech, Labov would go into a department store and ask about some goods on the fourth floor: 'Excuse me, where are the women's shoes?' Having received the required answer he would then pretend not to have heard and lean forward anticipating a more careful reply. In this way he was able to compare a casual pronunciation of words involving non-prevocalic 'r' with a careful one.

All of this goes to show that whilst linguists may preserve their honesty they have at times to be just a little cunning to get the required results. It's probably true to say, however, that most contemporary researchers, such as James and Lesley Milroy (see Further Reading), favour long-term participant observation, although this limits the range and number of people who can be observed and is invariably more time consuming.

Over-extension/generalisation. A frequent phenomenon in language development. It can be found not only in syntactic usage but also in word meanings. Very young children will sometimes refer to all animals as *dogs* or call all vehicles *cars* and, perhaps more disconcertingly, all men as *dad*. Discovering the limits of these words, what they do, and do not, apply to, is a useful way of penetrating the child's semantic system. It can take time for children to learn that words can refer to separate things. When a child refers to *milk*, for instance, does s/he mean the whole process of pouring it into a mug and placing it down, or does it have the restricted meaning we are used to? Children also over-extend word endings, saying *breaked* for 'broke' and *taked* for 'took'. Such over-generalisations indicate that children are not simply copying adults, since they will not have heard these forms, but generating rules of their own (*see* UNDER-EXTENSION).

Pidgin.   A pidgin is an auxiliary language that arises to fulfil certain limited communication needs among people who have no common language. The majority of pidgins around the world originated as trade languages; the word 'pidgin' is commonly thought to be from a Chinese word meaning 'business'. Probably the earliest pidgin was Sabir, based on Portuguese and used by the Crusaders in trading with Muslims.

Pidgins are all derived from a 'target' language, usually English, French, or Portuguese. In their initial stages, or **pidginisation**, they involve simplifying the target language by reducing the vocabulary and eliminating grammatical complexities such as TENSE and plural inflections. In many ways the process is similar to the one we all undergo when learning a foreign language. And just as we may import some English words and pronunciation patterns into our newly acquired language, so pidgins often absorb elements of the less dominant language. A word such as *okay*, for instance, is probably of West African origin imported into a local English-based pidgin. This is a process known as **admixture.**

The classic situation for pidgin formation, then, arises from a trading relationship between a group of European seamen and a local African or Polynesian tribe. This results in the formation of a **marginal pidgin**. A second stage begins when local tribes who speak different languages use the pidgin as a **lingua franca**. It then grows in vocabulary and grammatical structure and becomes an **expanded pidgin**. These kinds of pidgins exist all over the world where trading has taken place between Europeans and indigenous populations of other countries. The principal regions where we find them, however, are in the Pacific basin and along the coast of West Africa.

A further stage arises when expanded pidgins develop into **Creoles**. A creole is a pidgin that has become the mother tongue of a community. For this to happen it needs to acquire native speakers. A classic case is the development of African Creole in the Caribbean as a consequence of the slave trade. This major upheaval resulted in different language groups being forced to live together with pidgin as the only common means of communication. Not surprisingly, children soon acquired it as a native language, as a consequence of which the pidgin underwent **creolisation**. Similarly, in Papua New Guinea, where there are many different indigenous languages, the English pidgin known as 'Tok Pisin' is emerging as the first language of the country. Despite their derivation from other languages, creoles are languages in their own right. Their vocabulary, syntax, and stylistic range are greatly developed from the pidgin stage and enable them to be used in most formal and informal contexts.

A final stage often occurs if, as sometimes happens, the original 'target' language is re-introduced into the community. In many West Indian countries, for example, since independence, standard English has become the language of law, government, and in some cases, education. The effect of this is to cause the creole to unravel in a process known as **decreolisation**. This results in a **post-creole continuum** in which we get a range of possible forms from pure creole at one end of the spectrum to standard English at the other. So, as O'Donnell and Todd (1980, p. 52) comment, we find a number of forms in Guyana for the English sentence *I gave him*, ranging from *mi gii am*, *mi bin gii am*, *a di gi ii*, *a giv ii*, and so on up to the standard English form. It is likely that **black vernacular English** (**BVE**), of the kind we find in America and Britain, is not imperfectly learned English but a decreolised creole.

The processes of pidgin and creole formation outlined above enable us to see pidgins and creoles as languages in their own right, albeit, in the case of pidgin, of an auxiliary kind, rather than debased or corrupt forms of more prestigious languages. This is important to speakers of these varieties because of the recognition it affords to otherwise stigmatised linguistic forms. But it is equally important for linguists, for whom studying such processes has brought increased understanding of how languages generally are formed. The European languages French, Spanish, and Italian are, in a sense, all creoles, being descended from pidginised versions of Latin, and it is probable that when Old English met Old Norse, processes of pidginisation resulted in a leaner, less inflected, variety that eventually became modern English. More ambitiously, however, it has been argued by Derek Bickerton that creolisation provides vital evidence for the genetic inheritance of linguistic ability. According to Bickerton (1981) the rapid expansion which results when children become native speakers of pidgin happens because they are generating vital linguistic material themselves. If this is so it solves the vexed question of why creoles the world over are grammatically so similar. The reason is simply that children are operating what Bickerton calls the same 'bioprogram' (*see* BIOPROGRAM(ME) HYPOTHESIS). Needless to say, this view is contentious and there are many who have challenged it but, none the less, it provides intriguing evidence as to the continuing importance of this area of linguistics.

Prototype theory.   A theory that argues that people understand the meanings of words by reference to a typical example. So, for instance, if asked to say what a 'bird' is, most people would refer to a robin or black-bird, rather than an emu or a chicken. This is because robins and black-birds are seen as prototypical birds whereas the others aren't. The idea is that all categories involve members which are central to the category as well as those which are marginal. The central members are used by the mind as a way of assessing the right to inclusion of possible new entries.

Basic to these SEMANTIC procedures for class membership are what are termed **defining features** and **characteristic features**. Defining FEATURES are those which a member of a category must necessarily possess. In the case of birds these would include having feathers, two legs, two wings and being warm-blooded. Characteristic features, on the other hand, are optional properties that a member may, rather than must, possess. So birds usually have short legs, are small, can fly, and are able to sing, and so on. Prototypical birds, like robins and blackbirds, are those which, in addition to the defining features, possess most, if not all the characteristic features as well. According to prototype theory, people verify statements such as *A robin is a bird*, or *A chicken is a bird*, by checking the number of features which *robin* and *chicken* have against the prototype of *bird*. This explains why most respondents take longer to verify a chicken's status as a bird since, although it satisfies the defining features for *bird*, there are significant characteristic features which it lacks, or which are at least in doubt. Would we, for instance, describe the noise a chicken makes as singing?

One of the problems that besets prototype theory, however, is in deciding just what is a defining, as opposed to a characteristic, feature. Indeed, some characteristic features may seem more important than defining ones. Probably many people would initially think the ability to fly was an essential feature of birdhood rather than having two legs. And there are some categories where there appear to be no defining features, only characteristic ones. A case in point is 'fruit'. It's possible to list numerous typical features which various fruits possess, but very hard to find one feature which they all have. We're forced to say that fruit is a category not because of any defining feature which members have but on the basis of family resemblances. A prototypical fruit has many of these, a marginal fruit has less. It's on this basis that we can say that olives and tomatoes are borderline cases in that they share as many features with vegetables as with fruits.

The same is arguably true of some WORD CLASSES such as NOUNS and ADJECTIVES. Nouns have family resemblances, on the basis of which it's possible to categorise a prototypical noun as one which shares all the features that nouns are capable of. But there is no single, defining, feature that a noun categorically has to have to be a noun.

Register.   In stylistics and sociolinguistics 'register' refers to a socially, or situationally, defined style of language. Many FIELDS OF DISCOURSE, such as religion and medicine, have their own special language styles. These are **professional** or **technical** registers. In a more general sense, 'register' is also used to indicate degrees of formality within language use. A business letter, for example, will employ a more formal register than a domestic chat.

Most subjects can be talked about in a variety of different styles along a scale of more or less formality. This is partly because of the considerable stylistic variation that exists in the lexicon. Consider, for example, the terms for *horse:*

> *steed*
> *horse*
> *nag*
> *gee gee*

All of these terms are appropriate to particular situations: *steed* belongs to a poetic register, *nag* is slang, and *gee gee* would be used in the nursery. Another example is the terms for *home*:

domicile	(official)
residence	(formal)
abode	(poetic)
home	(core)
dwelling	(formal/archaic)
gaff	(slang)

It is usually the case with such scales that one term is more widely used than the rest. *Horse* and *home* fall into this category and can be identified as **core** terms.

This lexical diversity is largely the result of various historical influences on the language. Many of the more formal and technical terms are of Latin or French origin, and the humbler, vernacular ones, of Old English. So we find pairs such as *theft* (Old English) and *larceny* (French); *bleeding* (Old English) and *haemorrhage* (Greek). Register variation tends to be discussed principally in relation to choices in the LEXICON, but it is not limited to these. Any kind of utterance involves making syntactic and phonological choices as well. We can decide to adopt a formal or informal tone, passive or active constructions, abbreviated or full forms, depending on the situation. Part of the process of becoming communicatively competent involves being able to switch registers (**register-switching** or STYLE-SHIFTING) when the occasion calls for it. The casual style of expression we might use in a seminar discussion, for example, would not be appropriate in a discursive essay, which calls for tighter control of grammatical form and word choice. **Register-borrowing** and **register-mixing** are also frequent in more complex language forms. Register-borrowing can be encountered in many modern novels, which incorporate non-literary varieties such as newspaper articles, footnotes, and letters, in the text. Adverts also frequently borrow the registers of other forms of discourse. As for register-mixing, some forms of comedy deliberately mix formal and informal styles for humorous effect.

A good deal of work has been done by linguists interested in stylistics on identifying the various features that determine the particular register we choose to adopt in a given situation. The principal variables are FIELD or subject matter; MEDIUM (speech or writing); MODE, the particular genre (e.g. conversation, sermon, narrative etc.); CHANNEL, the technical means (e.g. telephone, radio, face to face); TENOR, the relationship between the participants; and CONTEXT, the situation, social, cultural, or institutional. Clearly, the permutations that are possible here are practically endless and we could be forgiven for thinking the task of classifying the registers available in the language futile. In practice, however, there are a small number of styles, or registers, which most adults use in everyday life. They have been described by Martin Joos (1962):

1. **Formal**. Informative and discursive. Used by lecturers, preachers, judges. Features:
   - grammar closely organised, complex structures
   - ample vocabulary
   - meticulous pronunciation, no slurring or contractions, neutral intonation

2. **Consultative**. Used for conversing with a stranger, and small group discussion. Features:
   - complete grammatical forms, major sentences
   - core vocabulary items, avoidance of elaborate terms and slang
   - clear pronunciation, friendly intonation

3. **Casual**. Easy conversation among friends. Features:
   - sentence fragments, fillers (*you know, I mean, actually*)
   - semantically empty words (*thingamajig whatsit*), slang
   - slurred, elided, forms of pronunciation, varied intonation

4. **Intimate**. Between people who know each other very well, lovers, members of an athletic team, and so on. Features:
   - non-verbal communication (shrugs, groans, raising eyebrows)
   - private vocabulary, reduced in range, special meanings, nonsense words
   - heavy use of stress and intonation, sometimes exaggerated, DIALECT broader

5. **Frozen**. Literary, religious, and legal works which are fixed in expression, e.g. scriptures, treaties, and initiations, wedding/funeral services. Features:
   - ceremonial language, sentence structures often archaic
   - vocabulary archaic, frequently latinised
   - pronunciation meticulous, intonation neutral, pitch raised.

Sapir–Whorf hypothesis. A celebrated hypothesis first put forward by the American linguist Edward Sapir (1881–1939) and later taken up, and developed, by his student Benjamin Lee Whorf (1897–1941). According to this view, the way in which we conceptualise the world depends on the particular language we speak. As Whorf puts it, 'We dissect nature along lines laid down by our native languages' (cited in Crystal, 1987, p. 15). Each language, in other words, imposes on its users a particular 'world view'.

Much of the evidence which Whorf used to support his hypothesis was gathered from work he is supposed to have done among Native Americans, principally the Apaches and the Hopis. Whorf claimed, for example, that the Hopis had a different way of conceptualising time than Europeans and that this was reflected in their language. Instead of visualising time in the mechanically chronological way of Europeans, they perceived it more organically, in terms of processes and change. More recently, however, these claims have been challenged and it has been shown that Hopi speech contains TENSE, units of time (such as days, weeks, months etc), and terms for quantifying time ('quick', 'long time', and 'finished'). They also have calendars and devices for measuring time. Probably the most direct attack on the hypothesis is by Steven Pinker in *The Language Instinct* (1994), who argues that Whorf took a fairly modest proposition of Sapir's about the relationship between language and thought and inflated it by means of flawed, even bogus, research, into a form of linguistic determinism. Whorf's views, he suggests, would mean that certain thoughts and perceptions would be denied to us unless our language allowed them. The classic case is the issue of colour perception. Languages do differ in their colour terms: Navajo, for example, uses the same word for blue and green, whilst Russian has terms that distinguish sky blue from dark blue. Does this mean that a Navajo can't tell blue and green apart, or that a Russian will see different shades of blue as separate colours? It has to be said that the evidence here is inconclusive. There are some indications from experiments that colour terminology can affect people's judgements about colour. On the other hand, it's impossible to prove that it's language that is the determining factor. Pinker argues quite firmly that it isn't: 'The way we see colors determines how we learn words for them, not vice-versa' (1994, p. 63).

As a consequence of these kinds of attacks on Whorf most linguists do not accept the hypothesis in the terms in which Whorf articulated it. However, many are attracted to a softer version of it, in line with Edward Sapir's first observations about linguistic relativism. Languages do differ in the way they relate to the experiential world, as we know from the difficulty of finding exact translation equivalents. It's only to be expected that these differences reflect cultural and social ones in some shape or form. But rather than language controlling thought, as the hard form of the hypothesis argues, this softer version would say that it 'influences' thought.

Style-shifting.   The ability to alter the style, or REGISTER, in which we are communicating, as the occasion demands. In broad terms, it usually means altering the level of formality or informality we are employing. See REGISTER.

Tenor.   In traditional literary criticism 'tenor' is one of a pair of terms – the other is 'vehicle' – which describe the twin parts of a metaphor. In linguistics, however, it's a term used in DISCOURSE ANALYSIS to describe the relationship between participants in a discourse. 'Tenor' is one of the factors which affect the style of language we adopt. This is particularly evident in situations which call for more, or less, formality. Two lovers will naturally use a different language style from an employee talking to his/her boss. There will be significant differences in INTONATION pattern, syntactic (see SYNTAX) structure, and the choice of lexical items (see LEXICON). The tenor of their relationship is intimate. Complications occur, however, if the boss and employee are also lovers. In this case there is a clash between two separate relationships, each with their own individual tenor. Many linguists cope with this by distinguishing between **personal tenor** and **functional tenor**. The first of these involves the degree of personal relationship between participants: whether they are friends, relatives, lovers, or just acquaintances. The second, involves the more public relationship they have. The ingredients here have to do with status, rank, and social roles. Wealth and fame are usually felt to increase a person's social standing, as does rising to a higher rank in the commercial world, the armed forces, or the class system. In addition, there are subtle nuances of functional tenor between doctor and patient, shop assistant and customer, teacher and student, as a consequence of the particular roles they play.

Situations in which there is a possible conflict of functional and personal tenors can be described as having a **complex tenor**, as opposed to the **simple tenor** of those which are controlled by only one set of constraints. Many novels and plays exploit the possibility of functional/personal clashes. In *King Lear* a king hands over power to his daughters, and in *Lady Chatterley's Lover*, a lady falls in love with her gardener. Along with CONTEXT, FIELD, MODE/MEDIUM, and CHANNEL, tenor is one of the main variables determining the style, or REGISTER, we adopt in everyday discourse.

Under-extension/generalisation.   Like its counterpart OVER-EXTEN-SION, under-extension relates to a stage in language development whereby children typically use a word without knowing fully its true limit. In this case, however, rather than using a word to mean more than it can – as in using *dog* to mean all animals – the child uses it to mean less. So, for example, Herbert and Eva Clark (1977, p. 491) report a child as using the word *car* at the age of nine months only for cars moving outside on the street but not for cars standing still or in pictures or in which she rode herself. And, generally, it's not uncommon for children to apply a term like *shoes* to their own shoes but not to anyone else's.

It's possible that under-extension might represent the first stage in the acquisition of a new word. So a child might begin by using the term *dog* to refer to one specific dog – the family pet. Later on s/he might extend it to other dogs, and then possibly over-extend it to animals generally.

References

Aitchison, J. (1992) *Introducing Language and Mind* (London: Penguin).

Aitchison, J. (1999) *Teach Yourself Linguistics*, 5th edn (London: Hodder Arnold).

Berko, J. and Brown, R. (1960) 'Psycholinguistic Research Methods'. In P. H. Mussen (ed.), *Handbook of Research Methods in Child Development* (New York: Wiley), pp. 517–57.

Bickerton, D. (1981) *Roots of Language* (Ann Arbor, MI: Karoma Press).

Bickerton, D. (1990) *Language and Species* (Chicago: University of Chicago Press).

Bickerton, D. (1995) *Language and Human Behavior* (Seattle: University of Washington Press).

Brazil, D. C. (1985) *The Communicative Value of Intonation in English*, Discourse Analysis Monograph, no. 8 (Birmingham: University of Birmingham).

Chomsky, N. (1965) *Aspects of the Theory of Syntax* (Cambridge, MA: MIT Press).

Chomsky, N. (1989) 'Some Notes on Economy of Derivation and Representation', *MIT Working Papers in Linguistics*, 10: 43–74; reprinted as Chomsky (1995).

Chomsky, N. (1995) *The Minimalist Program* (Cambridge, MA: MIT Press).

Chomsky, N. (2002) *On Nature and Language* (Cambridge: Cambridge University Press).

Clark, H. and Clark, E. (1977) *Psychology and Language: An Introduction to Language* (New York: Harcourt Brace Jovanovich).

Coupland, N. and Jaworski, A. (eds), *Sociolinguistics: A Reader and Coursebook* (Basingstoke: Palgrave Macmillan, 1997).

Cruttenden, A. (1986) *Intonation* (Cambridge: Cambridge University Press).

Crystal, D. (1975) *Prosodic Systems and Intonation in English* (Cambridge: Cambridge University Press).

Crystal, D. (1987) *The Cambridge Encyclopedia of Language* (Cambridge: Cambridge University Press).

Crystal, D. (1988) *Rediscover Grammar* (London: Longman).

Fabb, N. (1994) *Sentence Structure* (London: Routledge).

Fish, S. (1980) *Is There a Text in this Class? The Authority of Interpretive Communities* (Harvard, MA: Harvard University Press).

Fodor, J. A. (1975) *The Language of Thought* (New York: Crowell).

Fowler, R., Hodge, R., Kress, G. and Trew, T. (1979) *Language and Control* (London: Routledge).

Francis, N. (1967) *The English Language: An Introduction* (London: English Universities Press).

Freeborn, D. with French, P. and Langford, D. (1986) *Varieties of English* (Basingstoke: Macmillan).

Halliday, M. (1967) *Intonation and Grammar in British English* (The Hague: Mouton).

Halliday, M. (1978) *Language as Social Semiotic* (London: Edward Arnold).

Halliday, M. and Hasan, R. (1976) *Cohesion in English* (London: Longman).

Halliday, M. (1985) *Spoken and Written Language* (Melbourne: Deakin University Press).

Huddleston, R. and Pullum, G. (2002) *The Cambridge Grammar of the English Language* (Cambridge: Cambridge University Press).

Johnson, M. (1987) *The Body in the Mind: The Bodily Basis of Meaning, Imagination and Reason* (Chicago: University of Chicago Press).

Joos, M. (1962) *The Five Clocks* (New York: Harcourt, Brace & World).

Katz, J. J. (1972) *Semantic Theory* (New York: Harper & Row).

Katz, J. J. and Fodor, J. A. (1963) 'The Structure of a Semantic Theory', *Language*, 39: 170–210.

Lakoff, G. (1987) *Women, Fire and Dangerous Things: What Categories Reveal about the Mind* (Chicago: University of Chicago Press).

Lakoff, G. and Brugman, C. (1988) 'Cognitive Topology and Lexical Networks'. In S. Small, G. Cottrell and M. Tanenhaus (eds), *Lexical Ambiguity Resolution: Perspectives from Psycholinguistics, Neuropsychology and Artificial Intelligence* (San Mateo, CA: Morgan Kaufmann), 477–508.

Lakoff, G. and Johnson, M. (1980) *Metaphors We Live By* (Chicago: University of Chicago Press).

Lakoff, G. and Turner, M. (1989) *More than Cool Reason* (Chicago: University of Chicago Press).

Leech, G. (1983) *Principles of Pragmatics* (London: Longman).

Levin, B. (1993) *English Verb Classes and Alternations* (Chicago: University of Chicago Press).

Levin, S. (1977) *The Semantics of Metaphor* (Baltimore, MD: Johns Hopkins University Press).

Malmkjaer, K. (1995) *The Linguistics Encyclopedia* (London: Routledge).

McCarthy, M. (1991) *Discourse Analysis for Language Teachers* (Cambridge: Cambridge University Press).

Milroy, L. (1987) *Language and Social Networks*, 2nd edn (Oxford: Basil Blackwell).

O'Connor, J. and Arnold, G. (1961) *Intonation of Colloquial English* (London: Longman).

O'Donnell, W. and Todd, L. (1980) *Variety in Contemporary English* (London: Allen & Unwin).

Pinker, S. (1994) *The Language Instinct* (London: Penguin).

Radford, A. (1997) *Syntactic Theory and the Structure of English* (Cambridge: Cambridge University Press).

Saeed, J. (2003) *Semantics*, 2nd edn (Oxford: Blackwell).

Searle, J. R. (1976) 'The Classification of Illocutionary Acts', *Language and Society*, 5: 1–23; reprinted in *Expression and Meaning: Studies in the Theory of Speech Acts* (Cambridge: Cambridge University Press, 1979), 1–29.

Shklovsky, V. (1917) 'Art as Technique', in L. Lemon and M. J. Reis (eds) (1965) *Russian Formalist Criticism* (Lincoln: University of Nebraska Press).

Smith, N. (1973) *The Acquisition of Phonology: A Case Study* (Cambridge: Cambridge University Press).

Sperber, D. and Wilson, D. (1986) *Relevance: Communication and Cognition* (Oxford: Basil Blackwell).

Sweetser, E. (1990) *From Etymology to Pragmatics* (Cambridge: Cambridge University Press).

Trudgill, P. (1974) *The Social Differentiation of English in Norwich* (Cambridge: Cambridge University Press).

Trudgill, P. (1983) *On Dialect: Social and Geographical Perspectives* (Oxford: Basil Blackwell).

Trudgill, P. (1990) *The Dialects of England* (Oxford: Blackwell).

Wales, K. (1989) *A Dictionary of Stylistics* (London: Longman).

Further Reading

GENERAL READING

Aitchison, J., *The Seeds of Speech: Language Origin and Evolution* (Cambridge: Cambridge University Press, 2000).

Bex, T. and Watts, R. J., *Standard English: The Widening Debate* (London: Routledge, 1999).

Blake, N., *Introduction to English Language* (Basingstoke: Palgrave Macmillan, 1993).

Bolinger, D., *Language: The Loaded Weapon* (London: Longman, 1989).

Burgess, A., *A Mouthful of Air* (London: Hutchinson, 1992).

Burridge, K., *Blooming English* (Cambridge: Cambridge University Press, 2004).

Carter, R., *Language and Creativity: The Art of Common Talk* (London: Routledge, 2004).

Chomsky, N., *Knowledge of Language: Its Nature, Origin and Use* (New York: Praeger, 1985).

Crystal, D., *Linguistics* (London: Penguin, 1990).

Crystal, D., *The Cambridge Encyclopedia of Language*, 2nd edn (Cambridge: Cambridge University Press, 1997).

Crystal, D., *The Cambridge Encyclopedia of the English Language*, 2nd edn (Cambridge: Cambridge University Press, 2003).

Doughty, P. *et al.*, *Exploring Language* (London: Edward Arnold, 1972).

Finegan, E., *Language: Its Structure and Use*, 4th edn (London: Heinle, 2003).

Finch, G., *Word of Mouth: A New Introduction to Language and Communication* (Basingstoke: Palgrave Macmillan, 2002).

Finch, G., *How to Study Linguistics*, 2nd edn (Basingstoke: Palgrave Macmillan, 2003).

Fromkin, V. (ed.) *Linguistics: An Introduction to Linguistic Theory* (Oxford: Blackwell, 2000).

Fromkin, V., and Rodman, R., *An Introduction to Language*, 5th edn (New York: International Thomson Publishing, 1997).

Graddol, D., Cheshire, J. and Swann, J., *Describing Language* (Milton Keynes: Open University Press, 1994).

Graddol, D. and Goodman, S., *English in a Postmodern World* (London: Routledge, 1996).

Graddol, D., Swann, J. and Leith, D., *English: History, Diversity and Change* (London: Routledge, 1996).

Gramley, S. and Paetzold, M., *A Survey of Modern English*, 2nd edn (Cambridge: Cambridge University Press, 2003).

Greenbaum, S., *Good English and the Grammarian* (London: Longman, 1989).

Kenworthy, J., *Language in Action* (London: Longman, 1991).

Kuiper, K. and Allan, W. Scott, *An Introduction to English Language*, 2nd edn (Basingstoke: Palgrave Macmillan, 2003).

Milroy, J. and Milroy, L., *Authority in Language: Investigating Standard English* (London: Routledge, 1998).

Penhallurick, R., *Studying the English Language* (Basingstoke: Palgrave Macmillan, 2003).

Pinker, S., *The Language Instinct* (London: Penguin, 1995).

Poole, S., *An Introduction to Linguistics* (Basingstoke: Palgrave Macmillan, 1999).

Radford, A., Atkinson, M., Britain, D., Clahsen, H. and Spencer, A., *Linguistics: An Introduction* (Cambridge: Cambridge University Press, 1999).

Quirk, R., *The Use of English* (London: Longman, 1962).

Quirk, R., *Words at Work* (London: Longman, 1987).

Quirk, R., *English in Use* (London: Longman, 1991).

Saussure, F. de., *Course in General Linguistics*, ed. C. Bally and A. Sechehay, trans. W. Baskin (New York: McGraw-Hill, 1966).

Thomas, G., *Linguistic Purism* (London: Longman, 1991).

Thompson, N., *Communication and Language* (Basingstoke: Palgrave Macmillan, 2003).

Trask, R. L., *Language: The Basics*, 3rd edn (London: Routledge, 1995).

Trudgill, P. and Anderson, L., *Bad Language* (Oxford: Blackwell, 1991).

Wardhaugh, R., *Investigating Language* (Oxford: Blackwell, 1993).

Yule, G., *The Study of Language*, 2nd edn (Cambridge: Cambridge University Press, 1996).

PHONETICS AND PHONOLOGY

Ashby, P., *Speech Sounds* (London: Routledge, 1995).

Carr, P., *Phonology* (Basingstoke: Palgrave Macmillan, 1993).

Carr, P., *English Phonetics and Phonology: An Introduction*, 2nd edn (Oxford: Blackwell, 1999).

Collins, B. and Mees, I. M., *Practical Phonetics and Phonology* (Cambridge: Cambridge University Press, 2003).

Ewen, C. J. and van der Hulst, H., *The Phonological Structure of Words: An Introduction* (Cambridge: Cambridge University Press, 2000).

Geigerich, H., *English Phonology: An Introduction* (Cambridge: Cambridge University Press, 1992).

Hawkins, P., *Introducing Phonology* (London: Routledge, 1984).

Katamba, F., *An Introduction to Phonology* (London: Longman, 1989).

Kreidler, C. W., *The Pronunciation of English: A Coursebook in Phonology*, 2nd edn (Oxford: Blackwell, 2003).

Lass, R., *Phonology: An Introduction to Basic Concepts* (Cambridge: Cambridge University Press, 1984).

Shockey, L., *Sound Patterns of Spoken English* (Oxford: Blackwell, 2002).

Spencer, A., *Phonology: Theory and Description* (Oxford: Blackwell, 1996).

Trask, R. L., *Dictionary of Phonetics and Phonology* (London: Routledge, 1995).

SYNTAX

Aarts, B., *English Syntax and Argumentation*, 2nd edn (Basingstoke: Palgrave Macmillan, 2001).

Adams, V., *An Introduction to Modern English Word-Formation* (London: Longman, 1973).

Baker, C. L., *English Syntax*, 2nd edn (Cambridge, MA: MIT Press, 1995).

Bauer, L., *Introducing Linguistic Morphology* (Edinburgh: Edinburgh University Press, 2003).

Brown, K. and Miller, J., *Syntax: A Linguistic Introduction to Sentence Structure*, 2nd edn (London: Unwin Hyman, 1991).

Burton-Roberts, N., *Analysing Sentences* (London: Longman, 1986).

Fabb, N., *Sentence Structure* (London: Routledge, 1994).

Freeborn, D., *A Course Book in English Grammar*, 2nd edn (Basingstoke: Macmillan, 1987).

Greenbaum, S., *An Introduction to English Grammar*, 2nd edn (London: Longman, 2002).

Hudson, R., *English Grammar* (London: Routledge, 1998).

Hurford, J. R., *Grammar: A Student's Guide* (Cambridge: Cambridge University Press, 1994).

Katamba, F., *Morphology* (Basingstoke: Palgrave Macmillan, 1993).

Leech, G., *English Grammar for Today: A New Introduction* (Basingstoke: Macmillan, 1982).

Leech, G. and Svartik, J., *A Communicative Grammar of English* (Langenscheidt Schulbuch, 2000).

Matthews, P. H., *Morphology*, 2nd edn (Cambridge: Cambridge University Press, 1991).

Newby, M., *The Structure of English: A Handbook of English Grammar* (Cambridge: Cambridge University Press, 1987).

Poole, G., *Syntactic Theory* (Basingstoke: Palgrave Macmillan, 2001).

Radford, A., *Syntactic Theory and the Structure of English: A Minimalist Approach* (Cambridge: Cambridge University Press, 1997).

Radford, A., *English Syntax: An Introduction* (Cambridge: Cambridge University Press, 2004).

Thomas, L., *Beginning Syntax* (Oxford: Blackwell, 1993).

Valin, R. D. van, *An Introduction to Syntax* (Cambridge: Cambridge University Press, 2001).

Wardhaugh, R., *Understanding English Grammar: A Linguistic Approach* (Oxford: Blackwell, 2002).

Wekker, H. and Haegman, L. A., *A Modern Course in English Syntax* (London: Routledge, 1985).

Young, D. J., *Introducing English Grammar* (London: Routledge, 1984).

SEMANTICS AND PRAGMATICS

Aitchison, J., *Words in the Mind: An Introduction to the Mental Lexicon*, 3rd edn (Oxford: Blackwell, 2003).

Blakemore, D., *Understanding Utterances: An Introduction to Pragmatics* (Oxford: Blackwell, 1992).

Carston, R., *Thoughts and Utterances* (Oxford: Blackwell, 2002).

Chierchia, G., and McConnell-Ginet, S., *Meaning and Grammar: An Introduction to Semantics*, 2nd edn (Cambridge, MA: MIT Press, 2000).

Cruse, D. A. and Cruse, A., *Meaning in Language: An Introduction to Semantics and Pragmatics* (Oxford: Oxford University Press, 2000).

Cutting, J., *Pragmatics and Discourse* (London: Routledge, 2002).

Ferris, C., *The Meaning of Syntax* (London: Longman, 1993).

Goatly, A., *The Language of Metaphors* (London: Routledge, 1997).

Green, G., *Pragmatics and Natural Language Understanding*, 2nd edn (New York: Erlbaum, 1996).

Gregory, H., *Semantics* (London: Routledge, 2000).

Grice, H. P., *Studies in the Way of Words* (Cambridge, MA: Harvard University Press, 1991).

Hofman, T. R., *Realms of Meaning* (London: Longman, 1995).

Hudson, R., *Word Meaning* (London: Routledge, 1995).

Hurford, J. R. and Heasley, B., *Semantics: A Coursebook* (Cambridge: Cambridge University Press, 1983).

Iten, C., *Linguistic Meaning, Truth Conditions and Relevance* (Basingstoke: Palgrave Macmillan 2004).

Jackson, H., *Words and Their Meanings* (London: Longman, 1989).

Jackson, H., *Grammar and Meaning* (London: Longman, 1995).

Jeffries, L., *Meaning in English* (Basingstoke: Palgrave Macmillan, 1998).

Kadmon, N., *Formal Pragmatics* (Oxford: Blackwell, 2001).

Lakoff, G. and Johnson, M., *Beyond Cool Reason* (Chicago: University of Chicago Press, 1989).

Lakoff, G. and Johnson, M., *Metaphors We Live By*, 2nd edn (Chicago: University of Chicago Press, 2003).

Leech, G., *Principles of Pragmatics* (London: Longman, 1989).

Levinson, S., *Pragmatics* (Cambridge: Cambridge University Press, 1983).

Lyons, J., *Linguistic Semantics* (Cambridge: Cambridge University Press, 1995).

Mey, J. L., *Pragmatics*, 2nd edn (Oxford: Blackwell, 2001).

Peccei, J. S., *Pragmatics* (London: Routledge, 1999).

Portner, P., *Semantic Theory* (Oxford: Blackwell, 2004).

Ricoeur, P., *The Rule of Metaphor* (London: Routledge, 1986).

Saeed, J., *Semantics*, 2nd edn (Oxford: Blackwell, 2003).

Thomas, J., *Meaning in Interaction: An Introduction to Pragmatics* (London: Longman, 1996).

Tsohatzidis, S. L. (ed.), *Foundations of Speech Act Theory* (London: Routledge, 1994).

Waldron, R. A., *Sense and Sense Development*, rev. edn (Oxford: Blackwell, 1979).

APPLIED LINGUISTICS

Block, D. and Cameron, D., *Globalization and Language Teaching* (London: Routledge, 2001).

Candlin, C. N. (ed.) *The Applied Linguistics Reader* (London: Routledge, 2004).

Candlin, C. N. and Mercer, N. (eds), *English Language Teaching in its Social Context* (London: Routledge, 2000).

Coulthard, M. and Cotterill, J., *Introducing Forensic Linguistics* (London: Routledge, 2004).

Hall, D. and Hewings, A., *Innovation in English Language Teaching* (London: Routledge, 2000).

Halliday, A., Hyde, M. and Kullmann, J., *Intercultural Communication* (London: Routledge, 2004).

Holme, R., *Mind, Metaphor and Language Teaching* (Basingstoke: Palgrave Macmillan, 2003).

Nicol, J. (ed.), *One Mind, Two Languages: Bilingual Language Processing* (Oxford: Blackwell, 2001).

Olson, D. and Torrance, N., *The Making of Literate Societies* (Oxford: Blackwell, 2001).

Palfreyman, D. and Smith, R., *Learner Autonomy Across Cultures* (Basingstoke: Palgrave Macmillan, 2003).

Street, B., *Literacy: An Advanced Resource Book for Students* (London: Routledge, 2004).

Wallace, C., *Critical Reading in Language Education* (Basingstoke: Palgrave Macmillan, 2003).

HISTORICAL LINGUISTICS

Baker, P., *Introduction to Old English* (Oxford: Blackwell, 2003).

Baugh, A. C. and Cable, T., *A History of the English Language*, 4th edn (London: Routledge, 2002).

Blake, N. F., *A History of the English Language* (Basingstoke: Palgrave Macmillan, 1996).

Cable, T., *A Companion to Baugh and Cable's 'A History of the English Language'* (London: Routledge, 2002).

Fennell, B. A., *A History of English* (Oxford: Blackwell, 2000).

Fortson, IV, B. W., *Indo-European Language and Culture* (Oxford: Blackwell, 2004).

Freeborn, D., *From Old English to Standard English*, 2nd edn (Basingstoke: Palgrave Macmillan, 1998).

Gorlach, M., *The Linguistic History of English: An Introduction* (Basingstoke: Palgrave Macmillan, 1997).

Hughes, G., *A History of English Words* (Oxford: Blackwell, 1999).

Leith, D., *A Social History of English*, 2nd edn (London: Routledge, 1997).

Robinson, O.W., *Old English and its Closest Relatives* (London: Routledge, 1994).

Smith, J., *Essentials of Early English* (London: Routledge, 1999).

Watts, R. and Trudgill, P. (eds), *Alternative Histories of English* (London: Routledge, 2001).

SOCIOLINGUISTICS

Aitchison, J., *Language Change: Progress or Decay*, 3rd edn (Cambridge: Cambridge University Press, 2000).

Bratt Paulston, C. and Tucker, R., *Sociolinguistics* (Oxford: Blackwell, 2003).

Cameron, D. and Kulick, D., *Language and Sexuality* (Cambridge: Cambridge University Press, 2003).

Chambers, J. K., *Sociolinguistic Theory*, 2nd edn (Oxford: Blackwell, 2002).

Coates, J. (ed.), *Language and Gender: A Reader* (Oxford: Blackwell, 1997).

Coates, J., *Men Talk* (Oxford: Blackwell, 2002).

Coupland, N. and Jaworski, A. (eds), *Sociolinguistics: A Reader and Coursebook* (Basingstoke: Palgrave Macmillan, 1997).

Eckert, P. and McConnell-Ginet, S., *Language and Gender* (Cambridge: Cambridge University Press, 2003).

Fasold, R., *The Sociolinguistics of Language* (Oxford: Blackwell, 1990).

Holmes, J., *An Introduction to Sociolinguistics* (London: Longman, 1992).

Joseph, J., *Language and Identity* (Basingstoke: Palgrave Macmillan, 2004).

Marshall, J., *Language Change and Sociolinguistics* (Basingstoke: Palgrave Macmillan, 2003).

Milroy, J. and Milroy, L., *Real English* (London: Longman, 1993).

Milroy, L. and Gordon, M., *Sociolinguistics*, 2nd edn (Oxford: Blackwell, 2002).

Saville-Troike, M., *The Ethnography of Communication*, 3rd edn (Oxford: Blackwell, 2002).

Stockwell, P., *Sociolinguistics: A Resource Book for Students* (London: Routledge, 2001).

Trudgill, P., *Dialects of English* (London: Longman, 1995).

Trudgill, P., *The Dialects of England*, 2nd edn (Oxford: Blackwell, 1999).

Trudgill, P., *Sociolinguistics: An Introduction to Language and Society*, 4th edn (New York: Penguin, 2001).

Trudgill, P., *Dialects*, 2nd edn (London: Routledge, 2004).

Wardhaugh, R., *An Introduction to Sociolinguistics* 4th edn (Oxford: Blackwell, 2001).

Williams, G., *Sociolinguistics: A Sociological Critique* (London: Routledge, 1992).

STYLISTICS AND DISCOURSE ANALYSIS

Brown, G., *Listening to Spoken English*, 2nd edn (London: Longman, 1990).

Carter, R., *Language and Literature: An Introductory Reader in Stylistics* (London: Routledge, 1997).

Carter, R. and Simpson, P. (eds), *Language, Discourse and Literature* (London: Routledge, 1988).

Chilton, P., *Analysing Political Discourse* (London: Routledge, 2003).

Cockroft, R., *Persuading People*, 2nd edn (Basingstoke: Palgrave Macmillan, 2004).

Cook, G., *The Discourse of Advertising* (London: Routledge, 1992).

Cotterill, J. (ed.), *Language in the Legal Process* (Basingstoke: Palgrave Macmillan, 2002).

Coulthard, M., *An Introduction to Discourse Analysis* (London: Longman, 1989).

Crystal, D., *Investigating English Style* (London: Longman, 1973).

Fabb, N., *Language and Literary Structure* (Cambridge: Cambridge University Press, 2002).

Fairclough, N., *New Labour, New Language* (London: Routledge, 2000).

Fairclough, N., *Analysing Discourse* (London: Routledge, 2003).

Freeborn, D., *Style: Text Analysis and Linguistic Criticism* (Basingstoke: Palgrave Macmillan, 1996).

Haynes, J., *Introducing Stylistics* (London: Unwin Hyman, 1989).

Haynes, J., *Style* (London: Routledge, 1995).

Heath, S., McCabe, C. and Riley, D. (eds), *The Language, Discourse, Society Reader* (Basingstoke: Palgrave Macmillan, 2003).

Hoey, M., *Textual Interaction: An Introduction to Written Discourse Analysis* (London: Routledge, 2000).

Kelly-Holmes, H., *Advertising as Multilingual Communication* (Basingstoke: Palgrave Macmillan, 2004).

Knowles, G., *Patterns of Spoken English* (London: Longman, 1987).

Martin, J. R., *The Language of Evaluation* (Basingstoke: Palgrave Macmillan, 2004).

Salkie, R., *Text and Discourse Analysis* (London: Routledge, 1995).

Schriffin, D., *Approaches to Discourse* (Oxford: Blackwell, 1994).

Short, M., *Exploring the Language of Poems, Plays and Prose* (London: Longman, 1996).

Silberstein, S., *War of Words: Language, Politics and 9/11* (London: Routledge, 2004).

Simpson, P., *Stylistics: A Resource Book for Students* (London: Routledge, 2004).

Stenstrom, A., *An Introduction to Spoken Interaction* (London: Longman, 1995).

Wales, K., *A Dictionary of Stylistics*, 2nd edn (London: Longman, 2001).

Weiss, G. and Wodak, R., *Critical Discourse Analysis* (Basingstoke: Palgrave Macmillan, 2002).

Wright, L. and Hope, J., *Stylistics* (London: Routledge, 1995).

PSYCHOLINGUISTICS

Aitchison, J., *The Articulate Mammal: An Introduction to Psycholinguistics*, 2nd edn (London: Routledge, 1998).

Aitchison, J., *Words in the Mind: An Introduction to the Mental Lexicon*, 3rd edn (Oxford: Blackwell, 2002).

Dawson, M., *Minds and Machines* (Oxford: Blackwell, 2003).

Field, J., *Psycholinguistics: A Resource Book for Students* (London: Routledge, 2003).

Garnham, A., *Psycholinguistics: Central Topics* (London: Routledge, 1986).

Levelt, W., *Speaking: From Intention to Articulation* (Cambridge, MA: MIT Press, 1989).

Peccei, J. S., *Child Language*, 2nd edn (London: Routledge, 1999).

Pinker, S., *Language Learnability and Language Development* (Cambridge, MA: Harvard University Press, 1984).

Pulvermuller, F., *The Neuroscience of Language* (Cambridge: Cambridge University Press, 2003).

Stenberg, D., *An Introduction to Psycholinguistics* (London: Longman, 1995).

Sterelny, K., *Thought in a Hostile World* (Oxford: Blackwell, 2003).

Tomasello, M. and Bates, E. (eds) *Language Development* (Oxford: Blackwell, 2001).

Index

This index lists the terms, topics and authors discussed in the book.
Page numbers in **bold type** indicate the main discussion of an entry.